RURAL DEVELOPMENT
IN
SOUTH ASIA

RURAL DEVELOPMENT IN SOUTH ASIA

Jitendra Kumar Sharma

AUTHORSPRESS

First Published 2001
by Authorspress

E-35/103, Jawahar Park (Shree Ganesh Complex),
Laxmi Nagar, Delhi-110 092
e-mail: authorspress@yahoo.com

Typeset in NewCenturySchlbk by Chitra Computers

Rural Development in South Asia
ISBN 81-7273-045-4

Printed in India at Tarun Offset, Delhi.

Preface

The issue of rural development is an obstinate and longstanding challenge. The strategy for improving rural poor has undergone some important changes along with the changes in perception of the process of development. The philosophy of development is firmly anchored in the vision that growth alone would be a panacea for all social ills, including poverty eradication. The developmental process would entail regeneration and reinvestment of capital, expansion of productive forces, and absorption of the poor and the unemployed.

Rural poverty is a complex, multidimensional phenomenon and the poverty processes which entrap the poor are highly dynamic. There is no given prescription for solutions which are valid over time, between countries and even between different areas within the same region in any given country. The policy makers and development practitioners should develop specific instrumentalities in response to specific situations and adapt these to new situations.

In South Asia the new development paradigm centres around poor rural people, whose poverty must be alleviated if long-term, equitable development is to be achieved. Well-defined strategies are needed to help them, who suffer from multiple discrimination. They are not only poor, but also socio-politically marginalised, with little countervailing power to influence national decision making. NGO and local governments have a critical role to play in improving the socio-economic conditions of these vulnerable groups.

The burden posed by rural poverty to social cohesion has led to a more humanistic approach towards development with emphasis on satisfying basic human needs and putting in place various social safety nets to help the poor. These add-ons to the strategy of growth failed to bring about any substantive change in the scenario of rural poverty. Moreover, the tremendous pressure on public resources, arising from often too onerous extensions of the safety nets, caused a reduction in the overall growth, thus undermining the long-term development potential of poor nations.

Alleviation of rural poverty depends heavily on reversing the nature of the feedback between poverty and degradation of the environment. Resource conservation and enhancement must also be reconciled with development programmes and projects, and the planning horizon of individuals and governments. Projects to alleviate rural poverty must be designed and implemented within the framework of an internally self-sustaining, conservation-oriented strategy.

Development in fields of agriculture, habitation, health, sanitation, education, etc., must be taken care of at all levels of development, by monitoring their progress and allocating the required funds. The development programmes should establish the necessary mechanisms to promote local regional and international action plans and programmes for the economic advancement of rural women and children who are the poorest and the most vulnerable people in the world. Plans which centre around them are the key and hope for sustainable development and growth.

People's participation is a means and an end in development, whereby people become increasingly self-reliant economic agents in the decision making process. Participation also implies institution building at the grassroots, strengthening the institutions and organisations of the poor themselves; and at the local, regional or national level to sensitise institutions to the needs of the rural poor, and render them more effective in meeting these needs.

As passing through traumatic transitions such as ethnic nationalism, religious revivalism, separatism and external globalism, etc. in South Asia, developmental plans and programmes are getting less attention. The development experience in South Asian states have much to contribute their own and to each other's development by cooperating in all spheres and coordinating their plans and policies.

The present publication elaborately deals with the vast globally important subject of rural development in South Asian backgrounds. It includes the basic concepts, paradigms, policies, management and latest details about the subject in this region. It is an excellent discourse on South Asian rural development and is valuable to policy makers, researchers, scholars, students, and those who are involved in developmental activities.

Jitendra Kumar Sharma

Contents

1

Introduction

The seven SAARC nations accounts for nearly 1.2 billion people or one-fifth of the world's population. They share a common ecosystem and, except for Bhutan and Nepal, a common history of colonial rule. They also share a major burden, in the form of mass poverty, which saps their creativity and strength and hides the positive aspects of their civilisation. They share common roots in an ancient civilisation that has brought together various religions and been able to maintain its uniqueness and civilisation rhythm through the millennia, even while adapting to accommodate new values, new technologies, new forms of economic production and new social organisation.

In December 1991, at the SAARC summit in Colombo, the heads of states of South Asian regional grouping established an independent South Asian commission on poverty alleviation to look into the development options for South Asia, in the context of the staggering numbers of 440 million persons below the poverty line, nearly half a century after mainstream 'development' was initiated and in the context of its current opening up to the global economic system. The commission members submitted a unanimous report to the heads of states at their next SAARC summit. On the basis of the analysis and recommendations in the report, the heads of states reached a consensus on poverty eradication in South Asia by the year 2002. This chapter will attempt to elaborate upon some of the elements used in the report of Independent South Asian Commission on Poverty Alleviation.

The development strategies pursued by South Asian governments have for the most part failed to make a significant dent in the problem of poverty, mainly because they have tended to underestimate the complexity and magnitude of the problem. Similarly, the proportion of people below the poverty line declined since 1950. Despite all this, however, the problem of poverty still remains. Even at present a staggering number of nearly 440 million people live in absolute poverty in South Asia. It is simply too large a number for any society to carry. It puts democracy at risk. This "poverty overhang" is not only a problem in its own right, it is also an obstacle in the pursuit of other goals of human development.

The limitations of earlier developmental approaches are now being widely recognised and are leading to the formulation of a new two-pronged pattern of development in all the South Asian countries. The first prong, the conceptual and operational dimensions of which are fairly well understood, is the familiar one of economic liberalisation and structural adjustment which, in the longer term, aims to transform the economy into an export-oriented, internationally competitive one. The second prong, which is still mired in doubt and confusion, is that of poverty alleviation. In view of this situation what is needed is to give unambiguous attention and priority to poverty alleviation. It was in recognition of these concerns that the heads of states or governments of the SAARC countries decided to set up an Independent South Asian Commission on Poverty Alleviation and directed it to examine the causes and consequences of the resilience of poverty in South Asia, to distil the positive lessons from successful and sustainable experiences on the ground, to diagnose what went wrong with past development interventions and to identify critical, concrete and practical elements for a coherent strategy to alleviate poverty. The specific strategic thrust to achieve this result was based on a vigorous pursuit of a two-pronged-approach to development based on an open economy industrialisation strategy for longer term growth, with trickle-down and re-distributive justice; and a coherent pro-poor plan with social mobilisation in the shorter term, where the poor themselves being efficient could contribute to a more human and sustainable pattern of growth, initially at the base of the economy.

These two parallel strategic thrusts would have to be harmonised as the two processes evolved in their different time horizons. This more complex development paradigm was premised, not on *a priori* theorising or ideological orientations or on imitating the north. These "success cases" also showed that where South Asian countries had produced surplus food, pursued decentralised labour-intensive industrialisation vigorously, human development policies, including primary health care and primary education, the poor also benefited.

A pre-condition for this was, however, social mobilisation with real participation of the poor in development and their empowerment. Other critical elements were the non-predatory use of natural resources, financial discipline and the wise use of the various stocks of knowledge that were available to them. This was not a romantic distant dream, but a transitional strategy in the shorter-term which could become sustainable. It would also help avoid unmanageable chaos into which these countries could slide, as well as to buy time until structural adjustments took place in the north.

Solutions to the problem of poverty required a politically directed approach based on the lessons of past experience, taking into account the myriad examples of successful grassroots initiatives, as well as the proven macro-level successes and noting the failure of the overall pattern of development to make an adequate impact on the problem, the commission recognised that poverty eradication is a deeply political objective which cannot be achieved through purely technocratic means.

More specifically, a basic premise that has emerged from the analysis is that the major reason why the poor have been unable to overcome their condition of poverty is not so much the lack of initiative or knowledge on their part but rather the existence of institutionalised obstacles to effective action. The systemic obstacles requires both releasing the creative energies of the poor themselves as well as a lead role for the state. Sensitive support would need to be provided by a number of other factors as the process evolved. It is a fact that "the poor are efficient" in South Asia, not only in their ability to survive against insurmountable odds but also in their ability to contribute to growth through their creativity and strength.

Growth, human development and greater equity can be achieved in the same process. Therefore, the commission decided to focus its attention on ways and means of removing the institutional obstacles to collective action towards this objective. The strategic thrust for poverty eradication in the shorter-term, presented in the report however, would need to be harmonised, in a step-by-step manner, with the longer-term strategy of an open economy-industrialisation approach, as both of these clearly identified prongs in a new overall pattern of development evolve and mature in the South Asian context.

The harmonisation of these two prongs within a new overall pattern of development can be reinforced by economic cooperation among South Asian countries, leading to the building of a viable one billion strong South Asian mass market and a South Asian community.

The problems of poverty are further aggravated by various other social deprivations and discriminations from whicl. the poor suffer as well as by the spatial inaccessibility of outlying, remote and distant terrain which prevent the delivery of social goods and services. The structural adjustment policies, which accompany the open-economy-industrialisation strategy currently being adopted by most SAARC countries, are likely in the shorter-term, to put further strains on the poor.

South Asia has achieved an average growth rate of 3.1 per cent over the past ten years while several other regions in the south have had negative growth, such growth has failed to "trickle down" or be administratively redistributed to the poor, except in a limited manner. The magnitude of poverty remains, unacceptably high. Excessive dependence on the state for every lead in development curtailed the initiatives of the people. Obsessive preoccupation with capital accumulation, as the driving force in economic progress, resulted in neglecting the capacity of the poor themselves. Concentration on industrialisation/modernisation, as the dominant paradigm of development, created dualities in the system and wide gaps between rural and urban levels of living as well as further polarisation within these areas.

The poor, wherever they lived, faced the worst consequences of these processes. In making an overall assessment of the results of the adaptations made to conventional development wisdom by South Asian countries, however, there is evidence of a positive side, albeit a limited one, as far as the poor are concerned. For the last few years, all the countries in South Asia have been tentatively attempting to adapt their overall development plans to ensure that social polarisation and poverty reproduction are not exacerbated as their economies are liberalised and adjusted in pursuit of the open-economy industrialisation strategy. Some are attempting to further decentralise the process of development decision making, some are placing greater emphasis on social development, and still others are attempting to further increase the delivery of inputs to the poor more efficiently, streamline the administrative redistribution machinery and food systems, and introduce safety nets. A few have recently begun to initiate new bolder programmes of social mobilisation, which fall broadly within a new pattern of development, that enable the poor to contribute to growth and human development and also assert the right to resources intended for them. However, mere continuation of the conventional development pattern with marginal variations, greater efficiency in achieving these limited gains and ad hoc consultation with the poor in the name of participation would not be adequate to reverse the process of poverty reproduction.

The "trickle down" from the open economy strategy and structural adjustment with a human face policy couple with welfare programmes, a few fragmented safety nets and pro-poor projects are inadequate to respond to the poverty problem. The sheer magnitude and complexity of the task should not be underestimated. The eradication of poverty in South Asia would require a major political approach and a great deal of innovation based on the new lessons on the ground.

A sufficient body of new experience has matured at the micro-level in the South Asian countries which demonstrates that the poor participate as subjects and not as objects of the development process. An indepth analysis made of the hundreds of participatory processes on the ground confirm that the poor have contributed to growth and human development simultaneously under varying socio-political circumstances. They also demonstrate that, an relatively lower levels of income, it is possible for the poor to achieve a high level of human development. These experiences provide a material basis for the assertion that a qualitatively and quantitatively significant new element can be added to the strategic options for poverty eradication in South Asia.

The few success cases that have been presented in the report are merely illustrative of how poverty is being alleviated, savings and investment are being increased, assets are being created cost effectively. There is also evidence that where this process is supported sensitively with adequate resources and mechanisms, the process can be expanded cost effectively. A closer look into the experiences on the ground points to a number of common and specific lessons on what has been achieved through social mobilisation and participation of the poor in development. The limited positive results at the macro-level and the lessons from the ground have been combined to provide the new premises for action for a strategy of eradication of the worst forms of poverty within a given timeframe, leaving only a residual member to be carried by welfare and social safety nets, until they also can be brought into the mainstream. The perspective which should inform these new premises for action should be unambiguously pro-poor and culturally relevant. The new premises for action is a pattern of development which initially moves on two equally strong fronts, i.e., the open-economy industrialisation front and the poverty eradication front. These two parallel strategic thrusts, having longer and shorter term timeframes, can be harmonised as the two processes evolve.

The Report has concentrated on articulating the new premises that should inform the poverty eradication front. They are:

1) Poverty can be eradicated in South Asia by the year 2002, i.e., within a ten-year time frame, leaving only a residual number of poor who would need social welfare programmes. This latter category can be kept within manageable limits and be carried by society until they, too, can become part of the mainstream of development in wider human terms. This would involve a doubling of GDP per capita during this ten-year plan from the current US$ 300 to US$ 600 per capita (given a projected population growth rate of 1.8 per cent). This means a GDP growth rate of nine per cent per annum for the region. This growth rate of nine per cent is an ambitious target, but achievable. It can build upon the growth rate of three point one per cent in the 1980s which was achieved under very adverse conditions. Each SAARC country can phase its indicative planning targets according to its own potential. The major countries in South Asia and the world bank are claiming that the open economy can produce a growth rate of five to six per cent in the formal sectors. The poverty commission implied that two to three per cent growth was possible in the informal sector through vigorous social mobilisation and organisations of the poor. Then an overall growth rate of nine per cent need not be an impossible target.

2) Such an increase will have to be produced by a different pattern of development recommended by the poverty commission which requires an explicit sustained political commitment of the leadership and the participation of the poor in development. Such political commitment would have to focus on the two conventional targets of growth policy: lowering the incremental capital-output ratio from 4:1 to 3:1 or less

and increasing the marginal saving rates from the current levels to 27 per cent or more. Such a large shift would also require the involvement and participation of the poor through their own institutions and mobilisation of their own savings and that of the non-poor. Lowering of the capital-output ratio would involve a growth strategy based on labour- intensive development, with high productivity and human development. It would also require a new approach to food production, food security and rural development.

South Asian countries have little choice but to use labour, the factor in surplus.

The investment activity of the poor is effected mainly not in the form of monetary instruments but as asset creation by transforming labour into capital. Combined with proper organisation, it can help unleash new forces leading to efficient asset creation. The "sharing and caring" characteristics of the poor in South Asia and the values of "simplicity and frugality" can reinforce such an effort. Thus, in addition to the conventional accumulation process by the state and the private sector, there is a compulsion for a new accumulation process. All this requires a major effort at social mobilisation leading to the release of the creative energies of the poor and the building of their organisations. The new pattern of development must incorporate the following specific means of action:

3) Most of the poor in South Asia live in rural areas and depend directly or indirectly on agriculture; food security is an important component, not only of survival but also of the basic dignity and well-being of the poor. Thus a foremost element of the development pattern is to give a new priority to agriculture with emphasis on food production and a household food security programme. Where there is surplus food, its equitable distribution would also have to be ensured. This should be part of the new structural adjustment policy.

4) The designing of a strategy for small-scale, labour-intensive industrialisation for which South Asia has a

comparative advantage, forms a second element. This strategy would absorb the unemployed and underemployed poor, including youth, into productive activities. Labour-intensive industrialisation is a function of the product mix, technology choice, scale of activity, plant size and supporting institutions. New concepts of "work sharing", culturally relevant ways of "combining work and leisure", "employee management during privatisation" should deal with the transitional employment strategy in the harmonisation process.

5) An essential prerequisite of the poverty eradication strategy is human development which guarantees the right of the poor to participate in decisions that affect their lives, the right to food as a basic human right, the right to work and the right to all information services. Literacy, primary education, health, shelter and protection of children have also been included in this list of priorities. Defining and promoting the role and status of women in society and ensuring the full participation of all strata and groups in development decision making is necessary to make human development holistic. The ultimate objective of economic growth is to bring a higher level of human development within the reach of the poor and thus to expand the range of their choices. In this way development itself is made more participatory and equitable, where growth and human development need not be trade-offs.

Since they have different timeframes, this harmonisation could take place as the two processes unfold. South Asian regional cooperation to create a one billion strong market and a South Asian community can further reinforce the harmonisation process. The initial South Asian community will have to be characterised by austerity and simplicity of lifestyles, food security through the emphasis on food production and equitable distribution, and use of balance of payments surplus to expand the productivity base of the economy for sustainable human development.

In South Asia, again in imitating the Western paradigm of development, an attempt was made by the state to cushion the effect of the inadequate pattern of development on the poor, with various welfare elements. This took the form of direct subsidies to the poor or the "delivery" of various inputs such as primary health care and primary education. A strong initial trade union movement in some countries also helped to guarantee minimum wages and fringe benefits to organised labour. However, as in Western industrialised countries these paternalistic attempts at redistributive justice could not be sustained.

For poor countries in South Asia where the gap between the rich and the poor had widened to unmanageable proportions and the numbers of the poor had enlarged this kind of welfarism, a few subsidies and social safety nets were no longer the answer. A new social contract needed to be forged between the state and the poor. The report of the Independent South Asian Commission identified several elements in this social contract. The reported endorsement of the report and its recommendations by the heads of states in their historic "consensus on poverty eradication" at their summit in 1993 and again in 1995, initiated the political commitment and provided the political space for developing this social contract.

The elements in the new social contract which have emerged and need to be developed further are:

1) First, pro-poor values need to inform the pattern of development fundamental to South Asian cultures is the value of sharing and caring, where the benefits of development must be more equitably shared. This value is not merely the result of compassion. From the lessons on the ground, it is also evident that the poor are efficient. The efficiency permits them to initialise resources to which they are entitled to rationally. Hence, they must have access to resources. Where asset distribution has been shown as a result of past patterns, then asset redistribution also becomes part of the social contract. The efficiency of the poor is also demonstrated by the evidence on the ground that shows that when socially mobilised, they save, innovate, contribute to growth, create assets and set in motion a sustainable accumulation process at the base of the

economy. This accumulation process is accompanied by human development coupled with the release of their creative energies and together the two processes lead to greater equity and dignity.

2) Secondly, the new social contract needs to focus on the rights of the poor. These basic rights have been identified in the poverty commission report. They are:
   a) the right to participate as subjects and not as objects of development.
   b) the right to food, which can be guaranteed in a region which has food surpluses the right to work, with the right mix of work and leisure and the dignity that comes from creative and productive work.

Several other fundamental rights were also mentioned in the report such as the right to information, the right to health, education, and shelter.

The concerted efforts of the member states of SAARC towards eradication of poverty, institutional restructuring, agro-based reform will surely have impact on the standards of living in all member states. As we celebrate the first decade of SAARC, we are mindful of both the achievements and the impediments that prevent an acceleration in regional cooperation. We share the sense of frustration in some member states on the seemingly slow pace of development in some sectors. At the same time we realise that solid achievements can only be built on solid foundations.

India, as the largest country in South Asia, along with its preponderance, bears a special responsibility to move forward in the direction of normalisation through constructive action. This cannot be done by heightening tensions through military build-up, massive military deployments in disputed areas, or a feverish indigenous development of missiles and nuclear technology. Such aggressive attributes can only serve to heighten the threat perceptions of smaller states and place at risk the peace and security of the region.

The South Asian region has the potential of becoming the most vibrant region in the world, given its enormous resources in manpower, technology, agricultural and mineral assets, its history and civilisation, arts and culture. Intra-regional exchanges in the SAARC framework and trade among its member states can unleash much of this potential. Coordinated and concerted effort in international fora can lend a significant voice to the 1.4 billion people of the region.

The leaders of the nations of South Asia, as well as their privileged classes, will have to demonstrate a far-sighted statesmanship, indeed an attachment to the vision. Leaders will have to overcome historical inhibitions and stretch out their hands to each other to find meaningful and substantive solutions to bilateral and international disputes. We, in Pakistan, are waiting anxiously for a commensurate response to our many overtures from India, as our neighbour and as a partner in SAARC, to move out of the morass of security and political related entanglements which complicate our relations.

The challenge to the intellectual community in South Asia, ten years into SAARC, is to develop the elements in the "new social contract" further, using the political space created by the commitment of the heads of states. The "social contract" is not purely a legal matter, but mainly a political commitment which needs to be followed up intellectually and operationally.

2

Regional Planning in South Asia

More than 450 million people live in absolute poverty, nearly 400 million adults are illiterate, more than 250 million people do not have access to safe drinking water; so there, poverty is naturally the strongest of the shared concerns. It was at the Sixth SAARC Summit on December 21, 1991 at Colombo that the heads of states/governments decided to establish an Independent South Asian Commission on Poverty Alleviation consisting of eminent persons from each SAARC member state to conduct an indepth study of diverse experiences of the seven countries on poverty alleviation, and to report to the seventh summit, their recommendations on the alleviation of poverty in South Asia. The heads of states/governments welcomed the report, and committed their governments unequivocally to the eradication of poverty in South Asia, preferably by the year A.D. 2002 through an agenda of action which would, *inter-alia*, embody:

a) A strategy of social mobilisation involving the building of organisations of the poor and their empowerment through appropriate national support mechanisms, with the assistance of respective governments;

b) A policy of decentralised agricultural development and sharply focused household level food security through universal provision of 'Daal-Bhat' or basic nutritional needs;

c) A policy of decentralised small scale labour-intensive industrialisation with the choice of efficient and cost-effective technology;

d) A policy of human development, including the enhancement of the social role and status of poor women, the provision of universal primary education, skill development, primary health care, shelter for the poor and protection of children;

e) A policy to support the above initiatives with adequate financial resources.

The first meeting of finance/planning ministers took place at Dhaka in July 1994. The ministers reviewed the trends in the global economic situation and the economic situation in the South Asian countries, including the impact on the region of the emergence of regional trading blocks around the world. The ministers emphasised the need for policy convergence among developed economies for sustained and stable global economic growth. Recognising the unique opportunity provided by SAARC for sharing country experiences in poverty alleviation, they agreed that steps should be taken to bring about a closer interface between government agencies, NGOs and community organisations engaged in poverty alleviation so as to bring about convergence in action at all levels, particularly at the grass-roots levels.

The ministers decided to set up a mechanism which would act as a forum for exchange of information of experiences of SAARC countries in the implementation of poverty alleviation programmes, in the context of strategies adopted. This mechanism would be in the form of a three-tier institutional structure that would meet once a year. These three tiers would be:

a) the group of secretaries to the governments in the ministries/departments that are essentially concerned with poverty alleviation and social development;

b) the finance and planning secretaries of the SAARC countries; and

c) the finance and planning ministers of the SAARC countries.

The 'eighth SAARC Summit (New Delhi, May 1995) endorsed the recommendations of the finance/planning ministers' meeting which recommended the three-tier mechanism.

Thus, there is already a commitment among the nations of South Asia to work together towards the goal of poverty eradication by the year A.D. 2002 and a mechanism for coordination, exchange and cooperation already exists.

The need is to evolve a comprehensive South Asian perspective on development which is based on shared concerns and which reflects common aspirations. Cooperation on marching towards those goals will make a positive contribution to the speed with which the goals would be achieved by enhancing the ability of each of the member states to achieve those goals.

The poverty situation in the region, since then, does not seem to have improved much. Most probably in percentage terms, it has remained more or less the same. Given the regional population of about 1,200 million at present, well above 450 million persons of this region, are living below an absolute poverty line. Of these, over 250 million do not have access of safe drinking water. The average daily calorie supply per capita at about 2,300 in the region is much lower than the average for all developing countries.

Human development indicators in the region, except for Sri Lanka and the Maldives, are very low, and the worst is the situation in respect of literacy. There are selected human development indicators for countries in the region as well as some East and South-East asian countries. The gap in respect of adult literacy and education index between South Asia (excluding Sri Lanka and the Maldives in this respect) and the other Asian countries listed is very wide. Even a relatively low income-slow growing country like the Philippines has 94 per cent adult literacy. While poverty may be the cause of many other deprivations, low educational performance in South Asia may not be entirely due to poverty. It is clear that the development perspective for the region has to be strongly anchored in the goals of poverty eradication and human development. The imperatives of such a development strategy are:

a) high growth rate,

b) adequate employment generation with at least a certain minimum level of productivity and income,

c) adequate food availability,

d) large investments in education to achieve a minimum necessary level of educational attainment with a target period,

e) removing severe deprivations in respect of access to health, services, safe drinking water, minimum nutritional levels and shelter, within a timebound frame, and

f) developing institutions to bring about participatory development and empowerment of the poor.

Low level of income is a significant factor in poverty, even though the income distribution at low levels of income may be somewhat better. For example, let us compare India and China. China has the lowest per capital income among the five non-South Asian countries. India had a better income distribution than China in 1993. And yet the per capita GNP for the poorest 20 per cent of population in China was $746 as against $537 for India, a difference of 1.4 times which can make a significant difference in the levels of living of the poorer sections of population.

Thailand with its very high level of per capita income, and a high growth rate also shows a much more adverse income distribution. Yet in Thailand the per capita income of the poorest 20 per cent of the population in 1993 was PPP-adjusted dollar 1909, much higher than the average per capita income of the South Asia region. Report of the Independent South Asian Commission on Poverty Alleviation had projected a growth rate of nine per cent of the region, and on this basis had shown a large resource gap. Nothing much has happened in the recent past to encourage the view that nine per cent growth is attainable in the near future.

Since historically the incremental capital output ratios (ICORS) have been quite different in different countries of the region, even after moderation they are bound to remain different in different countries. It can be seen that investment requirements vary from 21 per cent of GDP is Bangladesh to 35 per cent of GDP is Sri Lanka. The resource gap varies from 5.4 per cent for India to 19 per cent for Sri Lanka. The most outstanding feature of the

South-East Asian economies and China's is a very high domestic savings rate.

The savings rates in 1993 were 40 per cent in China, 38 per cent in Malaysia, 36 per cent in Thailand and 31 per cent in Indonesia. These economies have been saving and investing at high rates for a long time. Economic reforms and structural adjustments are necessary for enhancing the domestic rates of savings and reducing the incremental capital output ratio.

Strengthening the functioning of various markets, particularly the markets in land and property, and making entry for business and entrepreneurs wide open and easy would encourage investment and provide a stimulus to further savings. Regional economic cooperation has a special role to play in this context for it would enhance the volume of trade and augment the production possibility frontier in each of the participating countries. The development experience of East and South-East Asia also has this lesson to offer that the objectives of high growth and poverty eradication are not conflicting but complementary and mutually reinforcing objectives.

The process of poverty alleviation and employment generation is also the process which spreads purchasing power widely and deeply, expands the markets and creates new opportunities for growth. Agricultural growth, in most successful economies, has provided a strong basis for further development, and rise in agricultural productivity has an immediate impact on poverty alleviation. However, in choosing the pattern of growth, employment generating potential of various industries has to be a prime consideration. The community of South Asian states have much to contribute to each other's development by cooperating in all the economic spheres and coordinating their plans and policies.

WOMEN AND DEVELOPMENT

Efforts to prepare reports on women's status, by either official or purely academic groups, had to confront the problem of invisibility of women's economic roles—in planning, economics/social science analysis, and in data systems. The order rested on three major foundations:

a) a rank order linked to occupational status and other qualities of groups (communities), rather than individuals;
b) careful preservation of distance/differences between diverse groups through controls over intermixing, marriages and acknowledgement of offsprings; and
c) subtle and sophisticated institutions to control and appropriate women's freedoms, sexuality and labour, designed and maintained successfully by the three most significant social organisations—the community (caste, clan, tribe, kinship, religions, sects, linguistic groups, etc.)—reflecting its position in the rank order; the family whose sense of belonging (identity) to a particular community, and the need for its support in times of needs or distress (security) required obeisance to the community's norms; and the state—through its gradual evolution within the region.

These institutionalised methods of control and subordination of women, currently referred to by women's studies scholars as structures of patriarchy, were, and are still, essential to the maintenance and continuity of the hierarchy. The forms of control or appropriation have kept changing over generations, but the dependence of the other two systems of social organisation on these partriarchal structures has remained basic to the social system as a whole. Colonialism and the entry of various forms of modernisation—in the economy, society and ideology through the new Western model education—did little to change these basic structural relationships.

The subcontinent has a long history of radical social movements which challenged the hierarchic and divisive, exclusive order. The medieval movements which cut across the religious and community divide, with messages of human equality, basic unity of all faiths and a firm position against violence, threw up the maximum number of women leaders—Hindus and Muslims—whose lyrics made the deepest impact on popular culture, and continue as part of the rich oral traditions of the region.

The power of the hierarchy, however, being stronger, latter day chroniclers successfully projected them as religious movements only, making even modern historians ignore the social content of this tradition. Political imperatives of the anti-colonial nationalist struggles on the other hand, had to oppose in principle, at least, all the three pillars of the inherited social order. Unity is also clear in the choice of alternative strategies for development, in the selection of key areas for organising and advocacy, and the increasing emphasis, even dependence on poor women at the grassroots level as the most powerful force and agency in breaking the hardened mould of the hierarchy-partriarchy combine that continues to dominate the social system.

Women and development studies had far-reaching consequences. They lead to:

a) discovery of rural and urban poor women's strengths, values and vulnerability (considerably different from the elite groups), and

b) questioning of the knowledge/education systems for their contribution to this invisibility.

c) researchers joined critics of development models of their advocates.

The latter, having marginalised and impoverished this majority through devaluation and appropriation of their labour, were ready to speak of 'integrating' them into the same mainstream.

Organising was necessary to challenge these establishments, and sharing of experiences was crucial. Regional cooperation in women's studies and development action has been a far greater reality than the cooperation officially committed by successive SAARC summits.

The targetting of the education system yielded some success in India by 1986, when the National Policy on Education committed the National Education System "to play a positive, interventionist role in the empowerment of women", and women's studies were accepted as legitimate area for research, teaching, curriculum development and community action. Shortly thereafter, Pakistan held its first workshop to examine possibilities for introducing women's studies at the school level.

The national literacy mission reports that 75-80 per cent of learners and a clear majority of teachers and mobilisers are women, and that women's response has been one of the most 'significant' outcomes of the campaigns. Regretting that despite this "signal success", gender bias continues in curriculum and campaign materials and within the organisations formed for the campaigns, the group makes various recommendations to ensure the participation and leadership role of women, especially of grassroots organisations in future phases of the programme. The group sees in the increased interaction between the non-literates, neo-literates and formal educational institutions some hope of ultimate reform of the educational process as a whole.

In South Asia, however, the discovery of peasant women's distinctly different attitude on environmental issues, compared to men from their own class began much earlier. Newly formed groups of poor peasant women, searching desperately for a secure livelihood and preservation of their life-support systems, initiated many ventures on wasteland regeneration, and mounted struggles against loss of community property resources (CPRs) in different parts of the region. An initiative to bring peasant women's groups together—to articulate their own perspectives on environmental degradation—through four summits in India, Nepal, Bangladesh and Pakistan—followed by a joint one in Lahore (February 1992) produced extraordinary results. In the dialogues with policy makers, the intermediaries took a backseat, and policy makers found themselves having to explain and justify their mismanagement of the natural environment to extremely peasant knowledgeable and angry women. Some of these voices did make an impact on a few sensitive ones among "the great men", as indicated in some clauses of Agenda 21, or the report of a UNICEF-UNCED-UNFPA symposium that preceded the Rio conference. Three most significant arguments of this symposium were:

a) Failure to recognise and draw upon the skills, views, experiences and indigenous knowledge of women as managers and stakeholders of natural resources would affect sustainability adversely;

b) Women's disenfranchisement rather than their fertility is the primary cause of environmental degradation, and

c) Technology/knowledge transfer should be a two-way process and should not contribute to further marginalisation of women's accumulated knowledge.

The South Asian summits on the other hand, emphasised the specificity of peasant women's experiences, functional specialisation and knowledge, thus avoiding an essentialist, biological view. All women are not environment conservers, especially with increasing urbanisation and consumption styles. Nor are all men or all science, destroyers of nature. South Asia's peasant women do not reject science or new knowledge. They only want a responsible and legitimate partnership, on terms of equality, with scientists and other learned and powerful persons.

The summits also demonstrated that 'as the largest group directly connected' with the environment-development matrix, peasant women can identify themselves with their counterparts anywhere, any place. Language, religion or national boundaries become irrelevant, because their problems, expertise, perspectives and aspirations are the same. "It is no longer adequate to talk about empowerment in general terms nor can the prerogative to define such empowerment be taken by any other group".

The politics of language is already active in South Asia. Most languages have gender-based terms for the traditional occupations i.e., fishing, dairying, weaving, etc. The inexplicable disappearance of the feminine term for peasant is one indicator. The other is the disappearance of customary use rights to productive resources of women among many of the peasant communities, including the tribals, in practice and in language.

During the two intervening decades, the focus had shifted increasingly from women's reproductive to productive and social participatory roles, beyond their familial and communal identity. It was a continuous struggle to persuade demographer and policy makers to look for non-demographic determinants of fertility, mortality, or migration within the socio-economic and value system, the historic shifts in women's productive roles and their valuation, and the negative impact of macro-economic policies on women's economic status.

In South Asia, Sri Lanka and Kerala were held up as examples where demographic transition had taken place, because of attention to such non-demographic factors—food security, land reform, education, public health and widening of women's independent opportunities. A thrust on collective organisations of women at the grassroots level, in rural and urban areas especially, within the informal sector, with acknowledgement of their entitlement to basic productive resources, training and credit, developed by three Indian planning groups received support from virtually all delegates to the NAM conference on women and development.

The programme of action of the mid-decade conference incorporated these ideas, as potential instruments for collective empowerment of women—to strengthen their assertive power in decision making at all levels—the family, the society and the polity. The organisations would also enable them to reach for services that they needed and wanted, including family planning, without the permission of the family or the community. Availability and quality of the services, were crucial. This umbrella approach reflected the knowledge that women did not require either propaganda or coercion for fertility control. Despite their subordination and bans propagated by all organised religions, women down the ages have tried to practise contraception and abortion, drawing on indigenous knowledge and services of traditional midwives and older women. The South Asian experience proves that formalisation of medicine and health services has destroyed the livelihood and much of the stored knowledge of these women practitioners, without ensuring women's access to formal services of any quality.

Legalisation of abortion in India or 'menstrual regulation' in Bangladesh has not reduced the scale of abortions performed outside the formal sector. What it has done however is to destroy the ethical content of the medical profession and medical education, rationalising commercialised anti-women practices like sex-specific abortions after sex-determination tests—as a patriotic duty.

On the other hand, alternative models of primary health care developed by South Asian doctors rebelling against the official model have great value in using semi- or non-literate rural women as 'frontline health workers'. Four decades of population control propaganda/policy has not promoted any serious measures to spread the scientific knowledge about what determines the sex of the unborn child, nor to convert the predominant son-preference, or to convince the majority of men regarding their responsibility for family limitation.

With the exception of a brief period during the national emergency in India the burden of population control by state policy in South Asia has been forced on women. And the instruments for fulfilling timebound targets, in sterilisation or implanting long acting, hazardous hormonal contraceptives are:

a) either the inadequate public health services, whose health functions and capacities have been steadily eroded by low budgets, over large jurisdictions, and the continuous pressure to utilise all personnel and energy to meet population control targets; or

b) the completely commercialised private sector of the medical profession for whom the new reproductive technologies, specially for sex determination or selection have proved to be money-spinners.

Twenty years before the Cairo meet the Committee on the Status of Women in India, while upholding the right to seek abortion as a woman's right to voluntary maternity, had clearly spelt out the dangers of using it as an instrument of population control, after listening to many senior medical educationists. At that time religious fundamentalism was not a serious problem in South Asia or elsewhere. In the context of the nineties, with women's rights under threat from such movements throughout the world, seeking an international mandate for abortion rights through the UN was politically unrealistic and futile.

During the last decade, however, the movement has had to confront the growing scale of political, ethnic or communal violence, raising serious questions regarding the movement's own capacity to deal with the problem. Social conflicts affect women on both sides, as powerless/passive victims, or as active participants. Feminism has still to probe adequately the layers and roots of consciousness that enmesh the individual woman's relations with her conjugal and natal families, and the class and generational variations in women's innate sense of dignity and degradation, or humiliation and a sense of moral worth.

Objectively, the spread of alcoholism, drug abuse and globalisation of the cult of violence and consumerism—actively promoted by the visual media—have loosened some cultural norms without replacing them by alternative ones, and provide a backdrop for increasing incidence of reported cases of domestic violence, frequently associated with dowry, but not confined to it.

Laws have been amended; some new mechanisms have been created—like crimes against women cells within police headquarters in some of the metropolitan cities—but the graph keeps going up; very few investigations end in conviction; and the role of the law enforcing agencies is increasingly doubted.

Brutalisation and corruption of the police have other causes—which make them a questionable ally for women victims of violence. One positive outcome is increased knowledge of law among women activists and the pressure that women's organisations are able to exert on the legal machinery.

In metropolitan cities, however, such interventions are most often *post facto*; follow up capacity is weak, and preventive and rehabilitative measures still weaker. Legal literacy among grassroots organisations of women in rural areas appear to produce more empowering effect on the women, enabling them to intervene more quickly and obtain some community support to ensure some rough and ready justice.

The credibility of governments has been greatly weakened by their inability to enforce laws, to prevent social and political tensions from escalating into violence, and the rolling back of welfare functions with increasing loss of economic sovereignty. The widening gap between governments and their people has been filled to some extent by NGOs. But not all of them are people-centred. Some are frankly extensions of the tertiary sector coming up during a period of economic stagnation and rising educated unemployment. Many are creations of fundamentalist, specific community oriented groups/parties/donors, whose real objectives are to win the poor and women to support the particular brand of ideology or politics they represent.

Some are undoubtedly humanitarian in outlook but do not necessarily share the ideology of collective empowerment of the people or women in particular. Their perpetual dependence on governments or external donors for funding does not always promote real autonomy or commitment to participatory development, and their accountability is often questioned. Despite these handicaps, the contribution of these development action groups remains one of most positive features of contemporary politics of South Asia. In India, Bangladesh and Sri Lanka they have enjoyed greater legal protection. In Nepal it is only since the restoration of democracy that such groups have been able to form and operate openly. In Pakistan their emergence in the face of active hostility and even persecution from the clergy, and the state has called for great courage and sacrifice, of which all South Asian women are proud.

Decentralisation of power and authority, development planning and responsibility and management of resources is the great buzzword, with widely varying interpretations. Two recent constitutional amendments in India make regularly elected local self-government bodies constitutionally mandatory. For the first time, one-third of seats in all these bodies are mandatorily reserved for women. While many in power, including state governments who have to enact specific laws to obey the constitutional mandate, would like to view these bodies as 'agencies for development', a growing opinion views them as the founding tier of democracy in India.

A coalition of the newly elected women representatives and grassroots organisations of poor women, legitimised, even supported by a quota within the anti-poverty programmes and the efforts of development activists, can create a force, that Mahatma Gandhi had dreamt of—"when women begin to affect the political deliberations of the nation". This is an issue on which South Asian experience led many of us to question "the head-counting approach" of Western feminists of trying to place women at the highest levels of governance. This region had thrown up some of the most powerful women rulers in the world. We have taken pride in their successful defence of national sovereignty and leadership role in defending third world interests in global fora.

Nor could they even begin the task of eliminating the subordination of women in the masses. If the South Asian women's movement needs a political figure as a symbol, it is more likely to be Aung San Suu Kyi, rather than the galaxy of women rulers that the region has produced. Unfortunately, the human development report has drawn its gender empowerment index from the state—ideas of women's movements which are weakening through co-optation and other reasons—and economists who do not really understand the logic of movement politics, however eminent or sensitive they are.

Women and children—girls and boys—were, and are the worst affected victims of these processes. The unequal power dynamics behind the economic processes that marginalised so many, reduced the common economic argument of "sacrificing for the future" to a mockery. What was happening was "sacrificing the future". The political economies within which women had struggled for equality had been "given". There were gaps between laws on paper and social reality, but there was space for struggle.

Individual women had challenged these gaps, only to discover that "solutions at the individual level were not of such use, even in one's lifetime." "The dynamics of consequences" made the emotional price too high. Individual liberation loses its gloss when women find "they have lost their freedom to rear their children". A search for collective solutions required understanding of the changing scenario, the new and hidden factors, their stakes in the power games being played, from the global to the grassroots levels, as well as ideological and conceptual clarity.

Some protested against frequent changes of 'jargon', especially by donor agencies and academe, making the tasks of grassroots activists difficult. Such conceptual changes (from 'women' to 'gender') did not reflect the priorities' concerns of women at the grassroots and their diversity by class, race, culture or migrant status, with increasing mobility of people within and across national boundaries. On the other hand, the increasing trend to professionalise 'gender-training' could be interpreted as an instrument to retain ideological control by the north, or as an effort to depoliticise the women's movement.

"Development is neither an issue for the south alone, nor an economic issue alone". How could any country/region claim a monopoly of humanist or feminist traditions, when most cultures had long histories of such traditions? Should people with histories of struggles against imperialism or racism be considered less developed than those who commanded more wealth? Some grassroots activists questioned the value of formal education or urbanisation.

Poor rural women were far more keen to seek strategies for change collectively. Some questioned the north's professed commitment to democracy or gender equality, when women's struggles to intervene in the political process in an organised manner were cold-shouldered as 'political', while no questions were asked of arms manufacturers or traders.

The academic activists had learnt ways of bridging gaps between disciplines, "the value of interdisciplinary thinking of demystifying social sciences" and the "difference between alternative and mainstream models of development". The "divide between theory and practice", many argued, was outdated and needed to be buried. Exposure to struggles at the grassroots and sensitivity to recognise even unlettered people theorising on the basis of their experience could help to reduce "the arrogance of learning", and encourage moving towards a different "language of discourse".

In South Asia, SAP was reinforcing existing forms of patriarchy. Increasing impoverishment of rural women who depend on land, forest and other natural resources for their livelihood affected their capacity to support their families, increased their vulnerability to domestic and social exploitation and precipitated breakdown of families. Views of certain analysts that Bangladeshi women had improved their economic conditions and life options by coming 'out' to work in factories ignored the 'atrocious, exploitative conditions' under which most such women had to work and their own views. "On whose terms are they better off? Not their own!" The group found the last question "funny", and ignored it. As a general strategy, it advocated mass action with a minimum agenda which could unite women without being affected by differences of class, community, etc.

"Resistance is difficult to operationalise, but time is very little". It is possible to begin at the micro-level and do "consensus-building" round issues, to promote mobilisation of grassroots groups, and a minimum agenda. In India, the inception of the new economic policy made people ask questions and start building data sets to work towards a minimum agenda. The fourth group decided to discuss issue by issue. Identifying TNCs 'as the fundamental aspect of globalisation', the group noted that their (TNCs) positive contributions were some new employment opportunities for women and improved personal hygiene for them.

The negative list included wage exploitation instability "increasing employment in one place means decrease elsewhere"—so some are bound to suffer. The social implications of large scale female migration invariably included increase in prostitution, sexual harassment and exploitation. All these are likely to increase with promotion of sex-tourism with higher risks of HIV infection and shortening of women's lives. Some types of technology transfer, e.g., contraceptives could improve women's choices, but the possibility of abuse enhanced their inappropriateness.

Profit-driven TNCs ignored such social contexts. On the potential role of TV and general media, the group felt that they could contribute to cross-fertilisation of ideas. However, their role in educational programme had often helped to reinforce stereotypes. Their use in selling products had promoted both consumerism and "alienation from people's own cultures".

The group found itself divided on the overall assessment of globalisation from a gender perspective. The last question, on the value of encroachments on national sovereignty was considered 'difficult'. There was a feeling that human rights law could benefit women, but the group had not been able to come to any conclusion about its implications or operationalisation. The discussion following the presentation of group reports revealed the depth of the identity dilemma that women face in defining their relationship with the state and their roles as citizens. There was little doubt that most governments, left to themselves, betray women's claims for justice and equality. But "romanticism about civil society" was no answer. Differences in approach to strategies indicated another dilemma. Women's oppression, exploitation/subordination stemmed from two sources:

a) inherited social systems, and

b) the global political economy.

How should one choose between a top-down, or imposed approach—say an international alliance, or invoking human rights treaties to achieve wage equality; and a bottom-up participatory approach from the grassroots, which could resolve some of the 'inherited' problems at the local level, using methods of collective bargaining and pressure politics? Would not the latter also strengthen democratic processes within countries? Advocates of strong grassroots organising appeared to be seeking for more effective models of accountability.

The "international architecture" of today's world, recent experiences of "unholy alliances in international fora", or the dominance of the "market-efficiency-reduced role/costs of the state" set of arguments in international development debates had hardly contributed to increasing women's faith in their accountability. Mainstream development models had increasingly emphasised upward accountability systems to the centralised state, to the "international community", to international funding agencies.

Most of these represented too distant, inaccessible figures to struggling women at the grassroots. To many, they symbolised the unknown, but oppressive other. A desire for downward accountability systems, within their reach, and accountable to them was understandable. To some of the participants, such a desire represented a political advance. In the context of globalisation without checks and balances, centralisation of state power could be viewed as a cause of erosion of its capacity to resist external pressures.

The contemporary trend in most countries is for governments to push the costs of 'social reproduction' back to the family, i.e., to women. To some extent, the contemporary anti-state beliefs provide a rationale for the state's retreat from welfare and the responsibilities of redistribution for the "common good". "Children must be seen as a common good"—part of "those things in which people must share to have a sense of society".

Globalisation, economic growth or recession increase these costs. But SAP, or the refusal of the international donor community "to put money into welfare, or develop a welfare policy", indicates their refusal to accept the responsibility of protecting "the common good in the public interest". Would these trends be different if women were represented in larger numbers in political and governmental bodies? The present evidence did not support such a hope. On the other hand, the shift in economic and political thinking against the welfare state took place in the 1970s, when the women's movement in the north was at its peak. Group discussions on these issues brought out even more questions about the character of the state. Was it a coalition of vested interests?

Some people tended to view the government as a "benevolent distributor of resources and setting developing agenda". Others saw it as "inefficient". For whose benefit should governance take place? If women were to be emphasised for the government's attention, which women?

There seemed to be agreement on what was needed. As one group put it: "Social justice and gender concerns add up to the social good, in opposition to vested interests".

The main challenge was to get governments involved in the lives of ordinary citizens, to reverse their top-down policies. It was also necessary to educate people that "they are the government". The other group placed "better quality of life for the majority", as the first priority. There was a consensus on "the need to resist donor models" and on re-educating 'experts'. Strategies suggested included "bridging gaps between women and politics, between local and national levels, between institutions and people"—by women's intervention—"to change power processes and make leaders of women"; legal literacy, and correcting the "anti-politics" discourse, because democracy could not be achieved without politics. Are political structures and processes "alienating" for women?

Why do so many women prefer to be involved in "community action", and share the "anti-politics" feeling? Why do so many people continue to differentiate between "hard" and "soft" politics, when all politics, in reality, is "hard"? "Social rights and entitlements are part of citizenship. Why then are women perceived as supplicants for some benefits when they are trying to assert their rights as citizens?"

"Women's agenda includes both day-to-day life (housing, health, etc.) issues, as also human rights, peace, etc. Why then should political structures be so resistant to them?" One answer was the combination of globalisation with "neo-conservative ideology", which "downplays the role of government in the economy" and distorts government's "notions of what it ought to be doing".

There was general agreement on the need to change political structures. But should this be attempted from the top or the bottom, from inside or outside? How to ensure that women's agendas were adequately representative of the concerns of diverse groups, differentiated by class, race, communities? Donor agencies' perspectives in regard to women have often been dominated by "basic needs". In the early years of the International Women's Decade, the tendency to project the women's issue in third world countries as the first and foremost one of basic needs, had been resisted by women from the third world, who invariably added to needs the "Right to participate". "Right to information" is essential for socio-economic needs and "Right to organise" is essential for life with dignity.

"The rights to life, education and health are essential to translate the rights of the child to reality". But having the rights on paper do not ensure their effectiveness, without citizens' action. Do international conventions, *per se,* impose responsibilities on the state? Opinion on this was divided. Some argued that the act of ratification itself involved the state's responsibility. Others felt that ratification had to be followed up by national legislations. This debate seemed to contain a hidden layer of argument.

National laws would make it possible for citizens to take a government to task for their violation within the country. Absence of such laws would require appealing to authorities/agencies/opinion outside the country, against the country's government, raising the spectre of erosion of national sovereignty. Similarly, the debates on customary vs statutory, or state-initiated rights raised the unresolved issues of culture and identity.

3

Dynamics of Development in India

Development has to be treated as an integral whole and as a cultural process taking note of natural environment, social relations, production, consumption and social well-being of the people. It is the "people" who have to be the main elements of development and it is their preparation and activation that should be the cause and consequence of development. This may suggest that development should spring up from the heart of each society. But the fast moving changes in the world economy during the last two decades or so, are not without significant effects on the development levels of the developing societies.

The world economy has changed from being intentional to transnational which has no political boundaries and impinges significantly upon the domestic economies of the national states. It is the flow of money rather than the trade in goods and services that shapes the transnational economy, and the economic politics of the sovereign national governments react sharply to the situations prevailing in the transnational money and capital markets. It is argued that in the transnational economy, the traditional factors of production, such as land and labour, and even money which is now universally available, have become secondary. Even the foreign exchange rates matter only for a short span of time. It is management now that has become the decisive factor of production.

The organisation and management of the same has been made possible by the information revolution and transnational enterprises. That would mean, newer transnational ecology and development of transnational laws to manage it. Even the recent far-reaching changes observed in the east European societies are indicative that they have failed to tackle their problems inwards and their economic compulsions have forced their national states' political systems to advocate and adopt structural changes encouraging democratic forces to operate in the decision-making processes.

Human needs, self-reliance and organic articulations are the foundations which support human scale department. Further, this strategy assumes a direct and participatory democracy. The basic postulate of human scale development is that development is about people and not about objects. It is considered inaccurate to view human needs as infinite, changing all the time and as different in each culture or environment as no effort is made to distinguish between needs and satisfiers of those needs. Except for the need of subsistence or to remain alive, no hierarchies exist within the system but the process of needs satisfaction is often characterised by simultaneities, complementaries and trade-offs.

The human need structure has been classified along axiological needs such as the needs of subsistence, protection, affection, understanding, participation, idleness, creation, identity and freedom and along existential needs, such as the needs of being, having, doing and interacting. These have been interacted to provide a matrix of needs and satisfiers. It is assumed that the fundamental human needs are the same in all cultures and in all historical periods. The changes observed over time and through cultures relate only to the ways or means by which the needs are satisfied. Unemployment and external debt are the two major problems of the third world nations. It is through a set of satisfiers that the above problems of a given society are taken care of.

The development options should move from the linear to the systemic approach and from efficiency to synergy. In other words, the human need structure and the associated roles and attributes of satisfiers as well as there should be permanent stimulations for creating synergy satisfiers and contribute to the fulfilment of other needs. This would usher participation of people and they would do the management of their needs through a self-reliant approach.

The invisible sectors or the micro-organisations and their economic activities may fill the gaps or spaces left out by the macro-organisations or formal economic structures and work towards increasing degrees of self-reliance for the transformation of economic and social relationships basic to the construction of a democratic culture. However, this should go along with the availability of resources for generation of economic surpluses, thus, making way for the reproduction and growth of these organisations. The state, on the other hand, should not consider this invisible world as a threat to its macro-organisational structures. Instead, the efforts should be to complement and supplement the role of these micro-organisations to have a sustainable, self-reliant and participatory development process through deconcentration and decentralisation of political power. A democratic country like India has to look towards a perspective based on human scale development for fulfilling the ideals of freedom, equality and social justice in developing its people.

India adopted planned development nearly four decades ago. Mixed economy was adopted to function as a planning process in which the private sector was formally recognised along with the public sector but this was considered a transitional stage. Ultimately it was hoped that the private sector would be replaced by the public sector. Efforts were made to establish the fundamentals of a socialist structure and to fulfil the democratic principles laid down in our Constitution through five-year plans and community development programmes. An examination of the planning process during the last four decades shows that although the initiators of planned development were inclined towards socialistic values like reduction of income disparities, equality and upliftment of the rural masses, yet in course of time, it turned out to be lopsided in terms of income distribution. Despite planned efforts during these years, a greater proportion of people are poor.

The path of mixed economy muddled through the development process and most of the decisions on economic issues and matter were influenced by private decisions rather than by the state. Further, economic progress became largely dependent on the development of the private sector. In order to determine the extent of private investments along with public investment policies of inducements and restrictions, but due to the lack of coordination of government policies, the private sector was given an edge over public investments for industrial growth and agricultural development. This has resulted in increased disparity of consumption standards among the people.

There was a visible trend of income disparities over the years and on increased concentrated of wealth and power within a segment of the population. In addition, institutional measures like land reforms could not be successfully implemented. Despite efforts to maintain consistency and uniformity in the approach to the mixed economy during the first three five-year plans, in reality the development process fell short of expectations. The growth and influence of the private sector over the years resulted in a plan holiday in March, 1966, after the third five year plan. This was a three-year planless period, the fourth five-year plan started only in April 1969. This plan period encouraged the private sector to further invest in certain important areas of economy like power, fertiliser and aluminium, which were reserved for public sector development according to the industrial policy resolution of 1956.

The sixth five-year plan was not allowed to take final shape and instead a timebound plan, a rolling plan to be renewed every year, was suggested in order to adjust the targets. Though the public sector still received official support yet the private sector grew and expanded not only in infrastructural areas but also in largest profit-making consumer goods and services. The subsequent sixth and seventh five-year plans claim to have lowered the population of people below the poverty line through special rural employment schemes. Apart from the increase in income disparities and concentration of wealth and economic power among the affluent in society, the Indian bourgeoisie got into league with the international bourgeoisie, giving a sterling fillip to the multinational corporations, the assets of which are reported to have increased manifold.

In the agricultural sector, the green revolution in the northern wheat-growing areas of India has led to increasing disparities between the rural rich and the rural poor. In addition to being affluent, the rich landowners, over the years, have become a political force to be reckoned with. Some scholars argue that the economic crisis of today is due to disproportionate expansion of public expenditure to the overall production. There is an unwarranted alarming increase in the non-planned expenditure, which includes expenditure on defence and administration. Increased investments by the private sector and decontrol of regulation on certain enterprises also resulted in generating a parallel black money economy and this has further widened the gap between the haves and the have-nots.

Only after 1962, when resources began to be directed towards defence that the national economy started developing strains. The economy was further adversely affected after the 1971 war. It is further stated that the concentration of investments in the urban areas is benefiting a small minority whereas a vast majority of the population (78 per cent) living in the rural areas is deprived of resources. Even the investments in the agricultural sector have benefited the large and prosperous farmers and the gap in the level of income and style of living is growing between the rich farmers and the landless labourers and marginal farmers. It cannot be said that planned efforts have not yielded dividends.

In terms of physical targets, India's achievements are appreciable but the development process has been skewed. Unless the process is reversed, there is hardly any hope of fulfilling the socialist values. Although India started with a 'bottom-up' approach to planning, this was soon concerted to 'top-down' multi-level planning. During the third five-year plan, grassroots planning was envisaged but the 'district' and 'block' plans could not become feasible or viable. The district plans remained a bundle of isolated, ad-hoc schemes prepared by various state departments. Most of these programmes launched through the five-year plans lacked flexibility. The programmes were uniformally structured throughout the country although different regions required special methods or approaches.

There was a lack of integration at the local level due to inadequate and faulty coordination. Factors like the spatial organisation of settlements in terms of providing efficient facilities and services and the need for human resource development were not given due attention. Even the planning for rural areas was devoid of its functional link with the urban centres. Further, the five-year plans were basically economic plans stressing on economic growth in terms of industrial and agricultural output, and did not focus on the social and cultural factors which were equally relevant to the total development process. Economic development and social change should be complementary processes.

If the value system and social organisation of the people are not changed, economic and technological advancements result in 'cultural lags' which are mainly responsible for maladjustments, tensions and disturbances. Of late, there has been a realisation on the part of planners of the importance of social, cultural and political factors in the development process.

Various factors seem to have complicated the socialistic approach to the planned development over the last four decades. These factors include the vested interests of the national bourgeoisie which increased the role of the private sector in areas reserved for public undertakings; the war with China and the subsequent two wars with Pakistan putting great stress on the plan expenditure shift of emphasis on the special area development programmes (CAD, SFDA, MFAL, DPAP, HADP, TDP, etc.); the declining importance of CD programmes; the failure of panchayati raj institutions in some areas and of these getting defunct in certain states; restricting democratic decentralisation and devolution of power due to rigid compartmentalisation between the bureaucratic structure and the development structure; elected legislators, parliament members and ministers, not willing to part with their leadership position and encourage new leadership; and reluctance on the part of bureaucrats to change their attitudes and give up their power functions to technocrats.

Other factors were the plan holiday, the ideological change in planning, politicisation of peasants, caste affiliations, concentration of wealth with the urban and rural rich, competition between the urban and rural rich to capture power positions in the state assemblies and parliament, consciousness of the rural rich and their politicisation to demand their rights *vis-a-vis* the urban rich, and the reaction of the urban rich towards peasant movement, traditions and cultural ethos embedded in religions beliefs, philosophy and dogmas, belief in *karma* and life after death, fatalism and destiny.

Adhocism, and adequate information system to generate reliable data for planning, ignoring scientific techniques for planning and over-reliance on value judgements, target-oriented policies of administrators, time constraints to meets targets, apathy on the part of the rural poor, illiteracy, marginality, caste and class factors, social and economic rivalries and party politics are some other factors which have resulted in marginal development of rural areas in our country. Further, the designing of five-year plans has been centralised. The Planning Commissions, in consultation with various ministries at the centre, has remained the sole agency for determining national priorities, has been influenced by the national leadership or party in power. The different states have hardly any leeway to lay down their priorities.

The various states have each set up a planning department, and they are actually looking after the utilisation of resources allocation and their priorities are in keeping with national priorities. The situation at the district level is much more confusing. Though district plans were conceived of as a part of planned efforts within the guidelines provided by the state, their implementation could not become a reality in view of inadequate resources and political interests of certain legislators and ministers.

Irrespective of the fact of whether one follows the evolutionary or revolutionary path of development, in either case the development goals are influenced and shaped by dominant personalities who usually keep the path of development chequered and nuclear. The goals set are invariably highly unrealistic and their accomplishments are illusionary. These are set purposively by such persons in order to keep themselves in dominant positions within the social system. When these people lose importance in the political scene, new ones take over and they ordain development goals and processes. Therefore, it appears to be psychological determinism which seems to interact with economic or ideological determinism while the value system and the social organisation of a society are employed as an instrument to relate development plans to the needs of the people.

One cannot eliminate elites even in the revolutionary system of development as party elites assume privileges and benefits which keep them distinct from the common mass. Depending upon their rank and length of service in the party, they acquire a differential status. Thus, the stratification system or the system of inequality, instead of operating on the vertical plane, becomes functional on the horizontal plane. However, the biggest advantage is that the income disparities are reduced in this system. Nevertheless, the hallmark of India's struggle for freedom has been the principle of non-violence preached and practised by Mahatma Gandhi. The democratic ideals of Nehru pervaded the Indian scene and did not allow the more militant plans of other leaders to fructify and gain popularity among the masses. The people accepted Gandhi's and Nehru's ideals as these seemed more relevant to the Indian tradition of passivity, persuasion, persistence and self-control.

DEVELOPMENT OPTIONS

The Indian tradition is characterised by a cultural ethos and a value system embedded in our religious philosophy and Hindu way of life. Some of the major values upheld in our society are conciliation or reconciliation, tolerance, sympathy, hierarchy, affection and warmth expressed through sentiments and emotions, belief in an *Almighty God* as a creator, preserver and destroyer of the universe, fructification of actions according to one's *karma* or deeds, spirituality and belief in reincarnation, mutual help or cooperation, hospitality and concern for the needy and suffering.

Modernising influences have affected some of these values, yet in practice preference is given to these over values of conflict, intolerance, hostility, rudeness, rationality and reward according to one's efforts, self-orientation and materialism. Not that these values are non-existent in the Indian society, but traditional values are still strongly upheld by a large segment of the population. Although India is the largest democracy in the world, yet democratic principles and ideals have not been allowed to function freely. Democratic principles need to be accelerated by educating individuals to make the right choices from the available alternatives.

The planning process during the last four decades within the framework of democratic principles and ideals failed to break down the social solidarity groups like caste and kinship. Instead, the social identities became more pronounced than before due to a lopsided development process.

Whether it is development of rural capitalism or development of rural collectivism, one thing is certain—that it is the "people" who have to be set in the centre of development. There is a need to evolve systems which empower people and which release their capacities and give them an incentive for change. Without these and without the deconcentration and decentralisation of power, investment and technology have no meaning so far as development of the developing nations is concerned despite the influences of the translational economy which has far-reaching consequences. Centralised planning has resulted in creating dependency among the people. This has to be changed in order to develop self-reliance, which is basic to the development of people. It is only through the participation of the people in development activities that one can ensure their commitment to development themselves as well as their community and to build up confidence in them to take decisions on their own.

To realise all this, a multidimensional paradigm focusing on institutional, technological, infrastructural, participative and service-oriented changes has been suggested to affect the village social structure in terms of occupational diversification, social mobility, reduction in income disparities, changes in values and social relationship for an integrated living. This can be effected through decentralised planning and the consequent involvement and commitment of community leaders. In the development of people, man and his institutions, man and his tools and techniques, man and his interests, and man and his justice should match and be compatible with needs, aspirations and motivations.

4

Rural-Urban Migration in Bangladesh

Migration is found to be generally beneficial for the well-being of migrants and their families, although the degree of benefits varies by age, education and gender. Migration is a cause and an effect of socio-economic change. It is also a behavioural trait that involves a balance in degrees of commitment to places of origin and destination.

Rural development through social and economic change can reduce the need for agricultural labour, generate aspirations for better economic opportunities and thereby result in out-migration. On the other hand, it may also improve local opportunities, expand jobs in rural locations, and hence reduce motives to migrate. The overall impact of rural development on migration will thus ultimately depend on the context or setting in which it occurs. Some researchers focus on the regional economic structure as the key contextual framework for the analysis of migration. Others prefer using a community development context to take into account broader contextual characteristics, community linkages, and intercommunity differences.

The decennial censuses conducted by the Bangladesh Bureau of Statistics (BBS) constitute the major source of population information in Bangladesh. However, the population estimates of the BBS are notorious for under-enumeration because of inadequate methods of data collection and data processing, improper supervision and logistic support, and inconsistencies in reporting results.

With regard to migration, a supplementary sample survey conducted with the 1991 census provides information on place of birth and year of migration to the present place of residence. But census data on birthplace and "duration of residence in the present place" fail to indicate whether the duration question refers to a move from the birthplace or from the previous residence before coming to the present place. Without a "place of last residence" combined with the duration of living in the current place, it is also difficult to detect non-permanent movements.

The electoral rolls failed to include slum and squatter settlement residents and grossly under-represented eligible voters (adults), including recent migrants. In general, there are methodological deficiencies in using a unidimensional definition to define type of migrant. For example, people may live their whole working lives in the city but remain committed to the village of origin where they have left their family of procreation and return there after retirement. The declared degree of commitment to the area of origin or destination is used to distinguish permanent and temporary migrants. A ten-year cut-off distinguishes the long-term from the recent migrants. Such a relatively long period is recommended to ensure a sufficient time period to investigate the consequences of migration.

Though the sample of temporary migrants was only about one-fifth women, it is sufficient to generate insights into the gender dimension of rural-urban migration. Data from non-migrants in areas of origin are desirable in the analysis of the determinants or consequences of internal migration. In selecting "stayers", the problem of locating purely non-migrant households was difficult.

To understand why people migrate and what impacts flow from their migration, it is important to analyse the context in which migration takes place. The relevant context refers to the economic, political, and geophysical structure of a social system within which the movements of individuals occur. Rural-urban migration in Bangladesh occurs in a setting marked by limited industrial, but rapid commercial, development, centred around metropolitan regions and the capital city in particular.

Rapid expansion of the commercial, transport, and construction sectors and a few specialised types of manufacturing activities, such as readymade garments, leather, and fish-shrimp processing, is drawing young adults from rural areas who otherwise would have remained largely underemployed. Such a setting is a common feature of societies predominantly based on subsistence production and consumption. The concept of setting can be explained by the macro-economic, political, and administrative structures of the capital and/or other metropolitan city in which the migrant earns a livelihood. An analysis of the macro-setting should be supplemented by the social situation of migrants represented by "modes of production, care and support in the rural homes".

In the urbanisation process in Bangladesh, Dhaka has a dominant role. It contains one-third of the total urban population. Two-fifths of the jute mills in Bangladesh are located in Dhaka, employing about half of all jute mill labourers. Similarly, a little over half of the textile mills and nearly one-third of registered factories are located in Dhaka. The rapid expansion of the garment industry, the fourth largest employer in the country, has been heavily concentrated in Dhaka. Dhaka is the preferred location for manufacturing and other industrial activities because of the relatively better developed infrastructure compared to other metropolitan cities and district headquarters.

Dhaka is the largest and fastest growing urban centre of Bangladesh. However, sheer numbers of inhabitants are not always a sensitive index of a centre's relative importance in an urban system. Centrality of a particular urban centre depends on the variety, type, or quality of the central functions available at that place. To assess centrality here, telephone connections are used, supplemented by information on city dwellers' access to transport and communications networks and amenities. Improvements in transport and communication networks have reduced the cost of all forms of travel, which in turn has enhanced mobility all over the ESCAP region.

However, through extensive fieldwork it was revealed that expenditure data also have problems and often suffer from the opposite problem of over-reporting. Thus slum and squatter dwellers tended to understate their expenditures while non-slum dwellers tended to overstate them. Through close observation, it was found that women in slum areas under-reported expenditures to conceal their husbands' personal expenditures on food away from the home as well as on drinking and gambling. Conversely, non-slum women tried to legitimise their higher incomes by overstating expenditures. Higher per capita income of the Dhaka city dwellers compared to the urban and national figure can be justified by higher expenditures on housing. To understand the migration process, the nature of movement and to link macro-causation to micro-stimuli, it is important to analyse the situation of the communities of origin of migrants.

Nearly half of all women migrants came as dependants compared to only about a tenth of males. Migration for education was a significant motive for both genders. Nevertheless, economic motives for migration were the predominant ones, accounting for over 62 per cent of male permanent migration and 83 per cent of temporary male migration. In contrast, economic motives accounted for under eleven per cent of permanent female migration, but 90 per cent of their temporary migration. Temporary migrants, whether male or female, young or old, came predominantly in search of employment. The most common premigration occupations of permanent migrants were agricultural and salaried services, with the proportions of students or unempleyed slightly larger. It is intriguing that the proportion of students was quite significant even for the 30-39 and 40-49 age groups.

A comparison of premigration occupational patterns of temporary and permanent migrants in their areas of origin shows that the proportion of unemployed, students, and housewives was significantly higher for temporary migrants. The role of the community context in determining out-migration can be assessed by examining the socio-economic development, physical facilities, social infrastructure, and the degree of accessibility in migrants' communities of origin. Socio-economic development refers to the level of living, which includes per capita income, job opportunities, types of jobs available, and scope for diversification. Physical infrastructure and social facilities include roads, schools, availability of electricity, and government services and non-government organisations.

Economic development rather than stagnation engenders population movement. The physical infrastructure and social facilities such as roads and markets were better in villages of temporary migrants than in those of permanent migrants. This may suggest that agricultural modernisation accompanied by infrastructure development in villages, rather than reducing out-migration, instead tends to give rise to an alternative pattern of migration, such as commuting, circulation, and other non-permanent forms of movement. Migrants are not randomly selected from the population in areas of origin, but few have examined the relationship between the selectivity of migration and its causes and consequences.

Temporary migrants were drawn here from supplementary censuses in the field while permanent migrants were selected mainly from electoral rolls, which suffer from gross under-enumeration of recent migrants. The latter may affect the age distribution reported for permanent migrants. Therefore, the age at the time of migration was retrieved for permanent and temporary migrants to determine migrant age selectivity. Only four per cent of permanent vs. 40 per cent of temporary migrants migrated to Dhaka before age 20. Between the ages of 20 and 29, another 50 per cent were added to the latter group vs. only 16 per cent to the former. The mean age of temporary migrants was 22 vs. 39 for permanent migrants, a striking difference. A comparison of the composition of the sample and the national population by age group also shows significant differences, while the ratio of children to adults was higher for the national population than for either the samples of families of permanent migrants in Dhaka or of temporary migrants in rural areas of origin. This is expected because migrants consist of a disproportionately large working age group, especially temporary migrants. The median age was similar at 21-22 for permanent migrants and the urban population in the country in contrast to 18 for the rural population. The sex ratio obtained from the migration survey and from the secondary sources reveals a concentration of males in the prime and middle-working age groups among long-term permanent migrants. The high sex ratio in the 40-59 age group is not unexpected because the mean age of the head of household overall was 45 compared to 35 for wives. The sex ratio is more balanced in poorer agglomerations than Dhaka city as a whole.

Families in places of origin with a high sex ratio are more able to adopt a strategy of labour allocation through non-permanent migration, which is a reason for the high sex ratio in families of temporary migrants aged 15-39. Hugo notes that the apparent increase in non-permanent forms of population mobility in general can be understood in terms of family survival and risk-maximisation strategy. Circular migration for work by a household member has the advantage of diversifying the range of income-generating sources, reducing vulnerability to the seasonal nature of jobs in rural areas, and lowering the risk of exposure to natural calamities, such as famine, flood, and drought.

The dependency ratio is defined as the ratio of persons in the "dependent" ages to those in the economically productive ages. In the present context, youth and elderly dependency patterns are used to examine the impact of rural urban movement on family welfare and support systems by comparing dependency ratios among city migrants with those of their rural families and with the total populations of rural and urban areas. A higher proportion of elderly live in families of temporary migrants than in either the rural or urban populations. Out-migration of temporary migrants is facilitated by elderly parents and adult relatives who care for their children and spouses and are active in household production. In these contexts, the elderly often made positive contributions. However, the high proportion of elderly also involves costs to society. The elderly in Bangladesh, as do their counterparts elsewhere in Asia, receive their primary material, physical, and social support from their children. Asian countries allocated only a small proportion of central government expenditures to social security in 1989-90. It is argued that with affluence, the younger generation has tended to become more materialistic and preoccupied with a youth-oriented Western culture, eroding the traditional respect for the elderly.

Contemporary migration research provides startlingly contradictory evidence on the consequences of migration. On one hand, migration increases interpersonal and inter-household inequality within and between villages, as well as between villages and towns. On the other hand, Kols consider that most rural areas gain more than they lose from out-migration, and their situation would have been worse had migration not occurred.

No single measure can capture the many dimensions that welfare has for individuals and their patterns of distribution across society. Aggregate measures, such as the Human Development Index of the United Nations Development Programme, demonstrate the acceptance of income, education, and health in determining well-being. Income includes per capita and household income, as well as household expenditures. This is because income is often under-reported. Education is also examined as a dependent variable since it is considered essential for "productive life in modern society".

Assessing the consequences of migration ideally requires a longitudinal study design in which migrants are followed from the time of their decision to move through eventual settlement in the city. Unfortunately the limited budget and timeframe made this impossible. Data gaps are partly compensated by case studies of stayers, return migrants, and families of temporary migrants in their areas of origin.

The nature of migration, temporary or permanent, makes a big difference in the expenditure pattern. Temporary migrants were found to spend only one-third of their consumption expenditures on food, compared to 46 per cent for permanent migrants. For clothing the estimates were 4.5 and 8.0 per cent, respectively. Expenditures by temporary migrants on remittances seem to have led to curtailment of spending on food and clothing. This is expected because, unlike permanent migrants who live primarily with their families, temporary migrants live alone in boarding houses, having left their families in the place of origin to earn in the city and spend in the village. Temporary migrants send up to three-fifths of their annual income to their home areas, mainly to meet consumption needs.

A multivariate regression model was formulated to analyse the determinants of income of migrant (permanent), non-migrant, and non-slum households in Dhaka. The income of a household was assumed to depend upon the composition of its members; the number of earning members and the dependents; the quality of labour; and investment in land and non-land assets accumulated by the household. Dummy variables were used to represent the different occupations. Government officers, engineers, doctors, teachers, and other professionals and businessmen were classified under the skilled category, for occupations which demand higher levels of skills and/or education.

Occupations which involve medium levels of education and some capital, e.g., employees of the service sector or medium or small businesses, were classified as semi-skilled occupations. Those occupations which depend exclusively on the physical labour of the workers, such as construction labourers, rickshaw-pullers, domestic servants, and scavengers, were classified as unskilled, which was used as the control. Finally, those who derive their income from rent and remittances were classified in a separate category since they were found to be among the highest income earners. In addition, the duration of stay in the city was assumed to influence the income of non-temporary or permanent migrants because they were considered to have greater knowledge of opportunities in the Dhaka labour market.

Regression equations are estimated in log-linear form. For education, completed years of formal schooling is used as a continuous variable. Independent variables in the equation were examined using a stepwise procedure which retains variables whose coefficients have, statistical significance at the five per cent level or better. Results reported are only for the final run with statistically significant coefficients.

For migrant and non-migrant households, the contribution of nonland assets to household income is high, the coefficients (indicating elasticities) being 0.28 and 0.30, respectively. These indicate that a 10 per cent increase in investment in non-land assets tends to increase household incomes by 28 and 30 per cent for the respective categories. The other variable which has a powerful effect on household incomes of migrant and non-migrant households is education, as expected. Its coefficient is the largest of all for both groups, and nearly the same (about 40).

Much of the difference in incomes of the two groups can be attributed to differences in mean education, recent migrants having more education than earlier migrant. As for the demographic variables, the coefficient of income with respect to number of workers is higher for non-migrant house-holds (0.25) than those of migrants (0.18). This can be explained perhaps by the higher labour force participation of adults in nonmigrant households (72 per cent) compared to 63 and 48 per cent for permanent and temporary migrants, respectively. Households with a higher dependency ratio also have lower household incomes. However, it is of course not only the number of earning members but the nature of their occupations that influences household income.

The contribution of a skilled worker is on average 25 and 13 per cent higher than that of unskilled workers in migrant and non-migrant households, respectively. Having income from rent and remittances and having a semi-skilled vs. an unskilled occupation is associated with significantly higher overall incomes among migrant households, unlike those of non-migrants. Of special significance for the present study, the impact of migration on household income over time may be inferred from the regression coefficient on length of stay in the city. With each additional year, household income increases by seven per cent. This means income doubles on average after ten years of living in the city.

For temporary migrants living alone in boarding houses, leaving their families in places of origin, it was not possible to run a regression to determine household income. While obtaining income data from all members of families was done in the cases of permanent and nonmigrant households, this was not possible for those whose origin families live in villages far from Dhaka. However, it was found that age and education of the head of that household were highly correlated with the level of income of temporary migrants.

The effect of the educational selectivity of migrants is mixed with regard to regional development. Educated migrants have the "potential to contribute to economic development in urban areas and also to alleviate the population pressure on land in the rural areas." Out-migration of young, educated and dynamic persons from rural areas is widely believed to impede rural development and create a vacuum in rural leadership. At the individual and family levels, the impact of education has always been beneficial. The remaining part of this section is devoted to examining the impact of the education selectivity of migrants on human resource development in Bangladesh.

An analysis of education patterns reveals that the benefits of education are unevenly distributed among region, gender, and classes in Bangladesh. At the national level, only two per cent of rural women have a high school or higher education compared to 12 per cent of women in urban areas. Therefore the low enrolment rates of children (of both genders) of recent migrants in Dhaka reflects a continuation of the rural pattern, while that of long-term migrants is similar to that of the urban population.

It is also important to note that rural-urban migration generates greater educational opportunities irrespective of the slum or non-slum residence of migrants. Half the children of slum households in the six-to-ten year age group were enrolled at the primary level, double that estimated in previous studies. Notwithstanding their higher enrolment, it declines with age, so it is important to examine retention rates through a longitudinal study. Enrolment rates were also found to be highly related to the education of the head among migrants, much more than among non-migrants. Hence, it can be said that the use of education as a "means to widening of choice" has been realised more by migrants than non-migrants, and transmitted into the creation of more human capital.

On basic ideological questions that govern gender relations, such as mode of marriage, inheritances of property, etc., a sizeable proportion of permanent migrants indicated in their responses to attitudinal questions in the survey a continuation of traditional rural values, except for those with high levels of education. However, higher levels of education, particularly among wives of permanent migrants, appear to expose women to more egalitarian values and liberate them from ascription-oriented traditional norms.

In contrast, only 30 per cent of well-educated male heads of permanent migrant households asked for similar entitlements for their daughters as their sons, almost the same figure as for non-migrants. Finally, fewer than 20 per cent of temporary migrants thought daughters should have the same inheritance rights as sons, or slightly less than the figures for permanent migrants and non-migrants, reflecting the persistence of traditional values among male temporary migrants. Respondent's attitudes towards women's education and working outside the home and towards the level of education that they aspire for their sons and daughters were also sought.

Almost all respondents expressed favourable attitudes about women's education, with wives more progressive than husbands. For example, one-fifth of male heads of permanent migrant households did not support women's higher education vs. one-tenth of their wives. Temporary migrants and stayers were more conservative than permanent migrants or their spouses, as one would expect. The proportion of permanent migrants, non-migrants in the city and temporary migrants who supported women's work outside the home was similar at about 90 per cent, or higher than support for women's equal education. It is important also to examine the justifications offered in support of women's education and outside work, that is, whether they are desirable to enable women to perform their reproductive and child-care roles better or to enhance their freedom and rights as individuals. Interestingly, about half of non-migrant and permanent migrant heads supported women's education for the former reasons vs. only one-third of their spouses for those reasons. At the same time, two-fifths of non-migrant wives and a quarter of wives of migrants offered functional justifications for women's education. Support for women's education as a means to enhance individual freedom was dramatically higher among educated wives of migrants and non-migrants than among their husbands. As with women's education, a majority of migrants and non-migrants offered functional justifications for women's work outside the home—for the family's solvency.

Temporary migrants' responses were more mixed, with more indicating the permission of their husband as a precondition (about one-fifth) for outside work; but at the same time, a sizeable proportion (one-third) accorded importance to outside work for ensuring women's freedom. It seems that the bilocality of temporary migrants induces conflicts between tradition and modernity.

The highly educated among migrants and non-migrants aspired to higher levels of education, professional careers, and delayed age at marriage for sons and daughters. In contrast, male bias is highly conspicuous in the responses of temporary migrants and rural stayers, irrespective of their own level of education. They prefer a secondary level of education for their daughters and for them to become housewives between ages 18 and 20. At the same time they aspire for higher levels of education for their sons, a business or military officer occupation and a minimum age at marriage between 25 and 28. The contrasts with the results above for long-term migrants indicates that a longer stay in Dhaka makes a person more modern in attitudes towards sex roles.

Unemployment among migrants was found to be lower at the destination compared to their premigration situation in rural areas, and incomes were much higher. And this holds despite the high level of urban poverty in Dhaka. Thus, although one-third of the GDP of Bangladesh is generated by urban areas, especially Dhaka, inefficient management and an unequal distribution system contribute to a high level of urban poverty. Moreover, the large urban slum and squatter settlements do not have access to the basic amenities provided by the formal institutions in Bangladesh.

Census questions based on the United Nations' prescriptions are not adequate in the current realities of Bangladesh, as is true for many developing countries. There should be questions on place of birth of the household heads and other members of the household, together with place of previous residence and either year of migration or duration at present residence. Questions on whether a family member or members are absent overseas or otherwise, the country or place of destination, duration of absence, and reason for leaving should be added to the supplementary survey schedule of the BBS.

Similarly, the census question on the institutional type of households should be extended to include boarding houses because they are common places of abode of temporary migrants. It would also be useful to include a question on place of work in the population census or its sub-sample survey to help identify non-permanent migrants. It is also possible sometimes to detect non-permanent movements by conducting interviews at (or near) the place of work. The labour force surveys conducted by the BBS should have questions on place of birth, current place of residence, and year of migration.

As people in Bangladesh are often involved in multiple income-earning activities, it may be appropriate to ask a question on time use to detect major and minor work and other activities. It also is recommended that along with the question on the materials used in housing, the census should have a question on land occupancy (government or private land) of the household to identify respectively the slum and squatter settlements which house a large proportion of the population in urban areas, including migrants.

In examining the impact of migration in places of destination, the probability of getting only successful migrants looms large. As in most surveys, there was no way to include repeat migrants who have moved elsewhere or returned to their areas of origin in the sampling frame, so the findings may suffer from selectivity bias. Since repeat migrants are often less successful, their exclusion leads to overestimating the success of migrants. This problem was addressed through thorough case studies of a few returned and "failed" migrants from migrants' areas of origin. Those studies generated insights into why and under what conditions some migrants fail to achieve their expectations, but they are too few to identify the characteristics and magnitude of return migrants. Therefore, for a comprehensive study on the impact of migration there is no substitute for a systematic survey in migrants' areas of origin and destination.

Non-permanent migration is assuming greater importance, especially among the younger population and women. A bipolar pattern of education selectivity among migrants suggests that relatively educated and illiterate migrants are involved in striving for a better future. The physical infrastructure and economic characteristics of the areas of origin of migrants indicate that migration is not usually an outcome of impoverishment.

5

Rural Women

The total number of rural women are living below the poverty line in developing countries. There are many reasons for the worsening poverty of rural women. Particularly important are: population increase; the present worldwide economic crisis; civil conflicts, natural calamities; degradation of the environment; changes in traditional values; the disintegration of families due to increased divorce, separation and desertion under duress and increased male migration, and an increase in single mothers leading to an increase in households headed by women; and a weakening of household survival strategies, etc. Rural women contribute to socio-economic development in three major ways: through the community and nation, at the household level and through the future generation. At the national and community level, rural women are a source of labour—their own as well as through reproduction, new additions to the labour force. They are also producers of marketed and non-marketed output, much of which is not accounted for in conventional national accounts, and source of savings and accumulation; they are often better savers than men. Household level, rural women take care of food and fuel security, domestic work and security for old age through their surviving male children. Finally, at the inter-generational level, women take responsibility for the care of children, their early education and the socialisation process and in passing on family vocational traditions.

Rural women are the vital link between the present and the future, between production and consumption, between savings and investment and between poverty alleviation and environmentally sustainable growth. Poor rural women should not be treated merely as the "target" groups of social welfare programmes; rather their principal role as agents of economic development should be recognised and enhanced. To elaborate on the economic role of rural women, they are the major food producers in developing countries and generate a large part of the family's cash income.

The improvement in household food security and nutrition and in food distribution between households, has, in many cases, proved contingent on women's access to income and their role in household decisions on expenditure. In general, women have a stronger voice in household decision making when they contribute cash income, as in many landless households, than when they do not earn any income. Resource-poor families are even more dependent than others for subsistence on women's labour in the food sector and/or on their earnings from waged labour and off-farm enterprises. While women's incomes are significantly and positively associated with children's nutritional status, especially in the poorer segments of the population, there is evidence that mothers' excessive labour burdens can have negative implications for child nutrition, as they are able to give less time to proper food preparation.

A preoccupation with the cash economy and methodological and attitudinal bias against the value of women's work make them statistically marginalised, though their contribution may be highly significant. The unpaid home and farm activities of women make a vital contribution to the economy of poor rural households in developing countries. The poorer the household and the country, the more hours women work and the greater are their contributions to the economy and to family welfare; however, rural women's non-marketed domestic activities such as cooking, childcare, water and fuelwood collection, food storage and processing and other household tasks are left out of official statistics that measure economic and agricultural output.

Improving women's productivity, income and quality of life therefore implies a multidimensional contribution to overall growth and development. As producers, women can contribute to alleviating rural poverty, to overall growth and to capital accumulation. Increasing the income of women consumers will result in an increase in demand for goods and services and contribute to the growth of other sectors, which will in turn raise demand for the products and services of the poor. The rural poor suffer from a significant gap between their potential and actual productivity, and the productivity gap of poor rural women is much wider than that of poor rural men.

Rural women will gain proportionally more if investment allocations and development efforts are shifted in their favour; they can go from a situation of being triply disadvantaged to one in which their contribution will have a multiplier effect, in the household, in the community, nationally and most important of all, in the future generation.

The status of poor rural women has to be assessed, economically, socially and culturally. Leaving aside regional differences, the common thread is that socio-economic and political power is unequally distributed between the sexes. It is necessary to place women's participation within the context of the family and social economy so that rural development projects can be accurately designed to respond to the needs of the target population. Women's non-market work subsidises the community's market work and their contribution is visible at all levels, in household chores, children and family subsistence, but has been treated as invisible and unaccountable. The challenge is to change the attitudes of society and individuals and introduce simple accounting procedures to give full recognition and support to women's role and work, creating a basis for investment and growth. It also means a recognition, at the micro-level, of the link between non-marketed domestic work and income-generating activities. Specific methodological problems which marginalise rural women's work include: data collection during short, pre-determined periods, which does not account for women's seasonal work; a narrow definition of economically productive work, which is biased against women; an arbitrary division between marketable produce and produce bound for home consumption, which renders many female activities marginal; gender-differentiated perception of male and female work, influencing data collection; and fragmentation of women's work in terms of time and tasks performed, which influence women's own perception of their activities.

Field work has demonstrated that the problem of women's statistical invisibility will not be resolved easily by using female enumerators and respondents. Methodological evolution must go hand in hand with changes in attitude. Rural poverty, the status of women, family well-being and national development are closely interlinked. The promotion of family well-being and national development depend on the vital link between women's productive and reproductive role to be given greater recognition and support. The starting point of reference is the household, followed by the community and the nation.

The definition of "household" need not be the traditional one which implies a husband, father or brother as the head, but a social one which includes households headed by women. The indicators used to measure the status of women represent economic and social factors which affect their productive and reproductive roles. Social and economic factors need to be realigned, so that they have a positive impact on women's productive and reproductive roles and these roles become more balanced. A more equitable sharing of decision making, responsibilities and resources is called for in the household to reduce the burden of women's reproductive role and enhance the efficiency and return of their productive work. Women's reproductive and productive roles are influenced by cultural and social biases, access to health care—maternal and child health and family planning included—and to sanitation as well as to water and fuel. Household decision making regarding the allocation of resources and sharing of household chores and responsibilities, including childcare, are vital to a more balanced role.

Childcare facilities and access to education and training enhance women's economic role. Other factors reflecting their status include access to income and employment, which is affected by labour market conditions and the female/male wage ratio, access to financial services, land and other farm assets, and markets and marketing services. Of equal importance is women's access to inputs, appropriate technology and extension services. Women's status in a society can be evaluated either by measuring separate indicators or by an integrated index.

An index of women's status has been developed which combines women's health, education, role in the labour force, contraceptive usage and female/male wage ratio. If relevant data had been available for a larger number of countries other indicators could have been included, to reflect such important factors as women's participation in decision making, ownership of assets including land, access to skill development and training, access to financial services, markets and so forth.

Information is still scanty on these aspects of women's standing in society. Following the methodology developed here, the index of women's status has been calculated for 114 developing countries and the countries have been ranked accordingly. The index takes values between zero and one. The closer the value is to one, the higher the measured status of women in that country. Does it really make sense to attempt to devise a quantitative measure of the status of women? The answer is yes, because qualitative assessment, while illuminating, does not allow comparative analysis between different situations. Quantitative indicators related to the well-being of women and their status in society are useful in designing appropriate intervention programmes. However, the content of such programmes cannot be determined without an indepth knowledge of the status of women, in order to decide on the most suitable strategy.

The female/male wage ratio gives only a rough guide to the situation in the labour market, since reliable data are difficult to come by. It is in any case a poor indicator of the overall relative earning status of women since a large part of women's work is unpaid family labour and receives no value in economic analysis. Therefore, in a sense, even this limited information on the female/male wage ratio overstates the earning status of women. Participation in the labour force, or lack of it, can be viewed as a measure of the under-recognition of the value of women's labour. For these 114 developing countries the female labour force participation rate was estimated at only about 30 per cent in 1965 and 1988; clearly most of the women in the labour force have remained invisible, not covered by formal surveys and censuses.

The female labour force participation rate has not changed significantly for any region except sub-Saharan Africa where it has gone down from 37 per cent to 29 per cent. It will be misleading to read this as real decline in women's labour force participation since it is due to women's moving out of, or not entering the formal labour market. For example, this decline in sub-Saharan Africa can be attributed to women being pushed out of the formal labour market due to cutbacks in public expenditures, due to structural adjustment programmes and also due to an increase in households headed by women which inhibits their participation in the formal labour market. Latin America and the Caribbean are the only regions where the majority of women are employed in the non-agricultural field.

Women's domestic conditions can be measured by the percentage of households headed by women and average hours spent in household work and in collecting water. However, because of problems of definition, measurement and data availability, these indicators have not been included in the calculation of the index of women's status. Data on the number of hours women work in the home or in collecting water were available for only a few countries. Also, the treatment of women's status as heads of households raises difficult questions about the concept of "head of household" and the distinction between households headed by women *de facto* and those headed by women *de jure*. Perhaps the most intractable problem relates to differences in the definition used by various agencies in collecting data in the field, which makes figures from different sources incompatible.

A majority of developing countries have signed the Convention on the Elimination of All Forms of Discrimination Against Women adopted by the UN's General Assembly in 1979 and many have been formally guaranteed equal political rights in national constitutions, progress in eliminating discriminatory aspects of civil and family law, labour legislation, and agricultural and financial sector regulations have been slow and uneven.

Women's explicit legal rights have improved substantially in Latin America over the past decade. In Asia and the Near East, progress in establishing women's formal legal rights have similarly failed to be adequately reflected in practice. Of particular importance to rural women is the development of legal measures and administrative regulations to improve their secure access to land. A second area of concern is the review of civil codes that treat women as legal minors, requiring, for example, their husbands' signature to open bank accounts or to obtain credit. Equally important for rural women, especially in Asia and Latin America, is new labour legislation supporting their equitable access to rural labour markets, mandating equal pay for equal work, and improving working conditions while enforcing legal standards.

A fourth priority is to improve rural women's access to informal sector markets by eliminating discriminatory licensing and price control measures. As heads of households, men not only control most household resources but are normally the direct recipients of project resources targeted at households. These principles hold even when men are not the primary source of household income and when women manage important household resources and conduct various household enterprises on a relatively autonomous basis.

In most societies there is still male control of land, major livestock resources, a large share of subsistence output and the bulk of "household income". Women are in general dependent on men for final decisions with respect to virtually everything that affects their lives and are therefore more vulnerable to poverty.

Many developing countries have legally affirmed women's basic right to own land, actual female control of land is practically non-existent. Administrative, economic, and cultural constraints combine to deny most rural women both ownership and effective control. Where land titles have been distributed, they are nearly always allocated to male heads of households. In Islamic law, women's land ownership rights are explicit, but they do not always control *de facto* land use. Under both the civil and the customary laws of Bangladesh adult women have the right to own property, either purchased with their own earnings or received as a gift.

Muslim and Christian women may inherit property, but Hindu women can take only a limited lifetime interest in inherited property. In India, women's right of inheritance is given by religious laws which are different between religions. Where the civil code exists alongside other systems of law, it is usually overhidden by these systems of religious law, as well as by custom. Steps have been taken to reform the personal Hindu laws to expand women's rights of access to land.

Subsequently, under the commune and production brigade and team system, women retained their right of access to land but were discriminated against in the form of lower work points and were considered as a labour reserve, to be used mainly when men were not available. Women were also deprived of the control of their income; the wife's earnings were automatically added to that of the husband and handed over to him as the head of household.

The Philippines' legal system is possibly the least discriminatory in the developing world with regard to inheritance law and property rights. This applies even to tenancy rights, which are usually inherited by the wife on expiry or in the case of incapacity of her husband. In Tanzania, the law gives women equitable access to land, livestock and productive assets. However, in practice such access is more often through male heads of households, while many rural women are not even fully aware of their rights and obligations. For example, under the Tanzania Village Development Act of 1975, women have ownership rights but in most cases customary laws of inheritance, ownership and control of property tend to prevail.

In African customary land allocation systems, for example, married women often have the right to cultivate specific types of fields on their own account. Such customary land rights enable women to sustain or augment family food security and to earn an independently controlled income. These rights, however, carry an implicit understanding that women will also contribute labour to male-controlled farming or livestock enterprises and that they will process and prepare food for husbands, children and other male kin. Rural women's customary land rights have been increasingly threatened by agrarian reform programmes which have tended to redistribute land titles primarily to men.

Although all the land reform legislation of Asia brought the land to the beneficiary "household" or "family", it allowed the allocation of land within the household to be governed by prevailing custom and law, which decreed the man to be the "head of the household". Land was allotted to the "tenant" or "tiller" who was always presumed to be a man. Thus, although the agrarian reform legislation of the period 1945-1985 did not specifically or explicitly discriminate against women, the application of the law in the context of existing customs and inheritance laws often resulted in their losing their right to land. Women's access to land has also been threatened when tenancy rights in resettlement have been accorded to male heads of households. A household headed by a woman with a number of adult male members theoretically qualifies for selection, but the formal allotment is often made in the name of the adult male son. A review of Latin American agrarian reform shows that in all countries, except Cuba and Nicaragua, only one member of the household can be officially designated as a beneficiary.

Women represented 25 per cent of the beneficiaries of Cuba's agrarian reform in 1985—a result clearly related to firm state policy to incorporate women and 15 per cent of parcel holders in Mexico's *ejido* or communal-based rural property system, primarily widows who inherited an *ejido* parcel. Nine other Latin American agrarian reforms have no data on the percentage of women beneficiaries.

Privatising customary land through adjudication, as in Kenya, has usually led to the loss of women's *de facto* control over productive resources. In most cases, land has been registered in the name of husband or sons. The impact of this on family food security is not clear. On the one hand, men will probably allocate a larger amount of land to cash crops, reducing women's food-producing land. On the other hand, since women will still have to carry out the responsibility of providing food for the family they may retain cultivating rights on an appropriate amount of land. Agricultural production in Gambia is predominantly based on subsistence farms.

The extended family is the main source of labour and the traditional farming system is a complex combination of collective and individual activities, each with corresponding decision-making authority. All activities, however, are essentially divided between production for family subsistence, *maruo,* and individual production, *kamanyango.* Under the first, decision making is traditionally vested in the male head of the compound although cultivation is carried out collectively by both men and women.

The second aims at complementing family subsistence or producing crops for sale at the discretion of the individual, who takes all decisions him or herself. *Maruo* crops are traditionally identified with wet season cultivation of coarse cereals in the uplands and rice in the lowlands. *Kamanyango* production is carried out in the uplands and constitutes an important realm of personal autonomy, especially for women. *Maruo* crops are sold to secure other items necessary for subsistence. *Kamanyango* crops are more often sold but may be transferred to *maruo* status, particularly in times of crisis.

Women were therefore to be the major beneficiaries of the improved swamp areas and irrigation. In the past, increasing the productivity of swamps through the use of improved technological packages had led to women's losing possession of the land they had traditionally tilled, because men had tended to take over the improved land.

In order to avoid such an outcome with the new project development, it was arranged with village communities that the swamps would be leased to the project authority, which would then redistribute them equitably to the original tillers after development. The redistribution was to be done by two land allocation committees with representation by both men and women. Initially, however, women were grossly underrepresented on the committees, consequently, land distribution was heavily biased in favour of men. IFAD intervened in the matter, in consultation with the government and local authorities, and the number of women members of the land allocation committees was increased to more than 50 per cent so that they represented the majority of leaseholders in the revised lists. Although these land allocation procedures formally assured women of their rights, subsequent developments, especially as they related to the *maruo/kamanyango* categories of production, demanded continued vigilance and care.

A significant number of the plots seemed to be evolving towards part *maruo,* part *kamanyango* use since a part of the crop was being assigned to home consumption purposes or disposed of by the male head of the compound. The reasons for these changes in the traditional farming system were manifold. Economies of scale, the physically heavy tasks of land improvement and the complexities of new and sophisticated technology may have made women depend on men in ways that constrained their decision-making power.

Another development was the presence of men working on the *kamanyango* plots and even undertaking tasks traditionally done by women, such as transplanting and weeding. This could be taken as a sign that men were moving in to take over, but the final interpretation must be based on fuller knowledge of the complex social context. Drought plays a definitive role here.

The survival of the members of the compound is an overriding concern for men and women alike. Thus, *maruo* obligations always have absolute precedence over *kamanyango*, and the importance of the latter in the local production strategies rises and falls with the difficulties of production which are essentially linked to weather conditions. Although this transfer is acceptable to women leaseholders, for whom food security is the priority, they do regret the erosion of their personal autonomy. As the project took over allocation responsibilities by leasing the lands from the local government authority, women began to come to the project management unit (PMU) for a replacement plot to be farmed as *kamanyango*. The PMU responded to these requests and allocated as *kamanyango* appropriate plots in the more recently completed rain-fed areas.

The Jahaly and Pacharr case provides important insights into several issues affecting women's access to land, especially in cases in which development efforts will fundamentally change the productivity and income-generating potential of this basic resource. Foremost, male resistance to changing the traditional terms on which women gain access to land and men's ability to assert rights to the monetary or physical returns to women's labour, can be expected to be significant. Land redistribution by development agencies offers an important way to improve the terms and security of women's access to land.

However, such interventions must be planned with a full understanding of the pre-existing social organisation of production and of the intricacies of gender-specific land rights if women's rights are to be effectively improved. Experience with modern forms of land titling and tenancy arrangements has shown that women's traditional land use rights and/or their rights to control output produced on traditionally designated "women's fields" can easily be lost if modern land rights are allocated only to families or households.

When development efforts anticipate a significant improvement in productivity and incomes, it is more likely that male cooperation can be fostered and male resistance to improving women's access to benefits diminished if ways can be found to share the benefits between men and women. In other words, an excessive and blind emphasis on helping women alone may in fact be less successful in supporting their needs than a more balanced approach. To do this, a great deal of effort will be required to sensitise government policy makers, local authorities, and project administrators—to the importance on gender equality in the access to project resource, so that the widely shared goals of improving food security and family welfare can be attained.

The formal assertion of women's rights through land titling is not sufficient to guarantee women's rights to permanent benefits, although it may be an important component of a larger set of strategies to improve women farmers' access to land.

Development projects and programmes should carefully investigate alternative measures, to guarantee and enhance women's access. It is also important to discuss beforehand with all potential beneficiaries any technological changes that will affect the value of land. This is particularly relevant for irrigation projects. Since pump irrigation may involve high costs for mechanised land preparation and pump maintenance, very high crop yields are often required to realise an acceptable return on the investment. Obtaining these yields may require a significant increase in labour and a strict adherence to the timing of labour inputs, requirements that may put pressure on women to neglect other tasks essential to their families or their personal welfare. Alternatives such as tidal or gravity irrigation technologies may also improve the yields of traditional crops and may be much easier for project beneficiaries to manage and sustain on their own. Just as importantly, these intermediate technologies are also less likely to incite men's interest in taking over land women have traditionally farmed.

Rural women are highly involved in the care of livestock. They often have traditional ownership rights to small ruminants and poultry and at times to cattle and larger livestock as well. Rural women's rights to livestock products allow them to improve family nutrition and to earn small personal incomes.

Cattle and draught animals are normally controlled by men, even when women may formally own a few cattle. Just as land improvement projects may erode rural women's access to land rights, their livestock rights and access to income from livestock products may be threatened by livestock projects, most of the projects which improve livestock breeding, health, and use of animal traction are directed at men. Commercialised processing of dairy products by private enterprises or parastatal organisations, and the introduction of quality regulations, have also been organised in a manner that eroded rural women's income from traditional milk-processing activities in Latin America and increasingly in Africa and the Near East.

Rural women's traditional functions and rights in the livestock sector must be studied and enhanced by aid agencies and women must be accorded access to improved resources and training, in new production methods if they are to gain rather than lose, from project interventions.

Women can be trained as village vaccinators and paravets especially for the type of livestock they own for. Women who head their own households, as well as married women, should have full access to credit for purchases of livestock and poultry, construction of pens and animals and inputs of feed or medical supplies. IFAD's experience shows that emphasis on developing the small ruminants owned by women creates additional income which they can control. Special efforts should be made to promote the cooperative use of animal traction resources within families.

Women's access to draught power may also be improved by facilitating cattle and oxen ownership by small groups of women who may decide to hire male labour for ploughing their own fields, or to rent out the animals to others. Such arrangements are particularly important where male out-migration is significant. Women's individual or collective ownership of oxen, donkeys or camels should also be promoted in order to improve women's ability to transport and market food and fodder crops, fuelwood and water.

Since few poor women have access to modern inputs which would enhance productivity, their incomes are primarily allocated to pressing consumption needs; also appropriate inputs and technologies are seldom available in rural areas. Rural women's activities in animal husbandry, food processing, crop storage and marketing are similarly bereft of modern technology. Development projects are major sources of access to improved inputs, technology, training, and credit for a wide range of farm and off-farm enterprises. Many studies have demonstrated that when men receive resources and training, the benefits rarely "trickle down" to women.

Women's own enterprises are improved only if women themselves gain access to new inputs, in order to break the vicious circle of low productivity. Such access, however, must result in improved incomes that women can control and use to purchase the inputs they require.

Women farmers face multiple constraints in obtaining access to improved seeds, new crop varieties, knowledge about improved cropping systems and other forms of technology. Since they are poor and most of their productive activities are not market oriented, project designers, credit officials and extension staff too often assume that women can afford neither to purchase modern inputs, nor to reimburse credit. Women's lack of legal rights to the land they cultivate also often circumscribes their membership to farmers' organisations and hence their access to inputs, services and credit, while women's crops, livestock activities, and especially crop processing and storage have received relatively little attention in agricultural research and technology development programmes.

A basic need in project planning is greatly improved knowledge of the gender organisation of production and the multiple sources of incomes in household economies; also, even more important, a willingness to recognise that poor women farmers understand their own potential and constraints, and are themselves an important source of knowledge and technology.

Projects may even provide men with new technologies that have the ultimate effect of eliminating or seriously undermining women's traditional income-generating activities, such as crop processing and small-scale marketing. For example, the introduction of traction and animal-drawn equipment, while reducing men's workload in land preparation, may increase women's workload in transplanting and weeding and relegate them to low-return jobs. Governments should be encouraged to protect women's interests under conditions of technological change. Many ideas are lost over time because they are not recorded and systematically passed on to the new generation of women.

The search for appropriate technology for women should lead to packages, judiciously combining traditional and modern ideas. Simplicity in use is desirable in technology for poor rural women, but all techniques should be amenable to upgrading to avoid confining women to the low-level technology trap. New technologies should always be assessed from this perspective before they are introduced. Women farmers also frequently have to pursue additional employment as a source of cash income and IFAD's sub-regional pilot project to develop and disseminate appropriate food processing equipment for rural women in sub-Saharan Africa aims to introduce them to new technology. This grant partially finances a pilot project to promote technical improvements in locally-produced food processing equipment which is adapted to women's needs and traditional work habits.

The project is being implemented through the United Nations Industrial Development Organisation (UNIDO) in cooperation with national and regional institutions in Burkina Faso and Mali. Links are being established with current IFAD projects to test and replicate the results of the pilot projects. The development and diffusion of technology appropriate to women's major tasks require increased research funds to be allocated to women farmers' traditional crops, small livestock and poultry, food processing and off-farm production. Problems are not limited to these areas alone.

New crop varieties are rarely tested or demonstrated on women's fields, so that agricultural researchers have learned little about women's specific problems with new varieties. This should change; research should be conducted on women's farms and research institutes and extension services should encourage the allocation of land to women's groups for demonstration farms on which new crop varieties and new cultivation techniques can be tested. Women often respond differently from men to new crop varieties because of their concern with problems related to processing and/or storage characteristics.

Women are often also limited in their ability to phase the process of cultivation of certain high-yielding varieties in the recommended manner. The overwhelming emphasis given in agronomic research to high yields often results in serious neglect of processing and storage and seasonal labour problems. As a result, appropriate technical messages to improve women's productivity are lacking. Also, technologies have to be developed to help generate women's off-farm employment. The IFAD has designed projects stressing time and labour-saving technologies for women, while seeking to ensure that these are environmentally sound. An example is IFAD's Artisanal Fisheries Project in the Aby Lagoon in Cote d'Ivoire. Here, assistance is given to women who not only do some subsistence farming (mainly growing cassava) but also earn cash income through smoking fish. Through the use of improved ovens, the project seeks to halve the time needed to smoke fish and also to conserve wood—the ovens run on coconut fibre. At first, due to a lack of proper awareness, the fish-smoking ovens were not adopted.

Women extension agents were appointed to strengthen the extension effort and promote the new techniques, which were then increasingly accepted by women. On the whole, Africa's female farmers have failed to benefit adequately from the introduction of new technologies. Lack of coordination in the variety of imported equipment can result in increased production costs, difficulties in maintenance and inefficiencies in equipment use. Also, a new technology may be inappropriate or may be disseminated in an unsuitable fashion, or may not take into account the limited purchasing power of women and their health and safety.

Women's full role in production-related activities needs to be brought into the mainstream of extension and training. This is a vital step in the process of commercialisation of women's activities. Both extension and training have to be geared to the total needs of women as producers, and this can be achieved only if programmes are designed to be gender-responsive. Evidence from different regions indicates that women farmers are rarely reached by extension services.

The basic constraints on women's access to extension in agriculture and livestock are: a relative lack of technical messages to improve the productivity of their agricultural activities, due to inadequate agronomic research traditional foodcrops; the very limited number of women extension agents trained in agricultural subjects: and, perhaps most important, a general perception that women are primarily homemakers rather than decision-making farmers, a perception that rationalises focusing extension services on male "farmers" who are expected to direct the work of female "family labour".

Women were the main recipients of agricultural technical messages under IFAD's National Extension Project, and they have shown themselves to be very receptive to agricultural innovation. The reorganisation of agricultural extension under this project brought agricultural assistance and advice to many women for the first time. The project has been successful in extending new technologies such as row planting, intercropping of maize with beans, fodder cultivation and improved pest and disease control in potatoes. Many women farmers started applying fertiliser for the first time, introduced zero-grazing, maintained better quality plants, and were reporting substantially higher coffee pruning, disease and pest control and weeding. The use of traditional village work groups to spread technical assistance has greatly improved women's access to the extension service as Kenyan women frequently form such groups for agricultural work, cottage industries and other joint enterprises.

Another important factor in the transfer of new technology to women farmers has been the improved link between research and extension. The agricultural extension services in nearly all developing countries are overwhelmingly male-dominated. The United Nations Environment Programme (UNEP) reports that less than one per cent of government employed "agricultural advisers" in Asia and the Near East are women, less than 3 per cent in Africa, and only 8.5 per cent in Latin America.

Where cultural constraints limit male extension agents' ability to work with women farmers, the small proportion of agriculturally trained women extension workers makes it particularly difficult to train women farmers in a new technology. Women farmers often feel more comfortable discussing their cropping problems with other women extension agents. In Zimbabwe, for example, more women were found to participate in extension activities when female agents were used. The outlook for the near future, however, is that women extension agents will remain a small minority.

The relatively low percentage of girls in secondary education has limited the intake of young women into agricultural schools. A study of trained manpower in Africa in 1983-1984 revealed that only 13 per cent of students enrolled in agricultural schools were women. Historically, training for women as rural extension agents has concentrated on home economics subjects: food preparation and nutrition, home-making and handicraft skills.

Agricultural training for women has been minimal or non-existent. Recently agricultural and livestock courses have been introduced and attention has been paid to off-farm income-generating activities, but many programmes are still very heavily oriented toward home economics. Women rural agents are often employed in ministries of social affairs or in community development rather than in the ministry of agriculture. In some countries women extension agents trained primarily as home economists are being retrained in agricultural subjects. Retraining is widely recommended as a means of making female extension agents knowledge and work more relevant to the major productive activities of women farmers, but in many cases even the best women extensionists and home economists find that their access to appropriate retraining, especially degree-conferring programmes that would facilitate career advancement, is extremely limited. Another important approach lies in retraining male agents to work with women farmers, particularly in the context of women's groups.

Agricultural extension supervisors and additional women technical specialists, particularly those dealing with women's crops and livestock, are needed to retrain and supervise existing male extension staff.

Providing appropriate extension to women is an acquired skill that can be practised by men as well as women where local customs permit. The shortcomings of existing training programmes have to be identified and, where necessary, new training programmes that are gender disaggregated should be developed to take into account socio-cultural differences among the trainees. Formal and informal training mechanisms may then be used to modify the existing roles of men and women. It may be desirable to implement, at the regional level, organised gender-specific training programmes for trainers, technicians and all personnel involved in agriculture/livestock and rural development projects.

The formation of women's groups may help to reduce the cost of training and extension services. More important, perhaps, is the creation of broader-based women's organisations in order to focus on their self-perception and identity. All too often, the language used by administrative officials in communication and training is alien to the target group, particularly if they are women among whom illiteracy is high. Joint efforts between trained personnel and others, including effectiveness of training for production and budgeting, family planning. The potential benefits beneficiaries, may improve the training and reduce costs. Women should include farm processing technology, planning accounting and auditing and implicit cost is justified by of such training, although there will sometimes be a need to provide grants for developing institutions for training and education. One of the primary objectives of gender-based research, extension and training should be a reduction in women's workload, both for domestic and marketed production and increase in their productivity.

The main obstacle for rural women in raising production above the family's subsistence needs is a lack of marketing outlets, more problematic for women than for men. Export crop marketing systems often bring marketing services direct to the village, while the marketing of foodcrops and other products of women's micro-enterprises must rely on informal arrangements with private traders or on the producer's own efforts to transport her output to local or urban markets.

Women farmers and small traders who market their own produce commonly face barriers related to state licensing requirements, quality or sanitary regulations that put them at a disadvantage in competition with large-scale producers, and they may even suffer police harassment on roadways and in urban and rural markets. Women traders are also constrained by insufficient working capital, and poor storage and transport facilities. Furthermore, information on market prices in various parts of the country is often unavailable to women producers and small-scale women traders; this reduces their bargaining power with wholesale traders and subjects them to unfair competition. Women also face other gender-specific constraints on their marketing activities. For example, patriarchal ideologies motivating men to attempting to control all household income may force women to hide their marketing activities; their access to more lucrative markets is thereby reduced.

Traditions of women's seclusion can make them dependent on men or children to market their output. Reliance on children restricts women to selling in markets nearby, whereas reliance on husbands may reduce their ability to control the income obtained. Projects have often paid insufficient attention to marketing issues and problems when attempting to improve crop, livestock and non-farm production. Market failure can easily lead to project failure if producers cannot realise an adequate income from market-oriented production.

Projects can aid part-time women traders and small-scale women farmers by providing credit for working capital and for crop storage to allow producers to avoid selling at low seasonal prices, by-helping to organise producer marketing groups and small-scale traders' cooperatives, by improving storage in local and regional markets and by providing information on marketing conditions and regional prices through radio broadcasts. Project marketing components should take particular care not to displace traditional women traders and should attempt to assure an adequate representation of women producers and traders.

Rural women's limited incomes, lack of collateral and social and economic-subordination drastically constrain their access to almost all forms of credit from financial institutions and government agencies. Women have comprised only seven to 11 per cent of the beneficiaries of these credit programmes in both rural and urban areas. Commercial banks will not make loans to poor rural women because they are unable to meet the banks' stringent collateral requirements.

Women's poor access to credit is also explained by their exclusion from cooperatives or other organisations through which credit is often channelled to farmers. Even comprehensive programmes of agricultural or seasonal credit in which group guarantees skirt the problem of collateral sometimes fail to extend credit to poorer women—and often poor men as well—fearing that poor subsistence fanners will jeopardise the group guarantee mechanism. Women's potential agricultural productivity and their ability to repay loans are often underestimated.

NGOs and international financial institutions such as IFAD have taken the lead in demonstrating that poor rural women can be reached through group lending and savings programmes. The repayment records of these women have often been superior to those of their male counterparts. Recent experience in the provision of credit to rural women via small group lending schemes, NGO-sponsored micro-enterprise credit projects, savings and loan clubs has demonstrated that poor rural women can make productive use of credit in a wide range of agricultural and non-farm micro-enterprises that they fit into or around their agricultural and domestic work.

The presence or absence of such links between women and credit has to be understood within the framework of their role and responsibilities in the social and economic systems. Social and household responsibilities claim an inordinately women's time, leaving them little opportunity to establish an interactive relationship with financial institutions and thereby strengthen their productive role. The situation is further aggravated by a lack of basic information on credit availability and procedures, as well as trained staff to deal with women's issues.

Inadequate training means women are unable to utilise credit effectively. They also lack the type of collateral required by financial institutions, and their illiteracy acts as a constraint to their entry into profitable economic opportunities and makes it hard for them to deal with the procedural formalities. For many women, previous experiences with regard to formal credit have been negative since institutions have not been fully responsive to their needs, in terms of the size, purpose and timing of loans; this makes them hesitant to avail themselves of the new opportunities offered by development projects.

Rural women's natural aversion to risk, poor institutional motivation and a lack of coherent government policies regarding credit for women, are other limiting factors. Two basic problems underlie the widespread perception that poor rural women are not appropriate targets for most credit programmes. The first relates to rural women's role as family labourers in many farming systems and the second to women's heavy involvement in the production of goods and services that are directly consumed within the family. When a major share of women's agricultural labour is performed as family labour on fields controlled by males, most project designers and credit administrators assume that it is only the male "farmer" who makes the cropping and input decisions and that only the "head of the household"—assumed to be male—should be the direct recipient of credit and the person responsible for its repayment.

Major rural credit programmes need to target rural women's multiple activities and make credit available to married women as well as to women who head their own households. A second problem in providing credit to rural women stems from women's primary involvement in the subsistence sector. Rural women's heavy responsibility for providing goods and services for family consumption not only limits the time they can devote to market-oriented activities, it also makes them appear as poor credit risks to financial institutions and other credit providers, including project designers and managers. However, raising the productivity of women's subsistence activities by new technology is essential to improving household food security and family welfare. The core of the problem in providing credit to purchase inputs for subsistence production is the inability of credit managers to imagine how loans for subsistence activities can be repaid. Credit officers normally assume that the activities for which loans are given must themselves produce an adequate financial return to sustain repayment.

A more realistic understanding of the functioning of poor rural household economies and particularly of rural women's dual participation in both subsistence and market-oriented activities is the key to breaking through the credit barrier. The use of productivity-enhancing inputs can increase the size of this marketable surplus. Women should therefore be seen not solely in terms of their subsistence activities, but rather as overall producers of goods and services. Poor women's earnings from such employment are, however, usually much lower than the imputed net return to labour that could be obtained from cultivating. Their own foodcrops, if yield were raised by using fertilisers, improved verified or other improved technology. Income to repay these loans may be generated either from an enhanced ability to generate a marketable surplus from subsistence-oriented production or from women's traditional off-farm income-generating activities.

The capacity of the financial intermediaries to reach the rural poor in general has to be strengthened and their personnel and procedures must be reoriented to be more sensitive to the needs of poor rural women. The staff of financial intermediaries should be trained to have a clear understanding of the economic role of women, both through marketed and non-marketed production and through their social and family responsibilities. The latter will help them to appreciate the fact that, in order for to have more time for production activities and for dealing with financial institutions, appropriate provision may have to be made for loans to support social responsibilities and household consumption during the loan period.

Loans for social responsibilities could be organised on a community basis, with group repayment, while individual loans could be guaranteed by women's groups mobilised for the purpose. For women to be viable recipients of credit, they must be given assistance to enter the market and gain bargaining power. Women's technical and market situation should be carefully analysed to ensure that their activities are financially profitable and that they have control over their production and income and how the household production system is organised. A generalised approach to credit delivery to a poor rural household will not guarantee rural women the necessary access, it may be diverted to production sub-systems dominated by male members of the household. Credit for poor women must encompass the diversity of women's current and potential productive activities. Women often need credit for small investments and working capital to support market-oriented production and trading activities.

Marketing studies and marketing support are critical to determine and ensure the profitability of women's enterprises. Allocating credit to both subsistence and market-oriented activities requires a fuller understanding of the interrelation between subsistence and market production in household economies and a careful targeting of inputs, training, and marketing services to meet the needs of women who must always balance their complex involvement in both sectors. Providing infrastructure, extension, training and marketing support to make women's enterprises more profitable is preferable to providing subsidised credit or resorting to the indiscriminate use of loan guarantee funds.

However, appropriate crop and livestock insurance may be devised to support women's credit-based activities. It will help if the interest rate remains stable during the life of the loan, if all loans include a grace period, preferably flexible, and if the amortisation of past loans includes repayment in kind where appropriate. Women's enterprises are critically import and consideration should be given to establish supervised credit schemes for them. This will help to encourage the demand for credit by rural women where such demand may otherwise lag.

In particular, supervised credit combined with extension and training can reduce both production and transaction costs and make the products of women's enterprises competitive, also in export markets. Financial institutions' approach to credit rural women has to be flexible in order encourage them to save and to respond to the wide range of credit demand that may arise from potential clients' diverse socio-economic needs.

Women are known to be good savers and in many countries informal savings associations are very active. The task is to establish a link between these informal efforts and formal credit delivery institutions. Equally important is the cost of credit delivery. Such costs must not be unduly inflate and passed on to the recipient of credit. It is therefore necessary to carry out a comparative analysis of the non-formal credit system—moneylenders, shopkeepers, NGOs etc.—in the areas which women often resort to. IFAD has demonstrated the effectiveness of reaching poor farmers with credit by linking village-based savings and loan groups with larger governmental credit programmes or with the banking sector.

For poor rural women in particular, banks' normal constraints on lending to women can be overcome by providing group guarantees to replace individual collateral and by providing an alternative mechanism for screening individual members' loan applications. Commercial or government banks often require institutional support and training to undertake this new form of lending to the poor, but once appropriate administrative mechanisms are in place credit programmes with links to formal financial institutions have good prospects for sustainability and replicability.

Rural women gain experience in dealing with financial institutions and those whose credit record is good may be able to obtain future loans on a retail basis by grassroots institutions: it is unrealistic to expect formal financial institutions to cover all potential female credit recipients in rural areas.

Creating and strengthening links between banks and government-sponsored seasonal credit programmes and village-based savings and credit groups is an extremely important means of increasing the availability of credit to poor rural women. Group liability for individual credit may need to be strengthened, with some form of disaster insurance provided from project funds and/or supplemented with group savings. Whether rural women are best reached through women's groups or through groups open to both men and women will depend largely on the degree of social segregation characterising the local culture and on the history and openness of existing groups in accepting poor men and women.

Women's groups may have the advantage of focusing credit and inputs linked to credit on the particular activities that characterise the women's economy. Potential women beneficiaries are probably the best source of information on this issue. They should be involved in discussions of all matters related to planning credit programmes.

An increasing number of women in developing countries are seeking to sell their labour. However, agriculture-based employment offers women only limited opportunities to earn adequate income. Quite often agricultural technologies adopted by commercial farms do not generate new farm employment opportunities. While opportunities for seasonal waged employment exist, their scale is not sufficient to absorb the large number of women seeking work.

Food processing and other agro-industrial enterprises do not guarantee regular employment and pay is usually low. The same is happening with the introduction of modern high yielding varieties (HYVs) in rice-growing areas of Asia.

Many rural women are marginalised into migrant labour work, floating between rural and urban and peri-urban areas as petty traders, street vendors, construction workers, domestic servants, and the like. Their working conditions need to be safeguarded and they should be accorded minimum wage protection under the existing law. Since the food security of poorer households is usually dependent on women's earnings, low-paying jobs and lack of regular employment for women often mean inadequate food security and poor family nutrition. Support for rural women should focus on generating off- and on-farm regular employment and on improving waged incomes. Improving the technical skills of women through better education and training also improves their access to better paid jobs. Poor rural women engage in micro-enterprises covering a wide range of activities, including food and beverage processing, producing and selling handicraft goods, and petty trading.

Micro-enterprises in informal sectors offer opportunities for entrepreneurial rural women, though official surveys and census data pick-up of these activities. Most go unrecorded. Many off-farm activities are becoming the exclusive domain of women entrepreneurs as men are out because of limited market and earning unities. However, these women receive little support from outside; their bargaining power is low and, particularly when they are they may have to depend on diaries to obtain inputs and market their products. The dynamics of off-farm activities are such that the benefits of labour intensity, local materials and local markets turn out to be constraints to product diversification and market expansion.

Other constraints on women involved in such micro-enterprises include interference by men, women's raiding of cash to meet domestic expenditure, fragmentation of profits, lack of infrastructure, appropriate inputs and technical services along the entire production and marketing chain, lack of appropriate managerial skills, competition with formal enterprises, and, most importantly, lack of access to credit and financial services. Considerable scope exists for expanding informal micro-enterprises. Such activities should be seen as linking agricultural and non-agricultural rural activities. Women's involvement in micro-enterprises has to be fitted into their domestic role, and in particular into their role as food providers.

Micro-enterprises should be compatible with, and linked at all stages to, the agricultural cycle. Such micro-enterprises have to be developed within an environment in which past initiatives, male or female-managed, have not necessarily performed well. This has not always been the fault of the enterprises themselves—it may be due to weaknesses in the support infrastructures and the capacity of the target population to deal with the complexity of such initiatives, especially where rural women are involved. Particular attention has to be paid to the value added of rural micro-enterprises in order to make them competitive with other household-based marketed and non-marketed production, and also to justify the allocation of resources to them as opposed to other sub-sectors.

Poor rural women should be encouraged to venture into micro-enterprise activities since they represent a more efficient allocation of individual family and national resources, land, labour and capital, than exists at present. National governments, donors and NGOs must work together to strengthen rural women's participation in micro-enterprises. The return for the existing activities must be improved and new opportunities created. Rural women must be given access to technology which they can easily absorb. Also steps have to be taken to salvage traditional technologies and improve upon them.

Appropriate technology for rural micro-enterprises managed by women should contribute, in particular, to increased employment and income-earning opportunities, faster production, manpower savings, less expensive raw materials, increased efficiency, reduced fuel costs, better product quality, consistent production flows, and optimum marketing conditions. Extension agents will also have to be trained to respond to the needs of poor rural women seeking to develop off-farm income-generating activities.

Since very little is known of successful rural micro-enterprises managed and operated by poor women, data banks should be developed on the various aspects of their operations. They will need particular support with respect to marketing, both domestically and externally. This is particularly crucial in the context of the recent trend towards market liberalisation. However, this trend, combined with the intra-regional trading processes which are under way in many parts of the world, is paving the way for new opportunities and markets.

Rural women's health is often seriously compromised by overwork, undernutrition, and repeated child-bearing. Among several indicators of women's poor health status in developing countries, perhaps the most dynamic is the rate of maternal mortality which is, at an average of four maternal deaths per 1,000 live births, over four times the average for industrial countries.

The World Bank's estimate of maternal mortality in low-income developing countries, excluding India and China, is six per 1,000 births, but countrywide averages go as high as 20 per 1,000 births in Ethiopia, where data are available only for births taking place in health facilities. Lack of adequate curative and public health facilities in rural areas seriously increases women's vulnerability to prolonged illness and early death. The availability and quality of health services are but one aspect of the myriad factors affecting rural women's health status. Rural women's ability to control family or individual incomes therefore has an important bearing on their access to health services and on their ability to influence the type of services provided. The same is true of public health services and infrastructure related to health.

Rural women's ability to contribute to the construction and maintenance of village water supplies, for example, will affect their availability, particularly in the current period of government expenditure reductions. Donors have often been active in this area, but have tended to neglect to involve women in planning and maintaining water points. Two projects in Ethiopia provide an instructive example of an innovative and effective means of involving women in a service that has exceptionally important benefits not only to public health, but in reducing the excessive labour burdens which threaten women's health. The Swedish International Development Agency (SIDA) and UNICEF have trained Ethiopian women together with men in the technical aspects of pump repair and pipe fitting. Both donors insisted that 50 per cent of those trained to maintain water points be women. Subsequent monitoring by these agencies in 1989 found that the pumps maintained by women were in better working order than those for which men were responsible. This illustrates the importance of involving women in planning and implementing project activities that have important implications for health, nutrition, and their own labour burden. With regard to maternal health care, information should be disseminated on the advantages of birth spacing, breastfeeding and family planning.

The education of the population in general and their sensitisation to women's needs and role in society may also help to eliminate cultural practices and taboos which may be harmful. These include female circumcision, young age at marriage, intra-family food distribution and nutritional taboos against eggs, milk and meat during pregnancy, as well as voluntary nutritional deprivation with the aim of having a small baby. The general health and well-being of women, their nutritional status and maternal mortality are affected by economic factors as well as social and cultural factors.

A dearth of health facilities and services, and heavy burdens on rural women, combine with social factors such as early marriages, repeated pregnancies and a traditionally low status in society to give a bleak outlook for rural women's health. These socio-economic factors have a strong impact on the health and nutritional status of women and they must be considered in any attempt to alleviate the situation.

Women's lower literacy limits their access to remunerative waged employment to decision-making positions in peasant organisations: and development projects, to certain types of modern technology, and to institutional resources require formal application procedures such as bank credit and government training programmes. Where rural women's access to economic and opportunities and their ability to participate in community decision-making processes are particularly affected by illiteracy, and especially in cases where women express a clear demand for literacy training, projects should aim to provide those literacy skills most essential to improving women's access to economic and social resources. Rural women's access to formal education has been growing, though slowly, in most countries, but here again structural adjustment has brought reductions in fiscal expenditure which threaten educational services at all levels.

Project designers must recognise that rural women have a rich traditional, knowledge of the production, processing, storage, and nutritional characteristics of a wide range of crops and wild plants, in methods of soil conservation and enrichment, and in issues related to livestock rearing. Agricultural and livestock research institutions have much to learn from rural women, although little has been done to investigate and build upon their knowledge and insights.

Participatory methods of project planning and management can help to open two-way communication between women farmers and livestock producers, and extension and research staff, so that more effective methods of cultivation, and management of the environment in general, can be developed and popularised. IFAD-financed projects focus primarily on raising the economic productivity, incomes and general welfare of poor rural women. It may be necessary to provide support for rural women's training and education, particularly as these relate to economic productivity, and the fund would first and foremost seek to mobilise the resources and expertise of external cofinanciers such as UNICEF whose mandate is closer to these areas of legitimate concern.

Under the community development programme, poor rural women are benefiting from literacy classes and training in health, nutrition and hygiene. External resources have also been mobilised by IFAD to finance rural women's education and training under the Belgium Survival Fund (BSF) for the Third World (a Fund established in 1985 by an act of the Parliament of Belgium), in which IFAD collaborates with WHO, UNICEF and UNDP in assisting the most vulnerable segments of the rural population in the five countries of the Horn of Africa. When no external cofinancing is available, and these components covering training and education may still be essential to the production and income objectives of IFAD's project, the Fund carries out discussions with the recipient government to obtain domestic financing to the maximum extent possible.

Literacy, numeracy and training in agricultural and horticultural techniques, as well as in savings and management of household finances, are being provided. In addition, this support is being provided for training teachers of primary and secondary schools and for more than 2,000 scholarships for girls to attend school. IFAD has provided the minimum indispensable finance for training and education of poor rural women in a number of cases, because of their contribution to economic objectives.

For example, under the Second North-West Rural Development Project in Cameroon, women will be provided with literacy training and bookkeeping skills within a component strengthening cooperatives and farmers' groups. In Gambia, under the Small-scale Water Control Project, the Fund is working with an NGO providing women's groups with literacy and numeracy training to strengthen them and help them partake of credit under the project. Participation in rural organisations such as peasants' associations, agricultural labour unions, cooperatives, and project beneficiary committees are means by which rural men and women increase their access to productive resources, information and training.

Membership of rural organisations also allows people to represent their interests to government authorities, project management and employers. Rural women's access to these organisations is, however, often severely limited. While there may not be any law which prohibits women from becoming members, they may still be excluded because membership is based on land ownership or a head-of-household extension. Even when a few women manage to participate in rural organisations because of their status as heads of households, or because government or project administrators require a minimal level of female participation, they usually form only a small minority of the membership.

Other factors, such as women's domestic labour responsibilities during the customary meeting time, or husbands' opposition, can reduce women's ability to defend their particular interests. Donor-financed projects have sometimes attempted to improve women's representation in beneficiary committees by requiring a certain level of female participation. Too often, however, these efforts are limited to stipulating that two or three women be appointed as members or women's representatives. Where customs of male and female segregation inhibit simultaneous interaction, or where women are expected to defer to men in public, separate women's organisations should be formed and accorded equal access to decision-making processes that affect the allocation of resources.

The formation of such groups also facilitates communication with the target population so that their needs can be better identified and their support and feedback enlisted. The group approach to extension, training, credit and marketing is featured in almost all IFAD's projects targeting women. For extension, it has been related to an attempt to better link agronomic research with farmers' needs through a two-way communication process facilitated by retrained extension workers.

The Bay Region Agricultural Development Project in Somalia is expected to conduct agronomic trials on farmers' fields and to reach women contact farmers and groups. Under the Farmers' Groups and Community Support Project in Kenya the number of women extension workers will be increased from 20 per cent to 40 per cent of the total and women farmers will be organised into groups to facilitate the dissemination of technology and improve credit delivery to poor rural women.

Mechanisms must be in place to gather gender-specific information at the household level and analyse it carefully. Women are particularly vulnerable to gender-specific impoverishment, therefore it is important to analyse the intra-household processes characteristic of a poor population. Of primary importance here are the extent of male control over household resources and the terms on which women gain access to those resources. Both qualitative and quantitative information should be collected.

Often, qualitative information is more revealing about the status of women than quantitative information.

No systematic information is available on household production systems and sub-systems run by men and by women. It is often not appreciated that the household production system consists of subsystems such as food and cash crop production, livestock production, processing and small-scale manufacturing which need to be separately analysed, with the links between them understood and reflected in support activities.

One practical way of determining women's access to resources is to study the nature of the tasks that men and women normally perform and the length and arduousness of their respective labour days. The tension is better understood if looked at in terms of the male sector, the female sector and the joint sector within the household economy. With hard data one can test the hypothesis that the male sector is formal, organised and closely integrated with the market, while the female sector is informal and less well organised, and linked only tenuously to the market. It is important for planning and project design to know who makes decisions within the household and who is in control of the farming cycle.

A second issue affecting women's welfare in households headed by males is the extent to which household income is pooled and women have influence over the allocation of subsistence and monetary incomes. Indirect indicators may provide much of the necessary information. For example, the relative level of men's versus women's and children's nutritional and health status as well as gender differences in the consumption of clothing, education, and consumer goods can provide information on women's influence over the use of household income and on the relative level of women's poverty. Difficulties in data collection should not be underestimated, particularly since historically very limited time and resources have been devoted to gathering data to evaluate women's work in and outside the household.

Rural women themselves should be involved in information gathering, but they have to be given minimum training for this. Above all, government institutions, and donor projects and programmes must open more direct channels of communication with rural women. Here the skills of development communicators and experienced rural development workers can be especially helpful. Survey methodology should be combined with other approaches to collect information on rural women. This type of analysis can both facilitate the identification of the poorest women in households headed by men, and help in identifying the most appropriate intervention in improving women's access to resources, their ability to generate income they can control, and their relative bargaining power in allocating household output and income to food and other basic needs.

6

Job Search Methods of Rural-Urban Migrants in India

This chapter presents a popular conception of rural to urban migration process in developing countries. In the earlier findings of village studies in India that there is a non-monotonic relationship between propensity to migrate and income: migration first increases and then decreases as origin income rises. The coexistence of urban surplus labour and substantial inflows of migrants from rural areas has been explained by economists in terms of probabilistic migration models in which the central idea is that migration proceeds in response to urban-rural differences in "expected" rather than actual earnings. In this class of models, migration is viewed as a two-stage phenomenon: migrants are attracted to the city by job opportunities in the formal sector, but may initially experience a period of time unemployed or working in the informal sector.

Employment in the informal sector thus serves as a means of financing the period of time searching for formal sector employment. An important underlying assumption is that urban-based job searching is either essential or more efficient than rural-based searching, that is, looking for work before migrating to the city. The implication is that migrants move on the basis of general labour market information, and obtain information on specific opportunities only after arriving in the urban centre.

Policies to tackle the problems associated with migration must also be based on information on the economic selectivity of migrants and the factors that alter the relative preferences of migrants for urban vs. rural areas. Many scholars expect the lowest strata of the rural society to demonstrate the highest propensity to migrate, and that therefore increasing incomes and the standard of living in rural areas must be the major policy instrument for reducing rural-urban migration. Analysis of migration motives has been the preserve mainly of sociologists. The shortcomings of data on migration motives reported in surveys are well known. In addition, economists have argued that the analysis of migration requires a detailed understanding of the conditions at the origin and the destination, and that motives articulated by migrants merely indicate that people migrate primarily for economic reasons.

A wide variety of factors triggers migration with different impacts on the rural community. For example, some migrants may have left the rural area because of loss of livelihood resulting from changes in agricultural technology, while for others migration may be seen as a wily way to earn income to finance investment on the farm. Migrants articulating these reasons come from different population subgroups, who are likely to react differently to policy measures. In the conventional economic models, migration is viewed as the consequence of the individual's decision to maximise his/her own net benefit.

In a large number of cases, migration does not involve movement of all members of the family and that often the wife remains in the rural area. It is important to study the urban-rural family links because the impact on the urban centre is much less when migration does not involve the movement of all members of the family. In such situations, the increase in demand for housing, education, and other services is much smaller. Close ties between areas also help ensure that accurate information on urban employment opportunities is transmitted to rural areas.

MIGRATION SELECTIVITY AND MOTIVATIONS

The propensity to migrate of non-landowning households was much higher than that of landowning households. However, the inclination of non-landowners does not represent the migration propensity of agricultural labourers. Besides agricultural labourers, the landless include professional workers, traders, artisans, and service workers. The propensity recorded for non-landowners is therefore the composite inclination of all these diverse subgroups.

Separate calculations for selectivity according to occupation show that the migration propensity for agricultural labourers was considerably lower than that for all non-landowning households considered together, though this propensity was higher than that for all farm-operating households considered together. The rising migration propensity noted over the lower range of farm size can be explained partly in terms of lower educational attainment migrants owning less than half an acre of land that had the highest proportion with no education and the lowest proportion who had completed high school.

However, it can be argued that the same factors which prevent individuals in the smallest farm families from receiving secondary education also directly constrain them from migrating to urban centres. Thus such small farmers and others with little or no surplus cannot finance the search costs and other monetary expenses involved in migration. They are also constrained from borrowing to finance search costs because of imperfections in rural capital markets. Finally, poorer families are likely to discount the future benefits of migration at very high rates, which reduces the attractiveness of moving.

Responses that indicated that the migrants were affected by natural calamities, or suffered lower economic returns than previously because of division of property, inability to lease land, business loss, etc., or faced an increase in the dependency burden have been lumped under the category "worsening of economic situation". "Aspiration factors" include responses such as "other family members could do the work", "brother had grown up and he could look after the land", or "wanted to improve the standard of living". About 22 per cent of the migrants cited indebtedness or need for cash as a reason to migrants. Nearly two-fifths of these, over eight per cent of the sample, were associated with marriage expenditures. This is consistent with the observations by sociologists that many rural households find it burdensome to adhere to the social norms for expenditures on lifecycle ceremonies and therefore get into debt. On the other hand, few migrants in the sample explicitly stated that they had migrated to obtain cash for investment in agriculture. Another fifth of the migrants moved because they did not want to perform agricultural work. Sociologists have pointed out that in rural India, status is inversely related to the performance of manual labour. Most parents therefore want their sons to obtain non-manual jobs. Thus rural youths who have had some education tend to move to towns since the scope for non-manual work in rural areas is limited or absent.

To gain insight into whether migrants citing different motives come from distinct groups, reasons for moving are related to the migrant's premigration characteristics. In the empirical exercise, for the purpose of normalisation, the motives "personality clash" and "other" are combined into one category with its coefficient set to zero. Thus, the estimated coefficients for each motive shown indicate the change in the log odds of citing that motive instead of a motive in the excluded category.

By ranking the coefficients of a given variable by size, we see the relative impact of the variable on the probabilities of citing a specific motive. We are constrained by the data set and the estimation procedure to restrict the independent variables to land ownership, education, age, and caste. It would be useful to examine the influence of marital status and region of origin on migration motivation, but these variables are excluded because for at least one of the motives they have no variance or are colinear. The results show that the probability of migrating to obtain cash or to repay debt is inversely related to the size of owned holdings, and that it declines sharply as the size of holdings exceeds five acres. This can be interpreted in two ways. First, it could be that smaller landowners are more prone to getting into debt, perhaps in their efforts to emulate the lifestyle and consumption pattern of the upper income and status groups, especially with respect to financing marriages and ceremonies. Second, it is possible that this has to do with imperfect capital and credit markets in rural areas whereby borrowing costs are high and land assumes the role of a critical collateral.

Migration can be viewed as a labour market response to the malfunctioning of capital markets. The results also indicate that scheduled caste migrants are more likely than those belonging to the upper castes to leave the rural area with the cash motive. The majority left to repay debt rather than seeking cash for other reasons. This reflects in part the tendency of scheduled castes to obtain credit from landowners in exchange for providing agricultural labour during the busy season. As for leaving the rural area because of "dislike of agricultural work", the probability of citing this motive increases steeply with middle school or higher education. Strong views are held in the rural areas regarding the types of work appropriate for persons with some schooling. Even persons who have merely acquired some degree of literacy by going through any school, or who have dropped out of secondary school before matriculation, often consider themselves educated and exempt from any obligation to work with their hands. However, this motive is less likely to be cited among migrants aged 25 or older at the time of their arrival.

The relationship between farm size and migrating because of a dislike of agricultural work is a U-shaped curve: the probability is highest among households with the smallest and largest size farms. This probably reflects the reality that the smaller farm households do not need all family members to work on the little land they have while the larger farm households have the means of using hired labour to replace the family member who migrates because of the dislike or agricultural work.

The likelihood grating because of a worsening of the economics situation is greater for those who are less educated and older. Among individuals who have studied up to matriculation or beyond, the probability falls sharply—as it does also for people who are above age 30. This motive has no significant relationship with caste or with the size of ownership holdings. Finally, those who migrate having secured employment previously are more likely to have higher levels of education, as may be expected.

Virtually all rural residents have general information on job opportunities and conditions of life in urban centres. Perceptions about urban centres are formed largely through the prior migration of relatives and co-villagers. The larger the number of migrants from its given area, the greater the awareness. Rural residents evaluate the attractiveness of urban opportunities on the basis of the performance of migrants in the city. The quality and quantity of information of potential migrants is considerably improved through personal visits to the city. Urban contacts can also be an important source of specific information. If an establishment is a small one and if the job does not require special skills or training, it may be possible for an employee to secure a job for the rural resident before the latter moves. Even if formalities such as a personal interview or medical examination are required, the contact can inform the prospective migrant and put in a good word with the employer. Recruitment through employee referral has advantages for employers as well, Employees tend to refer people like themselves and are usually wary of a referral who may damage their own reputation. Applicants referred by current employees are likely to be better informed about the characteristics of the job as this promotes job stability.

Rural residents may also learn of specific urban opportunities through formal channels. Vacancies for white-collar jobs are usually advertised in regional and national newspapers, and a large number of urban jobs, especially those in government establishments and public enterprises, are filled through employment exchanges. Therefore, rural residents with the required qualifications call search for urban jobs from the rural area by responding to advertisements and by registering with employment exchanges.

The survey data suggest that networks work better at the lower occupational levels. Among those who had listed urban contacts as a source of premigration information, 75 per cent had received information about manual jobs, with 46 per cent informed about a job with the same employer as their contact had. The tendency to receive information about the same job was inversely related to the status and skill of the contact's job. Migrants whose contacts worked in non-manual or skilled manual occupations were informed about the same job much less frequently than those whose contacts were engaged in unskilled manual occupations.

Migrants were generally successful in obtaining their expected employment in the first instance: the first occupation of 70 per cent of them tallied with their expectations. Still, those expecting to become clerical workers and peons were the least successful in locating their desired jobs. Even those who based their expectations for these two occupations on information from urban contacts were not very successful. This suggests that urban contacts overestimated their influence, or that their candidates lost to competition from perhaps more educated applicants.

For a fuller understanding, the choice of job search methods ought to be examined in a multivariate context. Search methods were classified into three categories based on using friends and relatives, formal application or interview, and personal search at the premises of potential employers. The cost and productivity of a search method depends on the skill and background of an individual and also on the nature of the job sought. Accordingly, we focus on the following variables: education, age at time of search, marital status, caste affiliation, region of origin, manual/non-manual nature of job, and sector of labour market in which the job is located. These variables capture demand side and supply side influences.

Migrants who are more educated, take non-manual occupations, and enter the formal sector are more likely to rely on formal channels of job search than seeking assistance from contacts or engaging in personal search. This is not surprising. Vacancies for jobs that educated persons seek, as well as job vacancies in the formal sector, are usually announced to the employment exchange and advertised in the press. Job applicants are usually required to appear for an interview and also may be required to sit for an examination. Knowing someone at the place where employment is sought may be important in competitive conditions, but the applicant has to achieve minimum standards set for the formal selection process.

The likelihood of obtaining a job through a contact falls with age and is far higher for the first urban job. Age at search proxies prior work experience and personal knowledge about labour market opportunities. Older job searchers are therefore more likely than others to engage in a personal search. By virtue of their longer work experience, they are usually better informed about labour market opportunities. Migrants who relied on contacts are more likely to enter the formal sector than those who engaged in personal search, but less likely to enter it than those who relied on formal channels of search; this is indicated by the smaller coefficient for the formal-sector employment variable in the equation for search through contacts than for the equation for formal application.

However, education, marital status, and manual/non-manual nature of the work have no significant effect on the probability of locating jobs through contacts relative to engaging in personal search. A *priori* one would expect scheduled caste migrants to shy away from personal search because of uncertainty about discrimination by prospective employers and co-workers. Instead, they should be more comfortable working for firms where friends and relatives are present who should already be aware of any discrimination. Scheduled castes are also likely to use job search through formal channels more often than those in the other castes.

The Indian government has an affirmative action policy under which a certain proportion of vacancies are usually reserved for the scheduled castes. However, results show that caste affiliation does not have a significant impact on the probabilities of using specific search methods; the coefficients of this variable are not statistically significant, though the sign is correct and the t-value larger than 1.0. We also find that place of origin of migrants does not have any significant effect on the choice of job search method. These results are encouraging in that they suggest that individuals from particular backgrounds do not feel disadvantaged in exploiting all channels of search.

In addition to help with job searches, migrants receive other forms of assistance from urban-based contacts on their arrival in the city, such as room, food, and money. The most common combination for both sources was "room, food, and job search", followed by "room, food, money and job search". Monetary help was the least common of the four types of assistance under consideration, but this does not necessarily mean that contacts were unwilling to lend money to new migrants. Rather, the data reflect the tendency of migrants not to ask for monetary help from their contacts.

Many urban households did not feel the responsibilities toward fellow villagers as toward relatives, and this difference was reflected in the patterns of help given to the two groups. In particular, urban-based contacts tended to confine their assistance to co-villagers' job searches, and that it was not common to give or lend money to co-villagers. This disparity, however, was not the experience of migrants in Delhi. When approached, co-villagers helped new migrants as adequately as relatives did. The pattern of help received by migrants who relied exclusively on relatives was similar to that received by those who relied on co-villagers only. In particular, the difference in the proportion who received monetary help was small—28 vs. 30 per cent. This finding can probably be accounted for by the widespread tendency among rural Indians and those from a rural background to attribute fictive kinship to fellow villagers.

Typically, rural Indians do not make a sharp distinction between "relatives" and "unrelated co-villagers". Rather, these individuals consider fellow villagers as a kind of relative, although not related genealogically, and commonly refer to them as "brother", "uncle", and so on. Given this attitude, urban-based contacts can be expected to give fictive kin from their village help similar to what they would give to close genealogical kin, though the degree of help may differ.

For migrants who received help from relatives and co-villagers, the patterns of help from the two sources differed considerably. Assistance from co-villagers was mainly aid-in-job search, while relatives provided all four categories of help. The type of assistance was determined mainly by the help seekers and not by the helpers. Migrants with relatives and co-villagers in the city tend not to approach co-villagers for help, and if contacted, only for limited help. New migrants prefer to obtain board and lodging from relatives if they are present.

URBAN-RURAL FAMILY LINKS

The behaviour of a multicentred family can be likened to that of a firm engaged in a multistage or multiproduct production process which finds it more profitable to set up its plants in various locations than to carry out the entire production process under one roof. Similarly, the family allocates its labour over space to maximise its net family gains.

The accumulation of surplus from migration may take place in either/both rural and urban areas. The urban-generated surplus is reflected in remittances to the rural household. The size of the surplus generated in rural areas, if any, depends on the premigration employment status of the migrant and the effect of his leaving on rural output and hence income. Connell et al. cite sociological studies which highlight the prevalence of two decision-making processes:

- The family head makes the decision on his own, and the migrant obeys this decision; and
- The family members arrive at the decision jointly.

However, the existence of multicentred families need not necessarily imply that migration is organised jointly by family members or in an authoritarian regime, and for the explicit purpose of meeting specific rural needs. Multicentred families would also arise if individuals migrated for the fulfilment of personal aspirations, and their utility function depended on the welfare of family members left behind in the rural household.

The presence of family members in the rural area was ascertained by asking migrants which members in their household were still living in the rural area at the time of the survey, and if the migrant considered himself to be a member of that rural origin family. Multicentred families were reported by those living as single-person or non-familial households and those whose urban household contained their nuclear unit, with the former being more numerous.

Among migrants, 44 per cent lived as non-familial units, over three-fifths married with their wives and children left in the rural area. The maintenance of rural links even by migrants who lived with their nuclear unit in the urban destination area reflects the pattern of family organisation in the rural area, and illustrates forcefully that family integration is not disrupted by migration. The likelihood of multicentred families is higher if migrants have a stake in rural property. Only a tenth of the migrants who came from families which owned land at the place of origin at the time of migration reported that they had no family members at origin, compared to a third of those who came from nonlandowning families.

The existence of strong ties between migrants and rural-based family members is not surprising given that other family members tended to be involved in the decision-making process. In over half of the cases, the migrants reported having consulted family members before leaving the rural area. One-tenth had left after receiving encouragement from a household member. For the rest, migration was an individual decision, in the sense that they did not consult any family member or receive suggestions from them; this does not imply that they were not concerned about rural-based family members. In many families the high degree of concern that members have for each other is supported by mutual sharing of resources. When a family acquires a multicentred character, economic ties are manifested in financial flows between the branch households. The survey data indicate that a substantial majority of urban migrants in the sample maintained economic links with the rural area through remittances. As expected, the proportion who maintained economic links was also the highest for migrants living as non-familial units.

The value of remittances tended to be related positively to urban earnings and also to the needs of the rural household, and negatively to obligations in the urban household. Also, there was no evidence of remittances weakening over time, although migrants who planned to settle in the city remitted less.

Conjugal separation is to be expected if migrants make the move alone and intend to be joined by their wives and other dependents after they have settled down in their urban jobs and found suitable accommodations. The separation of spouses in these cases is temporary and only lasts for the period required by the migrants to consolidate themselves in the city. Hence, as the duration of residence in the city increases, migrants are more likely to have their wives and children living with them. However, the "transition period" argument does not constitute a complete explanation for conjugal separation.

However, low earnings is not a valid explanation for conjugal separation. It suggests that the supply price for moving to the city with the conjugal unit is greater than the urban earnings of the affected migrants. That separation of the conjugal unit occurred suggests that these migrants were prepared to move with a lower supply price and also accept the psychic costs involved in the separation. Drawing attention to the low level of urban earnings, however, does not indicate what the actual reasons for moving with a lower supply price are. About 30 per cent of the migrants cited reasons that directly or indirectly implied that they were accumulating surplus for use in the rural area. Over one-tenth explained conjugal separation in terms of their wives having to do household work or looking after parents. For landowning migrants, another important consideration was protection of ownership rights. In 17 per cent of the cases of conjugal separation among landowning migrants, wives had been left in the rural area partly to look after the land. Except for this last reason, there was no difference between landowning and non-landowning migrants in the importance of reasons for conjugal separation.

The reasons for conjugal separation articulated by migrants reflect the subjective importance of the factors identified, and do not indicate how important these factors actually are. For this, it is necessary to consider all married migrants and compare migrants who brought their wives to the city with those who left them behind. This can be done by estimating a binary logit model in which the probability that a migrant brings his wife to the city is expressed as a function of a number of relevant demographic and socio-economic variables.

The empirical exercise confirms that the cash motive for migration and land ownership inhibits migrants from bringing their wives to the city. The size of the surplus is larger and the speed of accumulation faster if the migrant lives in a poor, non-familial household in the city, as is common. Thus an important source of saving is achieved through low expenditures on housing: the standard of housing acceptable to an individual living alone is lower than when living with his wife. As for the effects of land ownership, it can provide migrants income at old age and protection against urban unemployment. Thus migrants not covered by pension schemes, those whose urban earnings do not allow for accumulation of sufficient savings for old age, and those who do not have permanent employment all may want to safeguard their rights of access to land. If these migrants anticipate trouble in reclaiming their share of the land if it is left in the care of their brother or other relatives, they might leave their wives and children in the rural area.

The probability of a migrant's living with his wife in the city rises with the level of education. Educated persons are less likely to subscribe to traditional orthodoxy and probably place greater weight on living with their nuclear family. Further, educated migrants adjust to the urban environment more readily and tend to settle in the city permanently. Migrants with such intentions are not likely to leave their wives in the rural area. A set of regional dummies was also included in the estimated equation to capture the influence of distance and region-specific influences. Those who migrate long distances often have their wives with them. This can be partly explained by the high transport costs involved in making frequent visits to the place of origin to visit one's wife.

Migrants tends to move to urban centres after lining up a specific job, influenced by information received from urban-based contacts. Migrants are thus generally successful in obtaining employment, and the initial period of unemployment is short. Thus, it cannot be claimed that migration generally contributes significantly to urban unemployment and surplus labour.

7

Social Dimensions of Development in India

India is the largest democratic country in the world. The Republic of India has a federal structure with a written constitution. The Union of India consists of 25 states and seven union territories. For the governance of its affairs, the country follows the parliamentary system of government both at the union and state level. India achieved independence in 1947, after hundred years of colonial rule. In 1951, India initiated the process of planned development to raise the living standard of its people and to open up for them new opportunities for a richer and more varied life.

The country is committed to the achievement of rapid improvements in the quality of life of the people at large; growth with social justice, modernisation and self-reliance are the key elements of the strategy of development adopted for the purpose. In the mixed economy established by planning for development, private and public sectors co-exist and function as parts of a single organism.

India, among the developing countries, presents a unique case in terms of the sheer size of its population characterised by extra heterogeneity in respect of physical, economic, social and cultural conditions. Its population of 685 million accounted, in 1981, for about 15 per cent of the total world population with only 2.4 per cent of total land area. A number of social and economic institutions which formed a legacy of the colonial past have been transformed and modified in order that they serve better social purpose and aims of planned development. Land reforms aimed at providing landownership to the tiller, ceilings on land-holdings, distribution of land to the landless and nationalisation of insurance companies and banks are some of the important examples of institutional changes. The political system so established by the constitution leaves no scope for regimentation of any type. Human liberty and freedom of expression are zealously guarded by an independent judiciary.

The constraints imposed by the choice of democracy for governance of the country that is so vast, so diverse and so heterogeneous are quite obvious. Removal of poverty and reduction of social and economic inequalities have been at the centre of all its policies. The demographic trends witnessed during the period were a part of the overall changes generated by development; but it is also true that they in turn influenced the course of development itself. India's planning process, from its very start in 1951, recognised this interrelationship between population and the socio-economic development, that is, long before the country became a signatory of the world.

Since 1974, much greater attention has been paid to the integration of population policies into the development process, which has been increasingly concerned with the amelioration of the lot of weaker sections of the community. A review of the seventh five-year plan shows the progress achieved in several crucial areas, particularly economic growth, foodgrains production, resource mobilisation, health and human development and generation of employment. The energy sector has also recorded significant gains.

ECONOMIC DEVELOPMENT

The country's national income had been increasing less than 0.7 per cent per annum during the first half of the country. Modern industry existed on a nominal scale; factories establishments employed a meagre 1.8 per cent of the total working population. Since independence, India has travelled a long distance on the road to economic progress. It has achieved self-sufficiency in foodgrains, diversified its industrial structure and has made significant progress in science and technology. According to UNESCO's estimates, India has the third largest pool of trained scientists and engineers. Savings and investment have increased to 22.7 per cent and 24.2 per cent respectively from low levels of 10.2 and 10.0 per cent in 1950. The continuity of planning process has helped to widen the capital and human resources base to a substantial degree. During the first four years (1980-83) of the sixth plan the economy is estimated to have expanded at an annual rate of over five per cent. Despite the challenge of the drag, the determination of the nation to pursue development never flinched; the one indication of this is the increase in national savings measured as percentage of national income.

The total production of foodgrains increased from about 50 million tonnes in 1950 to a 3.3 per cent annual increase, well above the population growth rate. The limited land area of the country hardly offered any scope for expanding cultivated area. Decrease in food production during the last two decades is mainly the result of the modernisation of agriculture expansion of irrigation facilities and a package of improved or high-yielding variety of seed, chemical fertilisers, pesticides and mechanisation. Electricity consumption by the agriculture sector increased from less than one per cent (0.8 per cent) in 1960 to 17.8 per cent in 1982. Gains in agricultural sector have enabled the country to achieve self-sufficiency in foodgrains production at a higher level of foodgrain availability of 408 grams per day per person, about 25 per cent higher than the 1950 level.

The agricultural class or those who depend mainly on land or their living fell into two broad categories—the title holder and the actual cultivators. In between these two, there arose a third class who neither possessed any title to nor carried out any cultivation on land. They merely functioned as the link between the landlords at one end and the cultivators at the other. They squeezed the poor cultivators by levying high rentals and at the same time chiselled the landlords of their legitimate dues. They, thus, became the most important as well as the most ruinous class in the agricultural economy. Land reforms thus became not only necessary but urgent and unavoidable. The Planning Commission has laid down the basic principles of land reforms as follows:

a) the elimination of idle landlords and intermediaries;
b) a ceiling on holdings of substantial owners;
c) the confirmation of permanent rights to actual cultivators with the option for the lessee to purchase the holding outright at a fair price; and
d) fixation of fair rent.

The politicians capitalised on its egalitarian appeal as a powerful instrument to rope in votes for themselves. However, the most pressing question concerned tenancy and this was taken up first. Therefore, the first principle of land reforms to be put into operation in 1950-60 was land to the tiller. The law provides confinement of ownership rights in many states, security of tenure, fair rent policy, consolidation of holdings, etc. The law of ceilings 1960-61 and revision of ceilings 1970-71 have been brought into force under different stages of implementation.

The Ministry of Rural Reconstruction, formerly a department in the Ministry of Agriculture, was formed into a separate ministry in August 1979. The new ministry is to coordinate various functioning programmes of rural of developments, like the Small Farmers' Development Agency (SFDA), Drought Prone Areas Programme (DPAP), Command Area Development (CAD) and other rural-oriented schemes into an Integrated Rural Development Programme (IRDP), and generally to help the poorest of the poor in the villages to rise above the poverty line by earning substantial incremental incomes.

The Special Livestock Production Programme (SLPP) initiated in 1975-76, aims at providing employment opportunities to the weaker section of the rural population. The Desert Development Programme (DDP) was started in 1977 with the objective of controlling desertification and developing conditions suitable for raising the level of production, income and employment of the people living in these areas. The Council for Advancement of Rural

Technology (CART) has been set up under the Ministry of Rural Development to act as a nodal point for the transfer of appropriate technology, after its development, to all the villages of the country.

Industrial production has gone up by about five times during this period. Apart from the quantitative increase in output, the industrial structure has been greatly diversified, covering almost the entire range of consumer, intermediate and capital goods. The rate of industrial growth, however, has not been uniform during this period: the average growth rate of industrial production in three years during the 1980-83 period has been 6.9 per cent. The progress of certain key infrastructure sectors provides an idea of the scale of achievements of planning in the industrial field.

The more recent quantum jump in the output of petroleum products has been truly remarkable. Indigenous production of crude oil doubled during the last two years from 10.5 to 21.1 million tonnes in 1982. It recorded further increase of over 5.1 million tonnes in 1983. The changing character of the national economy is well reflected by the changes in the composition of the GDP. This encouraging trend in the composition of output is unfortunately not reflected in the structure of the country's labour force, the principal reason for this being the rapidity with which population and labour force have increased. India remains, therefore, a predominantly agricultural country with nearly 76 per cent of its population living in 576,000 villages and 70 per cent deriving their livelihood from agriculture.

The planning process started with the objective of rapid increase in GDP, but with the passage of time, unemployment acquired urgency and so, during the late sixties, the creation of employment opportunities gained importance and it became a part of planning. According to the 1981 census, out of the total population of 685 million, 222 million were main workers, i.e., those who worked throughout the year. More than 79 per cent of the main workers were males. In addition to this, there were 27 million marginal workers who did not work for the major part of the year preceding the census. Among the main workers, nearly 63 per cent of males and 70 per cent of females were engaged in the agricultural sector, while industry provided employment to only 12 per cent of the males and about eight per cent of the female workers. The inter-census comparisons are difficult; however, it is noticed that the shift away from agriculture has been slow. Unemployment has assumed a serious proposition in both rural and urban areas; the problem is particularly severe among the new entrants to the labour force, especially for the educated among them. In an agricultural country like India, the incidence of under-employment, too, is equally serious.

According to the thirty-second round of the national sample survey, 11 million persons were estimated to be unemployed in 1980. The net addition to the labour force was expected to be 34 million persons during the plan period (1980-85). The sixth five-year plan envisaged the creation of 14 million jobs during the period 1980-81 to 1984-85. Investment required for absorbing 45 million people in the manufacturing sector was Rs. 3,600 billion.

The restrictions on international flow of people do in fact contradict the philosophy of a free market based on free movement of both labour and capital. International migration, in quantitative terms has played an insignificant role in the total demographic situation in India. Certain streams of migration, however, deserve mention for their qualitative impact. The post-independence period witnessed a small but significant migration of skilled and semi-skilled manpower to the Middle-East and Gulf countries.

On the other hand, in the post-independence period, there has been some increase in migration due to two types of flows, viz., the return immigration of persons of Indian origin settled earlier in British colonies and those from the neighbouring countries. Though numerically small for the country as a whole, these flows can cause concern due to their impact on the local situation in certain border areas. According to the census of 1981, there were about eight million persons in India with place of birth outside India. An analysis of the total internal migration indicated that there is a significant rural-urban migration. There is preponderance of intra-district migration which accounts for nearly 65 per cent of the total internal migration. As for the cause of migration among females, marriage is the most important because according to the custom in India, the females, after marriage, live at the place of their husband.

The rural-urban flow is generally the result of population pressure and search for employment opportunities. It has been noticed that migration is mostly directed towards states with low density and areas with scope for industrial or agricultural expansion. The density of population in India according to the 1981 census was 216. The density of population varies from state to state ranging from 45 in Sikkim to 655 in Kerala.

During the colonial rule in the 19th century, a trend of de-urbanisation associated with decline of indigenous industries started and the population sunk to 10.8 per cent in 1901. Therefore, the trend of urbanisation has been one of increase. During the 1940s, there was a notable increase and the urban population reached a level of 17.3 per cent in 1951. Since 1961, there has been a continuous upward trend and the urban population increased to 19.9 per cent in 1971 and 23.3 per cent in 1981. Although India can still be considered as one of the least urbanised countries in the world, there are 218 cities with population above 100,000 and nearly 60 per cent of the urban live in these cities.

The corresponding percentage in 1961 and 1971 was 50.9 and 56.3, respectively. It is also notable that 26.7 per cent of urban population live in 12 cities having population of more than one million. Included among the largest cities are Calcutta, Mumbai, Delhi and Chennai with 1981 population ranging from 4.3 to 9.2 million. Sufficient focus was given to the country's development plans on urbanisation as an important aspect of the process of distribution of economic activities.

In the sixth plan also, the same approach was adopted and the thrust has been on provision of infrastructure and other facilities in small and medium concentrations of urban population in a few big cities. The government has also been taking steps to avoid excessive concentration of economic activities through a series of policies including industrial licensing with emphasis on appropriate location and dispersal of finance from public financial institutions for locating industries in backward and non-industrial districts.

The president of India is the constitutional head of the executive of the union. Though the Constitution vests executive power in the president, it also specifies that the said power is to be exercised in accordance with the Constitution. The real executive power thus vests in the council of ministers with the prime minister as the head. The Constitution distributes the legislative power between the union and state legislatures and provides for vesting of residual powers in parliament. The legislature of the union, which is called parliament, consists of two houses—the council of states (Rajya Sabha) and the house of the people (Lok Sabha). Each house of parliament has to meet within six months of its previous sitting and a joint sitting of the two houses can be held in certain cases. However, in India's bicameral legislature, the relative powers of the upper house (Rajya Sabha) and the lower house (Lok Sabha) follow the British, rather than American prototype. The upper house is only half as large, with twelve of its 250 members appointed by the president for distinguished attainment in arts and science, the others elected by the representatives of states.

The Rajya Sabha is not subject to dissolution, one-third of its members retiring on the expiration of every second year. The Lok Sabha is elected for five years, but may be dissolved by presidential decision. The membership of the Rajya Sabha, as constituted at present, is 244. Of these, 232 represent the states and union territories and twelve members are nominated by the president. The Lok Sabha is constituted of 544 members. Of these, 525 are directly elected from 22 states and 17 from nine union territories. Two members are nominated by the president to represent the Anglo-Indian community, if that community is not adequately represented in the house.

The allocation of seats in the present Lok Sabha is based on the 1981 census and, under the 42nd Amendment of the Constitution (1976), will continue to be so based until figures of the first census taken after A.D. 2000 become available. The Legislative Assembly (Vidhan Sabha) of a state consists of not more than 500 and not less than 60 members chosen by direct election from territorial constituencies in the states.

The legislative council (Vidhan Parishad) of a state comprises not more than one-third of the total number of members in the legislative assembly of the state and in no case less than 40 members, except the legislative council of Jammu and Kashmir. The legislative councils are not subject to dissolution but one-third of the members of the council are elected by members of the legislative assembly from amongst persons who are not its members, one-third by electorates consisting of members of municipalities, district board and other local authorities in the state, one-twelfth by electorate consisting of persons who have been, for at least three years, engaged in teaching in educational institutions within the state not lower in standard than secondary schools and a further one-twelfth by registered graduates of more than three years' standing.

The administration of the city vests in an elected council. There were 67 municipal corporations in the country in 1984. The Calcutta Corporation Act has been recently amended to provide for the system of Mayor-in-Council. The traditional caste panchayat may operate at three levels, these being house panchayat, a village panchayat, and a regional panchayat (the size of the region varies considerably). This is merely a formal description; the panchayat system is variable and these three categories do not necessarily exist in all parts of the country. However, caste panchayat may punish a violation of the rules of caste discrimination, but the law forbids caste discrimination. A panchayat is theoretically an assembly of five persons ('Panch'—five), but in fact there is no fixed number. Tradition and custom give it administrative and judicial authority. However, in several states the two-tier or even a one-tier system exists. The states design the structure of these institutions in the light of the local conditions. Different tiers of the Panchayati Raj system are originally linked up.

Special representation is given to backward classes, women and cooperative societies. Elected directly by and from among villages, the panchayats are responsible for promotion of agriculture, rural industries, provision of medical relief, maternity and child welfare, maintaining common grazing grounds, village roads, tanks, wells and provision for sanitation. Village panchayats exist in all the union territories except Lakshadweep and Mizoram. There are at present 2,17,319 village panchayats, 4,526 panchayat samitis (Council of Panchayat leaders), which in turn embrace the gram panchayats of their regions.

The Planning Commission noted that the chief purpose of this policy was to involve all the people in the rural areas to work for their own development. Nyaya-panchayats or village courts have also been set up to provide speedy and inexpensive system of justice to the villagers in some of the states. A comparison for convenience sake—the political parties are considered in different classes: the Congress Party as a 'centre left-wing' party; further left are the Socialist and Communist parties; further right are the various conservative parties and the local political personalities elected for different reasons and termed 'independents; in the parliamentary assemblies. Political parties play a significant part in elections held under the parliamentary system.

CONTEMPORARY SOCIAL TRANSFORMATION

The inter-structural autonomy of the social components in traditional Indian society has deeply influenced the nature and direction of its social change. Their role could be evaluated through various stages of historical transformation. The first stage coincided with the beginning of the Western contact through British Rule which set the pace for cultural renaissance, initial industrialisation and the growth of a new political consciousness culminating in the national freedom movement. These forces brought about major changes in the Indian society, especially in the areas of institution-building for a civic society, the growth of modern education and judicial administrative structures. It was marked paradoxically by a process of de industrialisation and ruralisation of the economy on the one hand and the emergence of a colonial mode of industrialisation and modernisation on the other. These innovations convulsed the traditional social structure, led to the downward mobility of several privileged classes and families, and the upward mobility of others drawn from the traditional business classes and feudal nobility.

The social mobility created new classes of educationists, administrators, professionals, businessmen, company agents and others who took advantage of the opportunities available in the early phases of colonial transformation. The emergence of these social groups, together with cultural awakening and reform movements in various part of the country, prepared the ground for political awareness and the national movement. This became a potent source of social and ideological mobilisation, intensifying the sense of collective self-awareness. A strategy was evolved, not only for political independence but for social, economic and cultural modernisation of society. The emphasis on the involvement of women, members of the weaker sections, peasants and workers reflected this ideological perspective. Political leadership at the local, regional, and national level emerged.

A substantial section of the middle classes comprising educationists, professionals, bureaucrats and businessmen had already set forth a new process of social mobility. This process of change, however, had a segmentary character. It did not affect large parts of the rural peasantry, working classes, scheduled castes, and scheduled tribes. The national movement too, in many ways, had a segmentary character, despite periods of mass mobilisation.

The inter-structural autonomy of the Indian social system was possible responsible for this. It made possible the selective modernisation to take place. Along with enclaves of rapid social transformation it left massive areas of society untouched by winds of change. This elitist or segmentary nature of social change had its positive features. It helped galvanise social energies of the people to fight against foreign rule without maximising internal schisms. The British policy of "divide and rule" only partially succeeded.

The evolution of a constitutional and democratic strategy of social transformation has been possible also due to this social feature. It kept the pace of transformation within the tolerance limit of culture and society.

After independence, a policy framework was introduced to strengthen institutions which served the objective of justice in a society. It meant also the abolition of the age-old principles of inter-structural autonomy in Indian society. The principles of inequality based on caste, birth, religion and sex were, in a normative sense, derecognised, though not successfully abolished. The new institutions which sought to replace them implied changes in society which had very revolutionary implications. The Constitution of India broadly lays down these objectives. In some areas, the policy of change began to show immediate results. These were electoral politics, agrarian reforms, industrial and economic expansion, and investment in education, science and technology. All these coincided with an expanding role of communication and media participation.

Electoral politics, apart from its liberating psychological effects on the mind of people, released new social energy in society. This was compounded by the abolition of intermediary rights in land and the introduction of panchayat raj and community development schemes in the villages. The rural areas were thus exposed to major forces of social change.

The nature of social change in India's village during the fifties and sixties indicates an uneven impact on its social structure. The domination of the traditional castes and classes continued despite social and economic reforms. The electoral challenges from the lower castes, the extenantry, working classes and the weaker sections did not alter the traditional power structure. The benefits of extension work in agriculture, animal husbandry, irrigation, marketing, credit and cooperative were monopolised by the traditional upper caste rich strata.

More significant changes in the power structure of the rural society took place in the southern stages than in the northern ones, because of the differences in caste demography. In this region too, spectacular patterns of changes emerged later as the investment made during the fifties and sixties matured in the seventies and eighties. Social mobility during the first two decades after independence was slow and mainly confined to the upper castes and classes. The poorer sections of peasantry, agricultural workers and harijans did feel the liberating impact of the new reforms, psychologically, and in some measure culturally but their overall impact on their social status and power and income remained marginal. Similar processes had been taking place in urban centres. The urban change during this period has been termed as "over-urbanisation". It meant city word migration of population without it occupational integration in the urban industrial workforce. It led to urban degradation, exploitation and impoverishment.

The increase in entrepreneurship and industrial investment was confined to the upper classes. The opportunities of education, especially in science, technology, medicine and professions continued to be the preserve of the privileged groups. Some openings were, however, found by the agricultural labourers, peasants, scheduled castes and tribes to send their children to the primary and secondary schools, and a very small proportion of them went to colleges or institutions of higher education. A few among them could survive up to the university level of education. Sociologically, however, even the school and college drop-outs severed an important function later as catalysers of social, economic, and cultural change in their society.

The changes during the first two decades after independence were also segmentary as in the past. There were, however, some major differences. The scope and potential of the social transformation now was much larger and the aspiration for social mobility had ceased to be segmentary. It had assumed a truly structural dimension engulfing the whole society. This, with the rising population, preponderance of the young in society, greater political participation, exposure to the media, such as radio, newspapers, magazines and public meetings led to a new social and political awareness.

The welfare policies of reservations for the scheduled castes and tribes, land reforms and developmental planning led to the emergence of a category of people from among the lower strata who were self-conscious of their deprivation, could assume a leadership role for their community and mobilise them for organisation and protest. The release of these social forces also coincided with major investment in science and technology, agriculture, industry, and health. The cumulative result of these showed results during the seventies and eighties. In many rural regions there took place the "green revolution", and the rise of new peasant middle classes.

In the urban-industrial domain, a new mercantile entrepreneurial class has emerged. However, in the realm of culture and national ideology, the values of secularism, social justice, consensus and participation have increasingly come under strain. These spell out serious consequences for the political culture and its future in India. We have to understand these forces, redefine our strategies and plan for the future. Today, the changes in rural India, which constitutes the dominant sector of our society, are bringing about a process of rapid social restructuration. It is leading to a breakdown in the segmentary mode of social change, a rise of new middle classes to power, massive absorption of science and technology in agriculture and substantial changes in beliefs.

The green revolution signifies not merely growth in agricultural production but also the use of new technology and new social relationships in production processes. These developments make this phase of changes in rural economy and society distinctive. A new interaction among technology, social relationship and culture is now taking place in rural society. This has resulted in social mobility, emergence of new power structure and mode of exploitation of the deprived classes. It has generated new contradictions in society. The green revolution has been basically a contribution of the middle caste peasantry, who have had traditionally, a strong attachment to land and agriculture as a mode of work and livelihood.

The green revolution marks a basic departure from the traditional pattern. The family mode of production continues, but authority has passed from the older to the younger generation. The new agriculture requires the skill in the peasant to negotiate with banks, revenue authorities, police administration, marketing bodies and block development administration. One is required to consult the experts and technicians for irrigation, social testing, fertilisers and seeds. This could not be handled by the older generation of peasants. This role is increasingly being performed by the younger generation, college or school educated or even a dropout from these institutions. This change is also reflected in the panchayat elections and the rural electoral politics in general. The green revolution has led to the consolidation of the status of the middle peasantry as a dominant class. But the rural poor too have become more organised. They too have now a youthful leadership which deals with agencies of development, political parties and institutions of law and order.

The upper caste-class groups who traditionally dominated have now been either replaced by the middle peasantry or have to compete with them to maintain their traditional status and power. They employ a variety of strategies of cooperation, compromises and occasional confrontations to remain in power. These triangular sets of social forces in rural society, which are particularly prominent in the northern states, lead increasingly to social polarisation, large scale migration to cities, social tensions, and erosion of political culture. The quality of relationship between the middle caste peasantry and the lower castes has particularly declined and is marked by exploitation and violence.

The peasantry have led a tradition of Bhakti movements or other reform movements in various parts of the country; their sub-culture has always had a strong ethic of workmanship, industry, frugality and conservative utilitarianism. These values combined with the social processes of upward mobility and social, political and economic dominance, have given birth to a cultural milieu which is more self-centred and antipathic to values of accommodation and social justice. Their relationship with the agricultural working classes, the lower castes and *harijans* is increasingly that of aggressiveness and antipathy. This is being reciprocated by the lower caste working classes as well, leading to a sharp decline in the cultural ethos of the rural society.

A situation is emerging in which the dominant classes do not take to policies of protective discrimination and the weaker sections do not accept the legitimacy of such reform measures either. The result is more conflict and less consensus on social issues. This happens when more and more mobility and development is taking place. We see in this process mixed blessing for society in general. It indicates a remarkable process of restructuration and social mobility. It reflects the rise of an economic ethic which is productive and generates surpluses and capital accumulation. It has already achieved a degree of shift of authority in favour of the younger people. It reinforces the resilience of the social system for selective absorption of technology, leading to high productivity and growth in agriculture. These changes have contributed to the upward mobility of the middle classes on the one hand, and on the other sharpened the self-awareness of the lower castes and poorer classes. They have resorted to large scale migration to towns, cities and other regions of India in search of employment and better opportunities. These developments, however, also coincide with negative social processes.

A change in the value system and ideology of people which promotes localism, casteism, and communalism has taken place. This results in a conflictual and exploitative relationship between the peasant classes and the rural poor. It also results in negative perceptions of the work, status and role of women. Its cultural outcome is that of the revival of masculinism, increase in the dowry system and cultural conservatism. Thus, social changes have also brought about conflict and maladjustment in the structure of society.

The massive investment in industry and technology which took place during the first two decades after independence has resulted in significant development in industrial activities and the rise of entrepreneurial classes in the urban areas. The size of the urban middle classes has more than doubled. The number of entrepreneurs of small and medium size, as also those having a broader social background, also have grown in substantial measure. This has come with the rise in commercial and industrial activities.

Compared to the traditional business classes, who largely had their social origin in the trading castes or communities, the new merchant class comes from a diverse and broader social background. It has contributed to the weakening of the segmentary social base of commercial and industrial capitalism in India, a process similar to that taking place in rural society. The growth in the size of the services, professions and the administrative or developmental bureaucracy reflects the social dynamism and mobility in the urban-industrial sector of life. Slowly, the process of mercantile capitalism is growing and maturing into industrial capitalism.

The rise in urban population, mostly of an unplanned nature, has put severe pressure on urban facilities, services, housing, sanitation, health, and ecology. It has led to proliferation of slums, over-urbanisation, increase in crime and other problems. The sheer weight of unplanned growth in urban population puts its civic culture and amenities in jeopardy. Speculative and clandestine commercial activities get linked up with exploitation of the urban poor. It breeds cultural anomie, and promotes sectarianism, communalism and regionalism. These negative aspects of urbanisation and industrialisation go together with a positive growth in entrepreneurship and industry. An urban middle class has also emerged with the rise of mercantile and industrial capitalism.

The social base of the middle classes has thus broadened both in urban and rural societies. The cultural background and ethos of this middle class has not, however, been studied fully, but it is obvious that it sets the trend for the contemporary process of modernisation. What is it—a modernisation ideology? This question assumes significance for an analysis of the existing patterns and future direction of social change in India. The cultural values of the emergent rural middle classes show sharper contradictions between their ideology and "national" goals of social transformation.

The historical context of the urban-industrial transformation today is different. The entrepreneurs and capitalist classes arose during the past three decades, and have a different value system. The traditional business classes had interacted closely with the national movement and its political and economic ideology. The new business classes, despite being a product of the national economic and social policies, have a value structure that is more inwardly directed. It is often governed by short-run business interests rather than long-term national economic and social goals commensurate with national policies.

The new capitalist class has grown under the protection of the nation's economic policies and has enjoyed political support, but its commitment to the cosmopolitan values of national development, social justice, welfare, liberalism and nationally has yet to be established. The evidence often suggests its negative or indifferent commitment to these values. Industrial capitalism has not successfully grown in any society without a strong national ethical tradition and its discipline in personal and public conduct. The ethical use of the emerging rural and urban capitalism has a complex character.

The processes of change in the family have also responded to forces of modernisation. The family system in India has not only undergone changes due to pressure of economic forces, social mobility and urbanisation, but has also contributed to the process of economic modernisation as such. In the rural areas, the green revolution has a strong base in the joint family mode of production. There is some evidence to suggest that the nature of family authority has also undergone changes in favour of younger sons who have some education due to the demands of interaction with new structures such as band markets, administrative and developmental bureaucracies, health centres and laboratories.

The older generation has seen wisdom in accommodating the younger male family members in decision-making roles in the family. The same process is also visible in the industrial and entrepreneurial activities. The positive relationship between the joint family system and the industrial entrepreneurship has been established by a series of sociological studies. It is found that in raising credit, managing family firms and ensuring efficiency, continuity and confidentiality in decision making the family members play a significant role. This reinforces the relationship between the family system and the industrial entrepreneurship in India.

Family culture and the values of sharing and sacrifice have strengthened the corporate values of the industrial entrepreneurial systems, and a breakdown in the same leads to day functions in the enterprise. Moreover, the milieu of the joint family and its pattern of role allocations ensure entrepreneurial innovativeness among members. Interestingly, both in the rural-agricultural and industrial sectors of our economy and society, the family system is seen playing a significant adaptive role in the process of change and modernisation. It is, however, not without tensions and contradictions.

The increasing strength of the joint family values together with economic prosperity have contributed to exploitation of women, increased violence against them and their marginalisation into work and status. This growth has contributed to the rise of a sub-culture of masculinism and neo-conservativism in rural and urban areas. This has caused inter-gender conflicts and led to demands of dowry and violence against women. The technological innovations, followed by economic development, are also seen displacing women from work more and affect their economic and social status. The family system in the process of change in the society brings out this dualistic direction of change as evidenced in most other sectors of social life.

A process of social restructuration is taking place in the urban and industrial sectors of our life. It symbolises social dynamism, mobility and growth and yet, it serves as a harbinger of increasing culture, disvalues and anomie. The increase in the social and ideological chasm between the urban rich-middle classes and the urban poor-weaker sections indicates it. It is compounded by the high degree of communication exposure, mass media participation, and political activism.

The professional and intellectual classes, who could normally perform integrative roles and catalysts of modernisation and positive social values have a fractured moral existence. Studies of the professions of medicine, law, science and technology, humanities and social sciences reveal a schismatic character of its ideology. Yet, there have been recently new cultural and ideological movements in India. The two important cultural sources which initiate this process are those of science and religious values.

The fear of social scientists that religious values in India would hamper the growth of science and technology has been disproved. Still, traditional values do retard the process of institutionalisation of science in our social life. The view that science would displace religions from human life too has been disproved. In India, as in many other societies, modernisation processes initiated by science and technology proceed along with adaptive changes in religious values and beliefs.

In most of the contemporary world, advancement in science has not been able to check the rise of sectarian, racial and other fundamentalist beliefs. The cultural transformation in our society, which has made successful adaptive synthesis between scientific, technological and traditional values, too, now shows tension of rising fundamentalism. The disvalues of religion or its narrow fundamentalist, communal and sectarian manifestations have their origin in a process of mystification. Mystification is rampant in the contemporary historical context of religion.

Mystification is defined as a process by which values that belong to the instrumental domains, such as economic, political, racial or communitarian values, etc., are lifted from their relevant contexts and transfigurated into categorical values by an interpretive fiat or demagogy. Thus, issues which normally belong to the instrumental or rational realm, and could be sorted out as such are withdrawn from this domain and passed on to the domain of unreason. This defines the character of fundamentalist ideology. One has to investigate the social conditions under which this transfiguration takes place to strike at the root of fundamentalism and its problems in modern society. Its origin lies in exploitation of people's anxieties and frustrations on account of their human conditions—existential, social, and spiritual. A major part of these anxieties arise from social inequalities and exploitation, and powerful vested interests who feel threatened by the maximisation of opportunities of social mobility and freedom.

The process of social restructuration going on in our society today is full of contradictions. We witness economic growth with increasing social inequalities, political freedom with foreclosure of existential opportunities, changes in values and definition of the self without elasticity in social structure or its power base and social mobility without a corresponding evolution of an organic consciousness.

The segmentary nature of traditional social structure with its inter structural autonomy had the advantage of encapsulating the impact of changes at the selective levels of social structure. That is how the first stage of modernisation could proceed in India without major upheavals in society. At the present stage of modernisation the very principles of inter-structural autonomy are breaking down. In fact, this is how it should be, in order to establish a democratic, free and just social order. But this process is relating social, cultural and emotional forces in society that render the rise in expectations so fast and intense, that the process of social restructuration cannot keep peace with this transition. Thus, it retards the growth of organic social and cultural consciousness.

The accelerated pace of social restructuration, which has enlarged the size of the rural and urban middle classes, encouraged entrepreneurial activities and the process of urbanisation, etc., has not, however, reinforced cultural values of secularism, justice, and equality. It has encouraged an ideology, that is non-cosmopolitan, and neo-conservative. Sham meritocracy, utilitarian opportunism and ethical fuzziness are its main features. The poorer and exploited classes perceive in this cultural profile of the middle classes a rejection of their identity. Their cultural perceptions suffer a semiotic break which leads them to "subalternity" or a search for counter-models of values. Insurgent ideology is a product of such subalternity. We have observed it happening in the ideology of the caste system.

There has been a movement among some scheduled castes to reject the brahmanical model of pollution-purity for one based on class exploitation. Such alienative cultural processes have obstructed the growth of cosmopolitan cultural tradition commensurate with our national ideology. Traditionally, the organic cultural values were sustained in India by a creative linkage between the folk art-forms, its rich oral tradition and the classical art-forms of the elite. There was a syncretic relationship between the two cultural traditions. The local and the cosmopolitan cultural traditions interacted together in their diversity and unity constituting a whole.

The pace of social restructuration, the emergence of new classes and the decline of traditional cultural institutions exemplify this process. Social mobility, migration and occupational diversification break the traditional institutional basis of art and culture. Society thus forces a dual cultural crisis: decline of the traditional forms and institutions on the one hand and on the other the feebleness of the new cultural institutions and forms. Here, the role of modern communication technology, both of the point and the electronic media, assumes immense importance.

8

Poverty Alleviation and Rural Development Programmes in India

Poverty reduction has been the fundamental goal of the Indian economic and social policy. Yet, the sixth plan estimated that in 1979-80 around 50 per cent of the entire population or nearly 340 million people lived below the poverty line, modestly defined as monthly per capita expenditure of Rs. 76 in rural areas and Rs. 88 in urban areas. Poverty in India is not related to inequitable distribution: those above the poverty line have a monthly per capita income of only about Rs. 136 per month. A recent analysis of the developing situation in India has concluded that there was no support for the hypothesis that the distribution of income here is getting worse. It has further concluded that the poorest 40 per cent are receiving a gradual but increasing share of the total national income and that the concentration of income is declining. The last decades have seen large scale public investment, benefits for the poor in terms of more easily available and cheaper food, higher incomes, employment opportunities and improved access to modern products and markets.

Higher investment and consequent economic growth have played a crucial role in poverty alleviation in India. Since the early eighties, public programmes especially directed at assisting the poor have played an important and supportive role. These can be grouped under three heads:

1) Minimum needs programme which widens access for the poor to the basic social services, education, health, family planning, water supply, shelter, nutrition, etc.

2) Targeted assistance for special groups or areas. Integrated rural development programmes, national rural employment programmes, programmes for backward classes, hill areas and drought-prone areas.
3) Pricing and regulatory policies like subsidies on food, and incentive to industries located in the backward areas and self-employment schemes.

For a country like India, where the rural poor constitute a sizeable fraction of its population, where agriculture provides 35 per cent of its GDP and where 65 per cent of the population depend on agriculture, macro-economic policies play a particularly important role in poverty alleviation. To remove poverty is to increase the real incomes of the poor. This can be achieved by (a) providing them with more assets such as land (for example, through redistribution) or skills (through education and training) which increase their income-earning capabilities; (b) increasing the value of their assets which is mainly comprised of unskilled labour, through increasing the demand for such labour; (c) reducing the cost of food on which the poor spend greater part of their incomes; or (d) increasing their incomes through transfer payments. All these call for policies for rapid economic growth and/or redistribution. The critical role of macro-economic policies in promoting growth and employment is well recognised. Given the size of the population under poverty, any redistributive programme, even a targeted one, will have significant macroeconomic incidence which cannot be neglected and some of which can in the long run even defeat the purpose of the policy.

India's Development Strategy

The objective of India's development strategy has been to establish a socialistic pattern of society through economic growth with self-reliance, social justice and alleviation of poverty. The institutional framework of a mixed economy is used where both public and private sectors co-exist and where a national planning commission sets targets for sectoral development and various social welfare programmes. During most of the past four decades the desired sectoral allocations were sought through industrial licensing and restricting imports only under import permits. Self-reliance was equated with import substitution and whenever a product was domestically available, imports were generally not permitted. India has followed a development strategy based largely on import substitution and only in the last few years has export promotion been considered a feasible and worthwhile option for accelerating development.

The strategy for industrialisation was based on a heavy-industry first strategy. Self-reliance also required that technology imports were restricted to one-time import and subsequent assimilation of the imported technology. Thus reduction in the import content, rather than domestic resource cost of production, became the guiding parameter of the drive towards self-reliance. This strategy led to what was obvious to some but what is now obvious with a 20/20 hindsight to most people a number of problems. The heavy industries involved hefty investment with high capital/output ratios and long gestation lags, and required large imports of capital goods. The gestation period was unduly long, owing to inadequate infrastructure, lack of experience and the necessity of learning by doing. Obviously these factors increased the cost which cascaded into all industries using these inputs.

In order to protect the high-cost domestic industry against foreign imports, trade was restricted and protection through high tariff and quotas was provided. To stimulate investment on domestically produced high-cost capital goods, capital was subsidised and factor prices got distorted resulting in choice of more capital-intensive techniques than would have been appropriate given the factor endowments of the country. Even if such a strategy was applied properly, a capital-intensive slow growth economy would have occurred naturally. Such types of economic policies encourage industrialists, traders, bureaucrats and politicians to go for rent-seeking activities that provide immediate financial benefits rather than going for long-term economic gains through efficient domestic production of goods. The domestic industry which was already protected from foreign competition through import restrictions against any domestically available product, and from domestic competition through industrial licensing, had thus no incentive to be efficient. The slow growth of the economy (35 per cent per annum on the average from 1950-1980) and employment did not help much in reducing poverty as the population kept growing at a rate exceeding 2.2 per cent per annum. This inward-looking development strategy implemented through bureaucratically controlled quantity restrictions (called the "permit-quota raj") started to move gradually towards liberalisation in 1980. Perhaps, liberalisation is too charitable a word. The policy changes over the 1980s are better described as a process of debureaucratisation in which licensing requirements were relaxed for increasingly larger levels of investments and in which more and more items were permitted to be imported without an import permit, though still with a substantial tariff. Even this has resulted in a significant increase in the growth rate of the Indian economy exceeding five per cent per annum over the 1980s compared to 3.6 per cent per annum over the previous three decades.

This higher growth rate has also resulted in reduced unemployment over the period in rural areas. In terms of number of person-days of unemployment, the rates have come down for both rural males and females. For urban males and females the rates have not shown any uniform trend since 1972/73 though over the 1980s it has come down for males and increased for females. However, in terms of persons employed by what is known as usual status, the situation has not improved in the 1980s. Why then has the regular employment not increased as fast as employment in terms of person-days over this period? For an answer we need to look at some aspects of industrial and labour policy.

INDUSTRIAL POLICY

Despite a buoyant growth rate of industrial output in the 1980s, the growth of industrial employment has remained low. Employment in the organised manufacturing sector grew at 2.42 per cent per annum from 1971 to 1981 and at 0.66 per cent per annum over the 1981-1986 period.

The slow growth of employment in the manufacturing sector can be ascribed to the broad development strategy pursued. It could be seen that the highly protected industries show a capital/labour ratio that is five times higher than for low protected industries. The low protected industries employed 77.7 per cent of total persons engaged while using only 43.1 per cent of the total fixed capital, while the high protected industries with 53.2 per cent of the fixed capital engaged only 18.5 per cent of total persons engaged. The output of some of the high-protected industries may not be easily tradable. However, if only 50 per cent of the capital from high protected industries were to use the same capital/labour ratio as the low protected industries, industrial employment would have been 40 per cent higher. This indicates the cost in terms of lost employment due to the adherence to faulty development strategy.

The World Bank claims that the estimates are fairly robust. They point to a significant trade-off between the real cost of labour and employment. It could be surmised that during the 1980s the organised sector employment growth slowed down due to the negative effect of increases in real cost of labour, which could not be adequately offset by the positive impact of faster growth in manufacturing value added.

The real cost of organised labour has been way above the costs of unorganised labour. A labour policy which protects employment operates in many ways. Labour laws make it extremely difficult to retrench any worker. Even economically unviable units are also not permitted to close down. In fact such units are often taken over by the government. Along with this job security, a number of other benefits such as one month's pay as annual bonus is given to workers as a deferred pay without linking it to productivity or even profitability of the enterprise.

As a consequence, entrepreneurs are forced to restrict regular employment. One can expect recourse to subcontracting and ancillarisation. The observation that, in terms of person-days, unemployment has gone down but has increased in terms of usual status is consistent with such an explanation. Thus in some sense, inspite of government policy, some benefits of growth do percolate as additional person-days of employment. This can be expected to have a positive impact on poverty reduction as is observed for the 1980s.

PUBLIC SECTOR

The public sector has been assigned a pivotal role in the development process, particularly in reducing concentration of economic power, providing large investments in basic industries and infrastructure, generating investible surpluses and serving as a model employer. Roughly 50 per cent of the capital formation in the Indian economy since 1965/66 has been in the public sector. It has reached the "commanding heights" in the sense that more than two-thirds of the employment in the organised sector is in the public sector and it generates around 55 per cent of the value added in the organised sector. Unfortunately, the public sector has failed miserably in generating surpluses and its gross savings have been less than 40 per cent of the investment in the public sector over the 1950 to 1985 period. All commercial public sector enterprises together showed an after-tax net profit of 4.7 per cent on their sales. For the non-financial enterprises, it was only 1.3 per cent of sales. Given the generally high capital/output ratio of these enterprises, this indicates a very poor return on investment. The gravity of this failure of public sector enterprises to generate adequate surpluses can be appreciated when it is noted that in 1983/84 the non-financial commercial public sector had a total net savings of Rs. 1,295 crores while its net capital formation that year was Rs. 12,766 crores.

The public sector has, however, fulfilled one objective, that is, it is a role of a model employer. This is true at least from the viewpoint of those employed by it but not from the viewpoint of economic efficiency. The public sector has become a high-wage island in the economy. In 1980/81, the public sector employees accounted for 6.8 per cent of the labour force who received as much as 39.8 per cent of the wages and salaries in the entire economy. The situation must have become even more skewed now after the revision in government pay scales in the late 1980s. The indifferent performance of the public sector has had serious consequences for the poor as it has significantly lowered the growth rate of the economy and has pushed wages higher in the organised sector as a whole. This has led to a choice of relatively more capital-intensive techniques and further constrained the growth of employment.

The location of public sector enterprises to promote regionally balanced industrialisation has also not been very successful. Politically determined locations involve some economic costs. While these may be considered acceptable from the viewpoint of regional equity, location of large public sector enterprises do not seem to have stimulated development of other industries in the area. Thus Bihar continues to remain industrially underdeveloped in spite of having many public sector heavy industry units and in spite of its large mineral resources. Perhaps a labour force spoiled by public sector indulgence does not attract other entrepreneurs.

In spite of the relatively poor performance of the Indian economy, poverty in India has been somewhat contained. This is because from the very beginning concern for the poor has been at the centre of Indian political debate. India's economic policy always had an egalitarian and redistributive bias following from the Constitution which valued a just social order and reinforced by Nehru's deep concern for the distribution of economic gains.

After a decade of planning, Nehru's government had to appoint a committee in 1960 under the Chairmanship of Professor P.C. Mahalanobis to study the distribution of income and levels of living in India. Even before this committee submitted its report in 1964, Pitambar Pant, then the head of the Perspective Planning Division of the Planning Commission, prepared a paper in 1962 outlining a 15-year perspective plan, the objective of which was to assure a minimum level of living for the entire Indian population by 1976. He argued that the central concern of our planning has to be the removal of poverty as early as possible. The stage has now come when we should sharply focus our efforts on providing an assured minimum income to every citizen of the country within a reasonable period of time. Progressively the minimum itself should be raised as development goes apace.

Pant rejected massive redistributions "operationally meaningless unless revolutionary changes in property rights and scale and structure of wages and compensation are contemplated." He argued that rapid growth is vital for poverty alleviation since "a comparison of distribution of incomes in different countries... at very different levels of development and with varying socio-political environments... follows a remarkably similar pattern, especially in respect to the proportion of incomes earned by the lowest three or four deciles of the population". However, he recognised that "on account of certain peculiarities of the Indian economy, it is, however, uncertain whether the distribution of income will remain stable with development or how it will change". Indeed, the paper elaborated on the Indian economy, with specific references to the poor living in remote rural areas and belonging to the vast reserve of underemployed labour force with limited mobility. It pointed out that this population was loosely integrated with the growing sectors of the economy and that economic development in itself was unlikely to lift it out of its poverty. For them income transfers were seen as needed. Taking all these into consideration the paper arrived at a growth target of seven per cent per annum by balancing what is desirable with what is feasible by way of rate of growth and income redistribution within a given period of time.

In the event, the perspective plan presented in Pant's paper was not adopted. Until Mrs. Indira Gandhi raised eradication of poverty as the main plank of her electoral platform in 1971, the Planning Commission did not formally propose a poverty-oriented component of five-year plans. The approach to the fifth plan postulated a specific objective of poverty eradication along with the elimination of net external aid on concessional terms, neither of which has been attained to this day. It included a "minimum needs" component which was an updated version of the notion of minimum levels of living of the Pant's paper which itself anticipated the few worthwhile elements of the late, but not so lamented, basic needs approach proclaimed by some international agencies. The sixth plan (1980-1985) included a number of poverty eradication measures such as programmes for rural works and self-employment and schemes for increasing the productivity of small and marginal farmers and rural artisans. The seventh plan (1985-1990) envisaged continuation of the various programmes of rural development but proposed enhancement in coordination and rationalisation of the various programmes. Midday meal programmes were introduced in a number of states under which school children were provided free meals at lunch time. The approach to the eighth plan (1990-1995) recognises employment creation as the major remedy for poverty and proposes a much greater decentralisation of programme planning and implementation.

FOOD PRICES AND INFLATION

Apart from the specific programmes for redistribution and employment creation, food and agricultural policies have also exerted a positive influence on the poor in the country.

Food policy plays a critical role in determining poverty in any country and particularly for a country like India where, for almost all consumers, expenditure on food constitutes about 70 per cent of total consumer expenditure. The dilemma posed by the need for high agricultural prices to provide incentives to domestic producers and the desirability of low food prices for the consumers has been sought to be resolved by the Indian government by a set of policies—low prices for agricultural products coupled with low prices for agricultural inputs such as fertilizers, water and electricity to protect producer interests. A dual pricing system, operated through a public distribution system under which a certain amount of food is given to ration cardholders at subsidised prices, is used to protect consumer interests. Agricultural producers are also protected against fluctuations in their incomes through price support operations of the PDS. Of course, the PDS contains food price rises in a bad agricultural year. These policies have by and large succeeded so far in containing food price rises to modest levels which has helped in containing inflation to single-digit levels for most of the past 40 years. Food prices for the urban industrial worker, who was a major beneficiary from the subsidised food distributed under the PDS till recently, have increased since the 1970s, if anything, at a slightly lower rate than the general consumer price index. In the absence of the PDS, it could have been expected to increase at a higher rate. From the Wholesale Price Index (WPI) for agriculture and the general WPI it is seen that the relative price of agricultural products has not changed dramatically over the years.

The barter terms of trade indicate that over the years there has been a modest decline in the barter terms of trade for agricultural producers. Thus the producers have not been fully compensated for changes in input prices by changes in output prices. However, in addition to subsidised inputs, agricultural producers also get other subsidies in the form of generous credit. In addition, agricultural income is exempt from central income tax. These should definitely compensate agricultural producers for loss in the barter terms of trade. Thus, the agricultural price policy in India seems to have managed to keep output prices to relatively low levels without affecting farmers' incomes adversely.

PRICES, PDS AND RURAL POOR

By and large, the poor in rural areas are net purchasers of food. In the poorest three expenditure classes that constitute 20.9 per cent of the rural households, the self-employed in agricultural occupations are only around 28 per cent of these households. The remaining 72 per cent of the households are therefore net purchasers of food. Even among the self-employed in agriculture some may not produce enough food for their own consumption and may be net purchasers of food. Thus low food prices increase the real incomes of these rural poor.

The PDS provides selected consumer goods to ration card holders at prices below the market prices. Consumers are free to purchase additional quantities in the open market. Till recently, the rationing system has worked mainly in urban areas, except in a few states where the rural coverage is also significant. Generally, in issuing ration cards, a means test is not applied.

In states like Kerala, Andhra Pradesh, Gujarat and Maharashtra, rural populations get benefits of some significance from the PDS. In fact, since the operation of the PDS has most likely raised the price of foodgrains in the open market, from which the rural poor who are not covered by the PDS buy their food, they may have been adversely affected by the PDS.

The agricultural price policy—of low input price, low output price and cheap rations—involves subsidies from the government's budget. These subsidies have been growing progressively and have now reached significant levels. These allocations cannot continue to grow for long. If the rising budget deficit is not contained, the rate of inflation will increase and its adverse impact on the poor will nullify the low food price policy and the accompanying benefits it brings to the poor. Since these subsidies are not targeted only to the poor but also go to the relatively better-off farmers, they can be trimmed without hurting the poor. In any case, for efficient management of scarce water and energy, better pricing of these inputs is needed. By rationalising input subsidies indirectly, by subsidising land improving investments and by better targeting the PDS, the strain on the government budget can be contained without harming the welfare measures directed towards the poor.

RURAL DEVELOPMENT PROGRAMMES

A range of rural development programmes undertaken in India aims not only to stimulate the growth of agriculture and the rural economy but also to provide employment. Thus, as mentioned earlier, an element of anti-poverty action has always been present in these programmes. In fact, some of them are primarily conceived as such. These programmes include area and resources development, and programmes related to works, training and provision of rural credit.

Panchayati Raj

Panchayats have been the backbone of the Indian villages since the beginning of recorded history. Gandhiji, the father of the nation, in 1946 had aptly remarked that Indian independence must begin at the bottom and every village ought to be a republic or panchayat having powers. Gandhiji's dream has been translated into reality with the introduction of the three-tier panchayati raj system to enlist people's participation in rural reconstruction.

73rd Amendment Act 1992

The passage of the Constitution (73rd Amendment) Act, 1992 marks a new era in the federal democratic set up of the country and provides constitutional status to the Panchayati Raj Institutions (PRIs). Consequent upon the enactment of the Act, almost all the states/UTs, except J&K, NCT Delhi and Arunachal Pradesh have enacted their legislation. Except Assam, Arunachal Pradesh, Bihar, NCT Delhi, Pondicherry and Goa (Zilla Parishad), all other states/UTs have held elections. As a result, about 2,27,698 panchayats at village level, 5,906 panchayats at intermediate level and 474 panchayats at the district level have been constituted in the country. These panchayats are being manned by about 34 lakh elected representatives of panchayats at all levels. Thus, this is the broadest representative base that exists in any country of the world—developed or underdeveloped. The main features of the Act are—(1) a three-tier system of panchayati raj for all states having population of over 20 lakh; (ii) panchayat elections regularly every five years; (iii) reservation of seats for scheduled castes, scheduled tribes and women (33 per cent); (iv) to appoint state finance commissions to make recommendations as regards the financial powers of the panchayats and (v) to constitute district planning committees to prepare draft development plan for the district as a whole. As per the Constitution, the panchayati raj institutions have been endowed with such powers and authority as may be necessary to function as institutions of self-government and contains provisions of devolution of powers and responsibilities upon panchayats at the appropriate level with reference to (a) the preparation of plans for economic development and social justice; and (b) the implementation of such schemes for economic development and social justice as may be entrusted to them.

Financial powers of panchayati raj

Institutions Article 243-G of the Constitution of India, introduced by the 73rd Amendment, deals with the question of powers, authority and responsibilities of Panchayats. It reads thus:

> Subject to the provisions of the Constitution, the legislature of a State may, by law, endow the Panchayats with such powers and authority as may be necessary to enable them to function as institutions of self-government and such law may contain provisions for the devolution of powers and responsibilities upon Panchayats at the appropriate level, subject to such conditions as may be specified therein, with respect to —(a) the preparation of plans for economic development and social justice; and (b) the implementation of such schemes for economic development and social justice as may be entrusted to them including those in relation to the matters listed in the Eleventh Schedule.

While Article 243-G of the Constitution visualises panchayats as institutions for self-government, it subjects the extent of devolution of powers and functions to the will of the state legislatures.

— As per Article 243-H of the Constitution, state legislatures have been empowered to enact laws;

— to authorise a panchayat to levy, collect and appropriate some taxes, duties, tolls and fees;

— to assign to the panchayat, some taxes, duties, tolls levied and collected by the state government;

— to provide for making grants-in-aid to the panchayats from the Consolidated Fund of the State; and

— to provide for constitution of such funds for panchayats for crediting all money received by or on behalf of panchayats and also the withdrawal of such money therefrom.

Article 243-1 of the Constitution provides for the constitution of a state finance commission (SFC) to review the financial position of panchayats and to make recommendations to the governor regarding the principles governing the major issues mentioned in Article 243-H. The State Finance Commissions of Andhra Pradesh, Assam, Gujarat, Haryana, Himachal

Pradesh, Karnataka, Kerala, Madhya Pradesh, Maharashtra, Punjab, Rajasthan, Tamil Nadu, Tripura, Uttar Pradesh and West Bengal have submitted their reports to the respective state governments. The states of Assam, Karnataka, Kerala, Madhya Pradesh, Punjab, Rajasthan, Tamil Nadu, Tripura and West Bengal have accepted most of the recommendations of the SFCs. Andaman and Nicobar Islands, Dadra and Nagar Haveli and Daman and Diu have received interim reports of the SFC on which states/UTs have yet to take action. SFCs of Orissa, Goa and Sikkim have yet to submit their reports.

The Constitution requires the Central Finance Commission to recommend measures needed to augment the consolidated fund of a state to supplement the resources of the panchayats, in the state on the basis of the recommendations made by the finance commissions of the states. The Tenth Finance Commission, for want of SFC reports, made an ad hoc provision of Rs. 4381 crores to the PRIs for the period 1996-2000. All the states were released grants amounting to Rs. 1095 crores during 1996-97 to be given to the three tiers of panchayats. However, releases during 1997-98 required the state governments to furnish utilisation reports. Kerala, Maharashtra, Himachal Pradesh, Tamil Nadu and Tripura were the only states which obtained all the four instalments during 1997-98. Andhra Pradesh and Uttar Pradesh have managed to obtain three out of four instalments. The remaining states have obtained either one or two instalments only. The state of Bihar was not released any grants during 1997-98 for want of elected PRI bodies.

The Eleventh Finance Commission which would recommend on the devolution of resources for five years commencing from 1 April, 2000, will be dealing with the mandatory subject of making recommendations for the panchayats. It is essential that expeditious action is taken by the states in terms of acceptance of the SFC recommendations as the Eleventh Finance Commission is expected to take into account the recommendations of the SFCs and recommend suitable financial arrangements in respect of the PRIs. A comprehensive paper on the requirement of finances of PRIs has been submitted to the eleventh Finance Commission by this Ministry.

A Conference of the Chief Ministers on Panchayati Raj was held on 2 August, 1997 at Vigyan Bhavan, New Delhi, under the chairmanship of the prime minister to review the functioning of the panchayati raj institutions where the outstanding issues like devolution of powers/functions and responsibilities upon PRIs, setting up district planning committees; implementation of the reports of the state finance commissions, linkage of DRDAs with zilla parishads, training to panchayati raj elected representatives/ functionaries were discussed in great detail. The Conference also called upon the concerned eight states to enact the required state legislation on the Provisions of the Panchayat (Extension to the Scheduled Areas) Act, 1996 before 23 December 1997.

Based on the detailed discussions, the Conference recommended setting up of two committees—(a) the Committee of the Panchayat and the Tribal Development Ministers of the eight states covered under Schedule V of the Constitution under the chairmanship of Minister for Rural Areas and Employment to examine and to give their recommendations to enact the state legislation in consonance with the Central Act, 1996 before the cut off date, i.e., 23 December, 1997; and (b) the Committee of the Chief Ministers under the chairmanship of prime minister to examine the issues regarding the devolution of powers, functions and responsibilities upon panchayati raj institutes (PRIs) and to recommend measures to streamline the panchayati raj system.

The Committee of Panchayat and Tribal Development Ministers of the Schedule V states and the Committee of Chief Ministers under the chairmanship of the prime minister have since submitted their reports which have been circulated to the states for appropriate action. The important recommendations of the Committee of Chief Ministers were:

— Leave selection of beneficiaries to gram sabha.
— Waive requirement of technical sanction for works up to Rs. 10,000.

— Innovate to provide adequate manpower support to the gram panchayats.
— Delegate total control over such manpower to gram panchayats.
— Zilla parishad chairpersons be made the chairpersons of DRDAs.
— Provide reasonable opportunity of hearing to the PRIs before suspension/dismissal.
— Gram panchayat president to be accountable solely to gram sabha.
— Expeditious constitution of district planning committees.

In order to ensure that panchayati raj institutions function as instruments of local government, it is important that their functional and financial autonomy is guaranteed and transparency in their functioning is ensured. This has to be accomplished in most of the states. The role of the gram sabha is, perhaps, the most important in ensuring the success of panchayati raj institutions at the village level. The role of local people in conducting social audit and fixing responsibility on panchayat functionaries will be effectively ensured with gram sabha becoming active. It is essential that the village community perceives meetings of the gram sabha as useful. The most important factor for that is the empowerment of the gram sabha.

An important factor for the success of the panchayati raj system is the need for transparency in the functioning of these bodies. Panchayats being closer to the people, their right to information and accessibility to the panchayats must be ensured.

The Ministry of Rural Areas and Employment convened a Conference of State Ministers of Rural Development and Panchayati Raj on May 13, 1998. This meeting was inaugurated by the prime minister. The resolutions adopted in the Conference held are—(i) a Task Force for studying the structure and functioning of the panchayats should be set up; (ii) provisions of 73rd Amendment Act and Central Act 40 will be complied with; (iii) gram sabhas should be convened on a single predetermined day every quarter and (iv) care should be taken to respect the autonomy and independence of each tier of PRIs and to build up capability of the village level panchayats. In pursuance of the resolution, a task force has been constituted under the chairmanship of minister of state (independent Charge), ministry of rural areas and employment to study the structure and functioning of PRIs.

The ministry intends to introduce a bill for amending Article 243-M of the Constitution to exempt Arunachal Pradesh from the requirement of providing for scheduled castes reservation. This will provide a legal and Constitutional basis for panchayati raj institutions in Arunachal Pradesh in accordance with the sociopolitical ethos of the state. The provisions of the panchayats (Extension to the Scheduled Areas) Act, 1996 came into force on 24 December, 1996. This Act extends panchayats to the tribal areas of eight states of India, namely, Andhra Pradesh, Bihar, Gujarat, Himachal Pradesh, Maharashtra, Madhya Pradesh, Orissa and Rajasthan, which intends to enable tribal society to assume control over their own destiny to preserve and conserve their traditional rights over natural resources. The state governments were required to enact their legislation in accordance with the Provisions of Act before the expiry of one year, i.e., 23 December, 1997.

All states barring Bihar and Rajasthan have enacted state legislation to give effect to the provisions contained in Act 40, 1996. However, there are certain problems, both with certain central laws and state legislations as have been passed in pursuance of Act 40 of 1996. Certain crucial issues arise:

— Definition of Minor Forest Produce—the Indian Forest Act, 1927 defines timber as including within its definition, bamboo as well as cane. The ministry of environment and forests define minor forest produce to exclude bamboo and cane. While doing so, they have decided to adopt the definition of timber as given in the Indian Forest Act, 1927. In most states, tribals have been traditionally depending on bamboo and cane for their livelihood. However, for the last so many years, forest corporations and forest departments have prevented tribals from access to bamboo and cane while at the same time giving these to private industry at highly concessional rates. In many cases, tribals have been driven to desperation on account of this policy of state forest departments. It is felt that the definition of timber in the Central Act, 1927 is neither scientific nor equitable. It is a colonial definition and goes against the spirit of the provisions of Act 40 of 1996.

— There are also issues arising from the interpretation by the ministry of environment and forests of the intention of parliament regarding vesting of ownership of minor forest produce in gram sabhas. The proposals made by the ministry of environment and forests interpret the intention of parliament as giving not ownership per se, but making available to the gram sabhas, residual profits of state forest corporations/federations. This necessarily means that according to the ministry of environment and forests, state forest corporations/ federations will continue to trade in minor forest produce and if there is any surplus, that surplus will be given to the gram sabhas. This ministry has already taken up these issues with the ministry of environment and forests.

— The continued application of the Minor Forest Produce (Trade Nationalisation) Acts of the states of Maharashtra and Gujarat contravene the provision of Act 40, 1996 in that, powers of control over minor forest produce vested in gram sabha is curtailed.

As a result of the elections of panchayats in all the states, there are about 3.4 million elected representatives at all levels of panchayats. Out of this, an overwhelming majority is new entrants, particularly from the weaker sections of the society, i.e., scheduled castes, scheduled tribes and women (33 per cent).

The Constitution having placed enormous responsibility on the gram panchayats to formulate and execute various programmes of economic development and social justice, elected representatives will have to acquire the required skill and given appropriate orientation.

The success of the panchayati raj system hinges largely on the extent to which their capabilities are built to perform these functions and responsibilities. Thus, a timebound and systematic training programme to provide orientation of the elected representatives on a very large scale is considered to be the most important prerequisite for the success of the PRIs. The states/UT governments are required to work out systematic and comprehensive training programmes for the entire ninth five year plan (1997-98 to 2002-03) to train PRIs and to generate awareness among the masses at the grassroots, level and to strengthen the gram sabha. The ministry extends limited financial assistance to the states in their effort to train and create awareness among the PRI elected members and functionaries.

The development functionaries working under the PRI framework are required to undergo a certificate course. The Indira Gandhi National Open University (IGNOU) has been entrusted with the task of preparation of the syllabus for the certificate course. The SIRDs/state governments are being requested to conduct these courses. IGNOU is also involved in the distance education programme. For IEC activities this ministry mainly provides funds for publication of "Panchayat Unnati" to the National Institute of Rural Development (NIRD).

The Research Advisory Committee headed by the secretary (Rural Development) also approves proposals on research and studies related to panchayati raj received from the voluntary organisations/institutions. This ministry has commissioned some reputed NGOs/institutions to conduct a number of research and evaluation studies.

National Social Assistance Programme

The National Social Assistance Programme (NSAP) which came into effect from 15 August 1995 represents a significant step towards the fulfilment of the Directive Principles in Articles 41 and 42 of the Constitution. It introduces a national policy for social assistance benefit to poor households in the case of old age, death of primary breadwinner and maternity. The programme has three components, namely:

1) National Old Age Pension Scheme (NOAPS)
2) National Family Benefit Scheme (NFBS)
3) National Maternity Benefit Scheme (NMBS)

These schemes were modified in 1998 based on the feedback received from the state governments. The salient features of these schemes in their present modified form are given below:

National old age pension scheme

Under this scheme, central assistance is available as per the following criteria:

— Age of the applicant (male or female) is 65 years or more.
— The applicant is a destitute in the sense of having little or no regular means of subsistence from his/her own sources of income or through financial support from family members or other sources.
— The amount of old age pension is Rs. 75 per month for the purpose of claiming central assistance.

National family benefit scheme

Central assistance is available under this scheme for a lumpsum family benefit for households below the poverty line on the death of the primary breadwinner in the bereaved family subject to the following conditions:

— The 'primary breadwinner' is the member of the household, male or female whose earnings contribute substantially to the total household income.
— The death of such a primary breadwinner occurs while he or she is more than 18 years of age and less than 65 years of age.
— The bereaved household qualifies as one below the poverty line according to the criteria prescribed by the Government of India.
— The amount of benefit available is Rs. 10,000 in the case of death of the primary breadwinner irrespective of the cause of death—natural or accidental.

— The family benefit is paid to such surviving member of the household of deceased who, after local enquiry, is determined to be the head of the household.

National maternity benefit scheme

Under this scheme, maternity benefit is provided as a lumpsum cash assistance to women of households below the poverty line, subject to the following conditions:

— The maternity benefit is restricted to pregnant women for up to the first two live births provided they are of 19 years of age and above.

— The beneficiary belongs to a household below the poverty line as per criteria prescribed by the Government of India.

— The amount of the benefit is Rs. 5.

— While the benefit should disbursed 8-12 weeks prior to delivery, in case of delay the benefit may be disbursed even after the child is born.

Under the modified guidelines the state government would be free to adopt any mode of disbursement of benefits, namely, cash, money order, bank account of beneficiaries in the post office saving bank/commercial bank. The benefit under NOAPS could be disbursed in not more than two instalments in a year. In case of cash disbursement, the payment shall be made in public meetings preferably of gram sabha in villages and in neighbourhood/*mohalla* committee meetings in towns.

The NSAP aims at ensuring minimum national standards in providing social assistance benefits to poor households. These are in addition to the benefits that the states are currently providing or might provide in future. The intention in providing 100 per cent central assistance is to ensure that social protection to the beneficiaries everywhere in the country is uniformly available without interruption. Accordingly, it should be ensured that central assistance does not displace states' own expenditure in this respect and states/UTs may expand their own coverage of social assistance independently wherever they wish to do so.

The NSAP provides opportunities for linking social assistance packages to schemes for poverty alleviation and provision of basic needs. Specifically, old-age pension can be linked to medical care and other benefits for the old and the poor. Integrated Rural Development Programme/Nehru Rozgar Yojana assistance may be provided in addition to the family benefit for the families of poor households who suffer the loss of the breadwinner. Maternity assistance can be linked to maternal and child care. The NSAP is implemented in the states/UTs through panchayats and municipalities. The panchayats and municipalities are encouraged to involve voluntary agencies to the extent possible in taking the benefits to the poor households for whom they are intended. The states/UTs have already taken various steps to appropriately implement the programme.

The implementation of the NSAP during the first year of its introduction was slow as states had to overcome several hurdles, both institutional and procedural. The institutional arrangements involved identification of nodal departments at the state/UT level, district-wise distribution of targets, constitution of state and district level committees, opening separate bank accounts at the district level to receive central grants, etc. The procedural aspects involved evolving procedures for issuing sanctions, audit and accounting mechanisms, etc. To ensure proper implementation during the following year, i.e., 1996-97 the concerned state level authorities were kept in constant touch and the performance of the programme was monitored regularly.

During 1997-98, a series of meetings was held at various levels with state government officials to review the progress of implementation of schemes and some of these states have since shown improvement in the implementation. The Central Advisory Committee under the chairmanship of Nirmala Buch met on 15 July 1997 to review the implementation of the NSAP schemes during the year. Since the beginning of the year 1998-99, special efforts have been made to ensure that the implementation of the schemes under NSAP improves substantially. Accordingly, the nodal secretaries of the states were invited in batches to New Delhi on 20 to 22 April 1998 for discussion and also to work out strategies for efficient implementation of the schemes in their respective states/UTs. The process continued for the whole year and the last batch of nodal secretaries was called for discussion on NMBS on 15 January 1999. An All India Review Meeting and Workshop of NSAP Secretaries was held at Yashada, Pune during November 1998. Two studies have been commissioned to assess the performance of the scheme in various states. Out of these two, the final report of the study carried out by ORG in eight states of the country has been submitted. Another evaluation study involving the two states (Rajasthan and Uttar Pradesh) is in progress.

Rajiv Gandhi National Drinking Water Mission

Provision of safe drinking water in the rural areas is the responsibility of the states. Funds are being provided for provision of the facility in the state budgets right from the first five-year plan period. The Accelerated Rural Water Supply Programme (ARWSP) was introduced in 1972-73 by the Government of India (GOI), to assist the states and union territories to accelerate the pace of coverage of drinking water supply. To ensure maximum inflow of scientific and technical input into the rural water supply sector to improve the performance, cost effectiveness of the on-going programmes and ensure adequate supply of safe drinking water, the entire programme was given a mission approach. The technology mission on drinking water and related water management was launched in 1986. It was also called the National Drinking Water Mission (NDWM) and was one of the five societal missions launched by the Government of India. The NDWM was renamed Rajiv Gandhi National Drinking Water Mission (RGNDWM) in 1991.

It was realised that the objective of supplying safe water would not be achieved unless the sanitary aspects of water and the issue of sanitation are addressed together. The Centrally Sponsored Rural Sanitation Programme (CRSP) was launched in 1986 with the overall objective of improving the quality of life of the rural people. It is envisaged that the two programmes, the ARWSP and the CRSP, implemented simultaneously would help break the vicious circle of disease, morbidity and poor health, resulting from water-borne diseases and insanitary conditions.

The Accelerated Rural Water Supply Programme (ARWSP) aims at providing safe and adequate drinking water facilities to the rural population by supplementing the efforts made by the state governments/UTs under the state sector Minimum Needs Programme (MNP). Keeping in view the different kinds of problems arising while providing potable water in the rural areas, 56 mini-missions (pilot projects) were identified covering all states/UTs. These pilot projects helped to evolve models that are replicable and can be incorporated in the on-going programmes.

The provision of drinking water facilities in the problem villages is based on the following norms:

— 40 litres of safe drinking water per capita per day (Ipcd) for human beings.
— 30 Ipcd additionally for cattle in the desert.
— Development Programme (DDP) areas.
— One handpump or standpost for every 250 persons.
— The water source should exist within the habitation or within a distance of 1.6 km. in the plains and within 100 metres elevation difference in the hills.
— Drinking water is defined as safe if it is free from bacteria contamination, chemical contamination, viz., fluoride, iron, arsenic, nitrate, brackishness in excess or beyond permissible limits.

Viewing the objective of providing safe drinking water facility in all the villages, there is need for a certain order of priority which is as follows:

— To cover the "Not Covered" (NC) habitations.
— To fully cover the "Partially Covered" (PC) habitations getting less than 10 Ipcd.
— To cover all habitations having water quality problems.
— To supply water to all habitations with per capita supply of less than 40 Ipcd at the rate of 40 Ipcd.
— To provide water supply facilities for the scheduled castes (SC), scheduled tribes (ST) and the landless agricultural labourers.

— To provide safe drinking water in every rural primary school.

Once the task of providing every village with at least one source of safe drinking water is completed, the enhancement and expansion process may be initiated to provide adequate drinking water.

The allocations are subject to matching provision by states under their MNP. States/UTs have to earmark 25 per cent as minimum outlay for SCs and 10 per cent as minimum outlay for STs, for taking up water supply schemes exclusively for them. The ARWSP guidelines state that at the time of scheme formulation, the coverage of SC/ST should be given first preference so as to ensure equal access to water supply facilities.

R.W S. sector supportive activities/programmes

The sub-missions were initiated with the objective of providing safe drinking water facilities in the water quality affected habitations. Excess brackishness causes the problem of taste and has laxative effects. Control measures include either providing alternate sources free from brackishness or supply of water with total dissolved solids within permissible limit of 1500 ppm (parts per million) by treating brackish water with the help of treatment processes like reverse osmosis, electro dialysis, etc. For treating brackish water, 194 desalination plants were approved by the RGNDWM and 150 plants have been commissioned.

Guineaworm is a water-borne disease caused by *dracunculiasis medinensis*. Efforts to control this disease were started in early eighties. It is a good example of how the coordinated efforts of organisations like National Institute of Communicable Diseases (NICD), RGNDWM, international organisations like WHO, UNICEF, and state health and PHE departments could attack and eradicate an otherwise difficult problem. India has approached the International Commission for Certification of *dracunculiasis medinensis* eradication.

Excess iron in the drinking water is prevalent in the north-eastern states. Consumption of water with excess iron causes constipation accompanied by other physiological disorders. Control measures include providing alternate sources free from iron or treating iron contaminated water (to within permissible limit I ppm) with the help of iron removal plants. For treating iron contaminated water, 16,415 plants were approved and 9,355 plants have already been commissioned.

Excess fluoride in drinking water causes dental and skeletal fluorosis. The problem is prevalent in 150 districts of 16 states of the country, including Delhi. Control measures include providing alternate sources free from fluoride or treating fluoride contaminated water (to within permissible limit 1.5 ppm) with the help of treatment processes such as Nalgonda technique or activated alumina process. So far 499 plants (fill and draw type and handpump attached type) have been approved by the mission of which 427 plants have been installed up to December 1998.

Contamination of ground water with arsenic was first noticed in eight districts of West Bengal, in the early 1980s. The first attempt to tackle the problem was made by the Government of India in 1988 by sanctioning an investigation project. Thereafter, the Government of India has sanctioned several R&D projects as well as field oriented projects in the arsenic affected areas. Four water supply projects costing Rs. 349.09 crores have been approved for control of arsenic/ providing alternate safe drinking water sources in West Bengal. Rs. 3,080 lakh have been released during 1998-99.

Ensuring sustainability is an important sub-mission for the success of water supply schemes, on a long-term basis. CGWB and NGRI have been engaged in the programme since the inception of the mission. With the introduction of scientific methodologies for scientific source finding, the success rate of wells has gone up considerably. Under the water conservation measures, funds worth Rs. 30.75 crores were approved against which Rs. 25.90 crores have been released and the expenditure reported so far is Rs. 20.67 crores.

For testing of the water quality and for water quality surveillance, 411 laboratories have been approved and 300 have been established up to December 1998. It is proposed to provide one laboratory in each district of the country. Twenty-two mobile laboratories have also been provided to various states.

In December 1994, the central government delegated full powers to the states/union territories to give technical and administrative clearance to schemes under ARWSP, subject to the same per capita cost ceilings as under Minimum Needs Programme (MNP). The powers for sanctioning and executing sub-mission projects were also delegated to the states with effect from 1 April, 1998.

Sustainable management of rural water supply and sanitation needs not only the engineering systems but also community participation and empowerment, together with adequately trained professional and sensitised planners, administrators and decision makers. To build up a human resource base of appropriately trained personnel to serve the needs of the rural water supply and sanitation sector, the National Human Resource Development Programme (NHRDP) was launched in 1994. The major objectives of the NHRDP are (a) to train at least one beneficiary, especially women, at the grassroots level in each village of the country, (b) improve the productivity of sector professionals through specialised courses, and (c) to introduce rural orientation in technical education sector coupled with publication of manuals on rural water supply and rural sanitation.

The implementation of the NHRDP involves:

— Creating a resource pool of trainers for training grassroots level trainees in the villages through the Indian Training Network (ITN).
— Establishing Human Resource Development (HRD) cells in all the states to undertake HRD activities in the state, based on trainer assessment.
— Networking with NGOs, teachers' training institute, community polytechnics, training institutes/ organisations, etc.
— Conducting specialised courses and experience sharing workshops for sector professionals, in India and abroad.
— Evolving courses, for introduction at diploma and

degree levels, to introduce rural orientation and appropriate technologies and practices.

HRD cells are functioning in 24 states. Up to 1997-98, a sum of Rs. 23.00 crores had been released to the states for HRD activities. An amount of Rs. 103 lakhs has been released for the programme during 1998-99.

Four workshops have been held so far for operationalising grassroots level training programmes. Four multimedia packages, focusing on four focal themes given below, have been prepared by the Technical Teachers' Training Institute for conducting Grassroots Level Training Programmes.

— Operation and maintenance (O&M) of handpumps.

— Construction of sanitary toilets and other rural sanitation facilities. Motivation for community support mobilisation.

— Health education and hygiene promotion.

Under the programme for development of capability of in-house training instructors, the course on Ground Water Development which was being conducted in United Kingdom through the Overseas Development Agency (ODA) assistance has now been fully transferred to the Gujarat Jai Sewa Training Institute, Ahmedabad, one of the seven key institutions selected under the ITN.

Two state government officers were nominated by the ministry for a short term training on Monitoring and Effectiveness, for improving community-based water supply and sanitation projects, at IRC, the Hague, Netherlands. It was realised that the objective of providing necessary scientific and technological inputs required to improve the performance, cost effectiveness and management practices of the on-going programmes would not be achieved without the Research and Development (R&D) input and support. A series of R&D initiatives have therefore been taken to provide the necessary scientific and technological inputs into the mission programmes.

A lot of valuable data and information is being generated under the sector related R&D projects being carried out by universities, R&D organisations, and NGOs. A number of field level activities that are in progress add to the available information base by their findings. There are also a number of developing countries that are engaged in R&D activities leading towards low cost appropriate rural technologies for rural environment.

The need for dissemination of and access to information on drinking water and sanitation globally was recognised and the mission entrusted the responsibility of conceiving, establishing and maintaining a documentation and information centre on drinking water and sanitation to the Indian National Scientific Documentation Centre (INSDOC), a national laboratory under the Council of Scientific and Industrial Research (CSIR), Government of India.

The awareness creation campaign programme of the mission, based on its Information, Education and Communication (IEC) strategy, is being implemented in the selected pilot districts of 20 states, at a total approved cost of Rs. 2,411.70 lakhs, to be released in two instalments. The main objective of the campaign programme is to inculcate hygiene sense and bring about a change in the concept/attitude of the people towards water and sanitation. The implementation stage of the programme in the states is at different levels.

The states of Andhra Pradesh, Kerala, Tamil Nadu and Uttar Pradesh have taken the lead in implementing the programme activities. In fact, Uttar Pradesh launched the campaign in the district of Kanpur Dehat in November, 1998 and the launch in the other three districts is scheduled in January-February 1999. The IEC, activities to be undertaken at the National level, as envisaged in the guidelines, are being carried out. Slogans/messages related to water and sanitation have been printed on postcards and inland letter cards in Hindi, English and ten other regional languages. Doordarshan is telecasting spots relating to sanitation (hand washing and latrine construction). Funds have been allocated to the states to meet the expenditure towards broadcast charges of similar films/spots related to water and sanitation. The information regarding rural water supply and sanitation is also disseminated through bi-weekly radio programmes sponsored by this ministry. Discussions regarding the prospect of using the railways (tickets) as a medium for propagating messages/slogans related to the sector are at a advanced stage with the northern railway (first phase).

The implementation of the programmes in the states is being monitored and evaluated at the national level. The Monitoring and Evaluation (M&E) focuses on the following aspects:

— Coverage of the Not Covered (NC) habitations-status, Partially or Fully Covered (PC/FC).
— Full coverage of PC villages.
— Population coverage, category-wise, i.e., SC, ST and general.
— Defunct status of schemes (handpumps/piped water supply, etc.).
— O&M status (physical & financial).
— Extent of community participation in O&M, capital cost sharing, planning and implementation of schemes.
— Issues and problems being faced by the community and the implementing agency.

Periodic studies are carried out by non-government agencies to evaluate the schemes and give an unbiased assessment of the implementation/coverage status. A monitoring and evaluation study of the RWS schemes (including sanitation) in selected districts of 13 States was carried out by seven organisations. The final reports are under submission.

The Integrated Rural Water Supply and Sanitation (RWS&S) Project in Maharashtra supported by the World Bank has been completed during the year 1998-99. The World Bank-aided RWS&S project in Uttar Pradesh and Karnataka is progressing satisfactorily. Fresh RWS&S project proposals from Tamil Nadu, Madhya Pradesh, Kerala and Andhra Pradesh, incorporating the features stated in the Generic Project Concept Document (GPCD) issued by the World Bank were received and these proposals have been forwarded to the World Bank by the Department of Economic Affairs, for possible funding.

The Management Information System (MIS) is extremely important for planning, effective monitoring of the implementation of the various components of the programme. It also facilitates the availability of data not only to the central and state governments and people's representatives, but also to the users. A quick to and fro flow of information between the mission and the states (including formations up to the division and subdivision level) is proposed to be established by using the state-of-the art Information Technology (IT). It will be ensured that public has access to habitation-wise data through NIC and there is effective communication system using NICNET. The MIS project consists of selection of hardware, selection of operating system, preparation of Software Requirement Specifications (SRS) Document, and Development of Customised Application Software.

Hardware for the project and vendor for the supply of the same for whole country has been finalised. A multi-user operating system has also been procured. The SRS defining the organisational objectives and priorities, user needs and establishing linkages within various organisations in all states/UTs have been taken up. The selection of application software is under process.

Rural sanitation

The Centrally-sponsored Rural Sanitation Programme (CRSP) was launched in the year 1986 with the objective of improving the quality of life of the rural people and to provide privacy and dignity to the women. The concept of sanitation includes safe disposal of solid and liquid waste including human excreta, personal, domestic and environmental hygiene. The central funds allocated under the CRSP supplement the state sources made available under the state sector MNP. The following are the objectives:

— Accelerate coverage of rural population, specially among households below poverty line (BPL), with sanitation facilities, complementing the efforts in rural water supply.
— Generate felt need through awareness creation and

health education involving voluntary organisations (VOs) and panchayati raj institutions (PRIs).

— Eradicate manual scavenging by converting all existing dry latrines into low cost sanitary latrines.
— Encourage cost-effective and appropriate technologies to support other objectives.

The following are the programme components

— Construction of individual sanitary latrines for households below poverty line with subsidy (80 per cent) where demand exists.
— Encourage other households to buy facilities through markets—including sanitary marts.
— Assist in setting up of sanitary marts.
— Launch intensive awareness campaigns in selected areas.
— Establish sanitary complexes exclusively for women.
— Encourage locally suitable and acceptable models of latrines.
— Promote total sanitation of village through construction of drains, soakage pits for liquid and solid waste disposal.

Construction of individual household latrines by persons below poverty line may be supported in cluster of 20 or more in a village. The unit cost of construction should be limited to Rs. 2,500 of which 80 per cent could be paid as subsidy to the selected beneficiaries below the poverty line. In case the unit cost exceeds Rs. 2,500, the additional cost should be borne by the beneficiaries or a specific approval of the Government of India may be obtained before execution. Out of the total annual funds a minimum 20 per cent should be earmarked for paying subsidy to the individual households from SCs and STs below the poverty line where the percentage of SC/ST population to the total population below the poverty line is less than 20 per cent. Where the SC/ST population, below the poverty line is more than 20 per cent of the total population, below the poverty line earmarking should be enhanced at least to match the percentage of SC/ST population.

The mission has already circulated the report of the Expert Committee, which has recommended a wide range of (27 Nos.) technical options, with cost estimates, keeping in view the concept of vertical upgradation, varying soil and hydrogeological conditions and acceptability and affordability of the beneficiaries.

In order to explore for additional models and to supplement the information provided in the report of the National Expert Committee on Technological Options for the implementation of the rural sanitation programme in the country, a committee has been constituted under the chairmanship of the mission director. The committee will suggest additional models/technologies to supplement the information provided in the *Handbook on Technological Options*, with special emphasis to waterlogged/rocky areas and the islands.

Though public latrines have not proved to be very successful in the past, in view of the difficulties experienced by rural women in some areas, where individual household latrines are not feasible, village sanitary complexes exclusively for women could be attempted, on a pilot basis. Up to 10 per cent of the annual funds can be utilised to provide public latrines in selected villages during the plan period, where the panchayats/charitable trusts/NGOs offer to construct and maintain village complexes exclusively for the use of women. The United Nations International Children's Fund (UNICEF) have successfully demonstrated the validity of the concept of sanitary marts by implementing the scheme through voluntary organisations in Uttar Pradesh and the Ramakrishna Mission in Midnapur district, West Bengal. Rural Sanitary Marts (RSMs) are outlets dealing with materials required for construction of latrines and other sanitary facilities. Besides, it also keeps the designs of various low-cost sanitary facilities showing estimated costs and the list of trained masons. Rural Sanitary Marts also serve as service centres. UNICEF provides assistance of Rs. 50,000 for each mart with a turnover of Rs. 2 lakhs per annum. Managerial subsidy is provided up to Rs. 18,000 per annum for a period of two years. One time assistance up to Rs. 12,000 is provided for publicity, etc.

Where UNICEF assistance is not available for setting up RSMs, the state governments/UT administrations can set up Rural Sanitary Marts with assistance from the central government through reputed voluntary organisations/ panchayati raj institutions in difficult areas where proper marketing facilities for sanitary components do not exist. Such voluntary organisations should be carefully selected, based on the assessment of their ability to carry out the task.

Other sanitation facilities such as drains, soakpits, solid and liquid waste disposals, etc., should be taken up as far as possible under the Jawahar Rozgar Yojana or any other programme for civic amenities in the panchayat. Where this is not feasible due to other priorities and non-availability of adequate financial resources, the facilities can be taken up under CRSP. While government machinery for publicity may be useful to some extent, a well orchestrated programme of publicity, health, education and creation of required facilities only can make any change in the attitude of the people. Support of the reputed local voluntary organisations, autonomous institutions, social, political and religious organisations who carry conviction with the people can be enlisted in creating the felt need. These organisations should be selected for their reputation for good and adequate infrastructure already available with them.

Assistance is also given to states to develop model villages under the programme. A model village is covered with facilities like sanitary latrines, garbage pits, soakage pits, drains, paved lanes, sanitary latrines in village institutions (school, health centre, panchayat ghar, aanganwadi), smokeless chullahs, clean tanks, ponds and surroundings, sanitary wells and safe drinking water sources with platforms for bathing and washing and drains.

So far, the states of Andhra Pradesh, Bihar, Assam, Karnataka, Kerala, Tamil Nadu, Madhya Pradesh, Maharashtra, Orissa, Rajasthan and Uttar Pradesh have taken up the model village scheme.

LAND REFORMS

The national government, since independence, has been

continuing to play its advisory and coordinating role in the field of land reforms as the subject is under exclusive legislative and administrative jurisdiction of the states as per Entry No. 18 of the List II (State List) of the VIIth Schedule of our Constitution. Even then agrarian reforms remained as a central issue of our national agenda for rural reconstruction ensuring social justice to actual tillers as well as landless rural poor and thus for creating sustainable base for the overall growth of industrial and tertiary sector of our economy. Generating greater access to land by the landless rural poor is also considered as an important programme for poverty alleviation in the rural sector. The Land Reforms (LR) division has been, since the first plan period, playing a crucial role of evolving national consensus at various stages for taking up major steps towards effective land reforms which include abolition of zamindari and all intermediaries since the beginning of the fifties, introduction of family ceiling from the mid-fifties, reduction of ceiling limit in 1972 and monitoring the progress of distribution of ceiling surplus land as a part of the 20-Point Programme of the government. It organised a large number of conferences of the revenue ministers, chief ministers, and initiated amendments of the Constitution 13 times for incorporation of 277 land laws in the Ninth Schedule. The last such amendment was the 78th Amendment of the Constitution to incorporate 27 land laws in the ninth schedule.

In addition to playing advisory and coordinating role on land reforms, the LR division acts as administrative division of this ministry for the purpose of administering the Land Acquisition Act including the issues covered under Entry No. 42 of the Concurrent List in addition to execution of certain centrally sponsored schemes.

This ministry being the administrative ministry in the union government to administer the Central Act on Land Acquisition, any proposal relating to amendment to the said Act by the centre has to be taken up by the division. The aforesaid Act was last amended by this division in 1984 and the current phase of amendment proposals to bring radical and pro-people changes has reached a culmination point and the Land Acquisition (Amendment) Bill, 1998 has been referred by the cabinet to the group of ministers.

"Acquisition and Requisition of Property" is a subject enlisted in Entry No. 42 of the Concurrent List vide VII Schedule of the Constitution. As per Allocation of Business Rules-1961 it is allocated to this ministry. The division has to examine and concur all proposals pertaining to the state governments for amendments of their Land Acquisition Act, 1894 as required under Clause (2) of Article 254 of the Constitution. All state legislative proposals covering any enactment on the subject of acquisition and requisition of property or any other state legislation having a bearing upon the acquisition and requisition of land, has to be examined by the division for the purpose of according Presidential Assent to such legislations as required under Article 200 (in case of Bills) or under proviso to Article 213(1) of the Constitution (in case of Ordinances).

The ministry being the nodal ministry in the union Government as regards to implementation of land reform programmes, all proposals for introduction of land reform legislations or amendments initiated by the states/UTs are referred to it for examination and comments particularly in the light of their conformity with the National Land Reforms Policy. The division processes all progressive land legislations for incorporating them in the ninth Schedule of the Constitution to protect them being challenged in any court of law on the ground of violation of fundamental rights (with special reference to Article 31 A and 31 Q) and moves the parliament for amendment of the Constitution for the aforesaid purpose. The Constitution of India has been amended 13 times so far to incorporate 277 land legislations in the ninth Schedule of the Constitution.

When president's rule is imposed upon a state, this ministry is required to discharge the responsibility of laying ordinances in parliament or enacting President's Act as and when powers of the state legislature are conferred on the president by the parliament under Article 357(1) In addition, any central ministry, whoever proposes to make legislation having bearing upon acquisition/requisition of land seeks comments/observations from this nodal ministry.

During the year under report, six central legislations and 27 state legislations were examined.

As per the direction of the cabinet secretariat, LR division, on behalf of this ministry, has been acting as an administrative division for drafting/formulating the national policy, packages and guidelines on resettlement and rehabilitation since 1992. During the current financial year the efforts of the division have reached a culmination point and the NPRR-1998 is under the final stage of examination by the cabinet. For providing statutory backing to the proposed national policy packages and guidelines, this division has initiated necessary amendments of the Land Acquisition Act. It has also initiated steps to prepare a national level RR database and to create necessary secretarial set up to support the proposed National Level Implementation and Monitoring Board to be constituted to overview the RR activities in this country.

To play an effective coordinating and advisory role in the matters of various land reform activities taken up by the states/UTs, the LR division specially monitors distribution of ceiling surplus land, government wasteland, bhoodan land, conferment of ownership rights to the tenants, prevention of alienation and restoration of tribal land, consolidation of holdings and other miscellaneous issues.

As per point no. 5A of the 20-Point Programme of the Government of India, the Land Reforms Division fixes annual target for actual distribution of ceiling surplus land and brings out quarterly progress report collecting QPRs from the states.

Since inception of the ceiling laws on agricultural holdings, according to reports received up to the 30 September, 1998, the total quantum of land declared surplus in the entire country was 73.74 lakh acres, out of which about 65.11 lakh acres have been taken possession of and a total area of 53.05 lakh acres have been distributed to 55.37 lakh beneficiaries, of whom around 36 per cent belong to the scheduled castes and around 14 per cent belong to the scheduled tribes.

In addition to the distribution of 53.05 lakh acres of ceiling surplus land, figures collected from the states/UTs show that an area of 147.44 lakh acres of Government wastelands have also been distributed amongst landless rural poor. However, the quantum of land reported by the states as distributed during 1998-99 till December 1998 is 2.48 lakh acres.

Similarly, the state governments are requested to send the latest figure both showing the cumulative figure as well as current year's figure pertaining to distribution of Bhoodan land. The Annual Conference of the Revenue Ministers held on 17 September, 1998 deliberated upon various issues connected with the implementation of the land reform programmes and the states were impressed upon to take new initiatives including special drives, to hasten the process of the aforesaid land reforms measures.

Legislative provisions have been made in extensive areas of the country providing for conferment of ownership rights on tenants or allowing cultivating tenants to acquire ownership rights on payment of a reasonable compensation to the landlords. Some of the states have acquired ownership of land from the landowners and have transferred it to the tenants who have to pay a certain amount of premium to the state. Sub-tenancies are generally prohibited except in certain cases, viz., widows, members of armed forces, minors, unmarried women, persons suffering from disabilities, etc. The programme for conferment of ownership rights to the tenants or otherwise protecting the rights of the tenants/sharecroppers from eviction-at-will is not getting adequate attention from the state machineries. The states are not giving specific figure on the number of tenants who have been conferred ownership rights on the tenanted land separately from those who have been only recorded to prevent eviction at will. Such separated figures could not be obtained.

However, 124.22 lakh tenants have their rights protected over an area of 156.31 lakh acres. Cumulative figure showing the total number of tenants and sharecroppers received ownership rights or protection from eviction-at-will in connection with land held by them under personal cultivation. Article 46 of the Constitution enjoins an obligation upon the states to promote the interests of the scheduled castes and scheduled tribes and to protect them from social injustice and all forms of exploitation.

The state governments have accepted the policy of prohibiting the transfer of land from tribals to non-tribals and for the restoration of the alienated land to the tribals. The States with large tribal population have enacted laws prohibiting alienation of tribal land and for restoration of alienated land. The legal provisions are however, generally applicable to the tribals living within the scheduled and notified areas. Though some results have been forthcoming in the efforts undertaken by different states for restoration of tribal lands, the task still remains unfulfilled.

As per reports received from 11 states on the aforesaid subject 4.65 lakh cases of tribal land alienation have been registered so far covering 9.18 lakh acres of land, of which 2.02 lakh cases have been disposed of in favour of the tribals covering a total area of 5.31 lakh acres of alienated land but only 4.61 lakh acres of land have been physically restored to the tribals.

With a view to prepare a draft model law on tribal land alienation, during 1998-99 steps were continued for the preparation of state-specific status papers after which a consolidated view is to be taken and the model law prepared in consultation with the ministry of welfare and the SC/ST commission.

Consolidation of agricultural holdings forms an integral part of land reforms policy and five-year plans have accordingly been laying stress on the importance of its implementation. This operation is considered necessary for planned development of villages and achieving efficiency and economy in agriculture. In pursuance of this strategy, a number of states have enacted legislation for carrying out consolidation of holdings. However, it appears that the programme of consolidation of agricultural land holdings has virtually stopped all over the country except in the state of Uttar Pradesh, where annually about 900 to 1,000 villages are being covered under the programme. So far an area of 1,583.45 lakh acres or 640.81 lakh hectares have been consolidated in the country.

The Central Sector Scheme was introduced in the year 1972-73. Under the scheme financial assistance is provided to various institutions/agencies for conducting agrarian studies on important aspects of land reform measures to have a concurrent evaluation of the impact of various land reform legislations in the entire country. During the eighth five-year plan a total amount of Rs. 92.76 lakh have been utilised for conducting agrarian studies through 45 institutions/organisations/subject-matter specialists covering various aspects like evaluation study on allotment of ceiling surplus land, impact of tenancy reforms, problem of tribal land alienation, gender discrimination in land laws, displacement and rehabilitation of families affected by land acquisition, impact study on computerisation of land records, etc. During the year under report, against the budgetary provision of Rs. 61.00 lakh, Rs. 58.00 lakh has already been utilised by 31.12.98 for conducting agrarian studies on various subjects including evaluation studies on the programme of computerisation of land records.

In addition to having a concurrent evaluation on various aspects of land reforms in India by the Land Reforms Unit, now known as 'Centre for Rural Studies' of the Lal Bahadur Shastri National Academy of Administration, Mussoorie, the said unit has brought out a number of good publications on various issues pertaining to land reforms written/edited by eminent personalities in the concerned field. During the financial year 1998-99 funds to the tune of Rs. 25 lakhs were provided to the Academy which have been fully utilised by the Academy under the programmes/schemes/activities suggested by the ministry.

During 1988-89, pilot projects for computerisation of land records were taken up as a sub scheme of agrarian studies and up to 1991-92 a total amount of Rs. 5.02 crores was released to cover 24 districts under the programme in various states.

During the eighth plan period the budgetary provision for both agrarian studies and computerisation of land records was Rs. 65.00 crores, out of which funds for computerisation were separated from the total allocation, providing Rs. 48 crores for the computerisation programme exclusively. Out of the aforesaid amount, the expenditure under the scheme was Rs. 59.42 crores on financing a total number of 323 projects in various states/UTs.

During 1997-98 against the allocation of Rs. 20 crores, under the programme funds to the tune of Rs. 20.19 crores were released to the states/UTs to cover additional 177 new project districts in addition to providing second/third/fourth/final instalments for the ongoing projects and for operationalisation of the programme in 470 tehsils /blocks. Thus by 1997-98, 500 districts and 470 tehsils in the country were covered under the programme. The number of districts covered under the scheme also include districts which have been bifurcated by creating new districts by the states.

With a view to develop an 'online' land management system in the country, in addition to computerisation of land records, it was decided to take up computerisation/digitisation of the existing cadastral maps. Accordingly, during 1998-99 the budget provision under the scheme was increased by Rs. 10 crores from Rs. 20 crores during 1997-98 to Rs. 30 crores. Out of this budget provision, up to 31 December 1998 funds to the tune of Rs. 12.84 crores have been released to the states by covering 28 new districts under the scheme and by operationalisation of the programme in 275 tehsils/talukas/mandals. In addition, four pilot projects on digitisation of existing cadastral maps have also been sanctioned. The balance funds are proposed to be provided to the states by operationalisation of the scheme in more number of tehsils and by sanctioning more pilot projects on digitisation of cadastral survey maps.

In spite of correspondence, field visits and national level conference held in connection with speedy and effective implementation of the programme of computerisation of land records, the physical and financial progress reported by the states are not satisfactory. The reasons forwarded by the states include late delivery/installation of hardwares by the NIC, delay in constructing computer rooms at district/tehsil

/headquarters, deficiency in training input and lack of necessary infrastructure at tehsil/block/mandal levels. However, the states have been urged to take up appropriate and corrective steps to improve upon the process of implementation of the programme.

To have an evaluation of the programme of computerisation of land records, eight studies have been entrusted to eight reputed non-governmental organisations during the year. The results of the studies are expected to help in initiating effective steps for better implementation of the programme.

The Centrally Sponsored Scheme for Strengthening of Revenue Administration and Updating of Land Records (SRA&ULR) scheme was first approved by the cabinet during 1987-88 for states of Bihar and Orissa. In the year, 1989-90 the scheme was extended to other states and funds were released to various states during 1989-90, 1990-91 and 1991-92. The expenditure under the scheme up to 1991-92 was Rs. 36.63 crores towards central share.

The eighth plan provision for the scheme was Rs. 175.00 crores. However, the expenditure under the scheme was Rs. 98.23 crores. The main reason for this lower level of expenditure has been that the state governments have not been able to provide their matching share in time which results in accumulation of unspent balances with them towards central share and non-release of further funds to them. During the year 1997-98, against the budget provision of Rs. 18.80 crores, the expenditure under the scheme was Rs. 18.83 crores.

During the financial year 1998-99, keeping in view the increased requirement of funds under the Computerisation of Land Records Programme and that the overall allocation under the Land Reform Schemes remaining the same, the budget provision under this Scheme was reduced from Rs. 18.80 crores to Rs. 8.80 crores which has almost been utilised by providing funds to the states for strengthening their revenue administration and updating of land records by way of induction of modern technology/equipment in the field of survey and settlement, strengthening of training infrastructure of the revenue, survey and settlement staff, creation of facilities for maintenance and storage of land records, purchase of basic office equipments for the offices of revenue/settlement department at the lower levels, etc.

The states/UTs have been advised to expedite expenditure, submit utilisation reports as well as seek funds on schemes having higher priorities and also to enhance state budgetary provision to avail more financial assistance under the scheme. The states have also been requested to take up resurvey and settlement operations by preparing necessary schemes and programmes to adopt new technology in the field of survey, settlement, updation/ reproduction of maps and revenue records which include use of photogrammetric system, global positioning system, total station, use of scanner and digitisers for preservation, updation and reproduction of cadastral maps, etc.

During the last few years, the programme division has allocated major amount of funds under this scheme for development of infrastructures for revenue administration as well as to meet training need of the revenue officials. Some states have, with such financial assistance, developed state-level, regional level and held level training institutes or have upgraded the same. Further, some states have constructed record rooms for proper storage of land records.

RURAL ROADS

Rural roads are defined as those roads, which connect villages. They constitute Other District Roads (ODRs) and village roads in the hierarchy of the system of roads. The ODRs are feeder roads serving the rural areas where agriculture is the predominant occupation, providing them with outlets to urban market centres. These roads also play a significant role in opening up backward areas and accelerating socio-economic development. The systematic development of these roads received fillip during the fifth plan when construction of these roads was made a component of the Minimum Needs Programme.

During the fifth plan, the programme envisaged connection of villages with a population of 1,500 and above with all-weather roads. Against this, the sixth plan laid down the target that all villages with a population of 1,500 and above and 50 per cent of villages with population between 1,000 and 1,500 should be connected with all-weather roads by 1990. In respect of villages in hilly, coastal, tribal and desert areas, separate norms and targets were adopted. The Minimum Needs Programme on rural roads was continued during the seventh plan also. The total expenditure on rural roads under the Minimum Needs Programme from the fifth to seventh plan was Rs. 2,976,39 crores.

The eighth plan envisages linking of all villages with a population of 1,000 and above with all-weather roads. There are about 1.3 lakh such villages. It is estimated that about 86 per cent of such villages have been connected with all-weather roads by the end of the plan.

The MNP outlay for rural roads during the eighth plan was Rs. 3,066 crores. Against this, the expenditure incurred during the period was Rs. 2,679.83 crores.

Apart from the MNP outlay, funds were also available for construction of rural roads under Jawahar Rozgar Yojana (JRY). Works having a wage to material ratio of 60:40 are taken up under this scheme. Though no specific earmarking of JRY funds is made for rural roads, a substantial part of JRY outlay has been spent for rural road works in the past.

The working group on roads for the ninth five-year plan has estimated that an amount of Rs. 14,040 crores would be required for construction of rural roads to achieve the target of covering 85 per cent of villages with a population above 1,500 (1991 census basis). Of this, Rs. 4,410 crores would be required for construction of 49,000 kms of roads in villages with population of 1,000 and above, Rs. 9,000 crores for construction of about one lakh km. of additional roads in villages with less than 1,000 to ensure connectivity of 85 per cent of village population and Rs. 6.30 crores for black topping as mentioned above. However, the working group has proposed only an outlay of Rs. 10,540 crores for the ninth plan recommending a smaller outlay for villages with less than 1,000 population.

The scheme, "Roads in Special Problem Areas" is centrally sponsored and its implementation is limited only to the dacoity infested areas of the states of Uttar Pradesh, Madhya Pradesh and Rajasthan. The scheme is being implemented from 1985-86 onward and the Government of India and state governments share the cost of the works in the ratio of 50:50. In February 1992, the progress of the works sanctioned under the scheme was reviewed. It was found that the progress in respect to this programme was very slow and the States are not evincing adequate interest in it. The implementation of programmes is done by the public works department of the state governments, whose response to this programme was lukewarm. It was also observed that the original objective of improving communication facilities in dacoity prone districts has become less significant as the problem of dacoity has been practically eliminated.

In view of this, the state governments have been requested to complete only the ongoing works and no new/additional works should be taken up. Therefore, from the first year of the eighth plan, i.e., 1992-93, the funds available each year are being released to the states to meet the central liability for ongoing works depending on their progress.

AGRICULTURAL MARKETING

Agricultural marketing is a process which starts with a decision to produce a saleable farm product and involves all aspects of market structure or system, both functional and institutional, based on technical and economic consideration. Though agricultural marketing is a state subject, the Government of India has an important role to play in laying down general policy framework, framing of quality standards, conducting survey and research studies and in providing guidance, technical and financial support to the state governments. The central government is aided and advised by two organisations under its control, namely, the Directorate of Marketing and Inspection (DMI) and the National Institute of Agricultural Marketing (NIAM), Jaipur.

The main functions of the Directorate of Marketing and Inspection are:

- Rendering advice on statutory regulation, development and management of agricultural produce markets to the states/union territories;
- Promotion of grading and standardisation of agricultural and allied products under the Agricultural Produce (Grading & Marking) Act, 1937;
- Market research, survey and planning;
- Training of personnel in agricultural marketing; and
- Administration of Cold Storage Order, 1980 (except regulatory functions) and Meat Food Products Order, 1973.

The National Institute of Agricultural Marketing started functioning at Jaipur (Rajasthan) with effect from 8 August 1988. It is an autonomous body under the administrative control of the ministry of rural areas and employment, and is registered as a society with 30 members in the general body. The minister-in-charge of the ministry of rural areas and employment is the president of the general body. All the executive and financial powers of the Institute are vested in the executive committee subject to the directions of the Government of India and the general body. The director general is the chief executive of the Institute. The main objectives of the Institute are as follows:

- To augment the agricultural marketing infrastructure of the country through programmes of teaching, research and consultancy services;
- To design and conduct training courses appropriate to the specific identified needs of the personnel and enterprises and institutions that they serve;
- To undertake research to demonstrate and replicate better management techniques in the field of agricultural marketing;
- To provide consultancy services for formulating investment projects and for problem solving advice; and
- To offer educational programmes in agricultural marketing for supplementing the existing facilities.

The Institute has constructed a new office building complex at Jaipur to which it shifted on 2 April 1997. The DMI, as a central advisory organisation, has been providing technical assistance and advice to the states in framing suitable market legislation. For this purpose, the DMI has framed a "Model Act" which not only provides guidelines for framing of legislation but also intends to bring about uniformity in state legislations. Due to constant endeavour of DMI, all states and UTs except Manipur, Kerala, Andaman and Nicobar Island, Lakshadweep and Dadra and Nagar Haveli have enacted legislation. The Jammu and Kashmir Assembly has passed the Bill on Market Regulation in its state. The DMI is pursuing with remaining states/UTs for enactment of necessary legislation. Out of 7,245 wholesale assembling markets in the country, 7,062 markets have been brought under the ambit of regulation as on 31 March 1998.

The DMI is presently conducting 20 market surveys for various commodities and the reports are likely to be brought out soon. Four studies relating to the planning of wholesale markets for fruits and vegetables are also at various stages of completion. The Marketing Planning and Design Centre (MPDC) of DMI prepares a state master plan for the development of agricultural produce markets and imparts training to the personnel of state governments/marketing boards for the preparation of a state master plan. The draft of the master plan for market development in Mizoram state is almost complete. So far, DMI has brought out 325 reports on market surveys for various agricultural and allied commodities.

The NIAM has also taken up the formulation of state master plans for the development of agricultural produce markets for Goa, Himachal Pradesh, Andhra Pradesh, Jammu and Kashmir and Sikkim. Further, the Institute has taken up case studies on post-harvest management of various commodities and formulation of integrated action plan for promotion of handlooms and handicrafts in Varanasi and Nadia districts in collaboration with the Institute of Rural Management, Anand, during the year 1997-98. Apart from this, NIAM has taken up research projects on the Action Plan for Horticulture Produce Marketing and an all India Research Study on Cost and Spread of Margins in Vegetables—A case of Tomato. The NIAM has also taken up case studies on the following subjects:

- Study of chilli production, procurement and marketing in Tonk district of Rajasthan.
- Problem areas in the development of spices in Rajasthan.
- Marketing practices and problems of fruits and vegetable growers in Jammu & Kashmir.
- Study of oilseed production of Rajasthan.
- Spatial distribution of markets in southern Jaipur.
- Organisational and functional pattern of Chaksu market.

Besides this, studies are undertaken under the scheme of research grants and a total of 35 research studies are going on. Under this scheme, an amount of Rs. 72.19 lakhs has been released to various research institutions/universities throughout the country. A scheme for estimation of marketable surplus and post-harvest losses in foodgrain was launched by the ministry during the year 1995-96 in 100 selected districts of 25 states. An amount of Rs. 3.43 crores has been released to designated state agencies for conducting the field survey under the scheme.

The NIAM has conducted six training programmes on various aspects of agricultural marketing during the year 1997-98. During 1998-99, the DMI imparted training to 169 personnel from states/UTs, cooperative societies, marketing boards, etc., in different courses upto 31 December 1998.

The Agricultural Produce (Grading and Marking) Act, 1937 empowers the central government to fix quality standards, known as 'Agmark' standards and to prescribe terms and conditions for using the seal of 'Agmark'. So far, grade standards have been notified for 159 agricultural and allied commodities. During the year 1997-98, new grade standards have been formulated for five commodities, viz., caraway seeds, vermicelli, macaroni and spaghetti, cloves, mace and large cardamom.

The Cold Storage Order, 1980 which was uniformly applicable throughout the country except in the states of Haryana, Punjab, Uttar Pradesh and West Bengal, was promulgated under Section 3 of Essential Commodities Act, 1955 to ensure hygienic and proper refrigeration conditions in the cold storages all over the country. This has been repealed with effect from 27 May, 1997 with a view to remove the controls laid down in the said Order in the areas of licensing, price control and requisitioning of cold storage space, etc., and allow functioning of free market mechanism for demand-based growth of cold storage industry in the country free from all kinds of administrative interference.

The objective of the Meat Food Products Order, 1973 is to ensure quality control and hygienic manufacturing conditions of meat food products for domestic consumption, and the order is applicable all over the country. A total of 128 licences have been issued to the manufacturers operating under the order up to December 1997. Necessary amendments are being proposed to be made in the order to streamline the implementation of the order in a broadbased manner, keeping in view the interests of the manufacturers and license holders in the meat food products industry.

A high power committee on agricultural marketing was constituted in January 1992 under the chairmanship of Shri Shankarlal Guru, former chairman of Council of State Agricultural Marketing Boards (COSAMB), New Delhi, to review the present State Market Acts and working of various agricultural marketing bodies, and to recommend appropriate measures for streamlining and strengthening the set up for marketing of agricultural produce. The committee in their report has submitted 81 recommendations to the government, out of which 58 recommendations have been accepted and 21 recommendations rejected. The accepted recommendations have been communicated to the state governments/UT administrations for implementation.

TRAINING

Training is one of the tested tools for performance improvement as well as upgradation of knowledge and skills of the personnel. Organisational motivation and moral, as reflected in the attitudes and administrative culture, are rendered relevant and sharply focused through effective training programmes. Training has thus constantly gained an important position in rural development activities in the various poverty alleviation programmes which call for an efficient and motivated stream of government as well as non-government functionaries. As training, research and development are inextricably linked, continuing education of both policy makers and programme implementers is imperative. Towards facilitating this, the National Institute of Rural Development (NIRD), an apex training and research institute was set up in 1965 to impart training to the rural development functionaries as well as panchayati raj institutions through classroom interaction and field work. Thereafter, 25 State Institutes of Rural Development (SIRD) and 87 Extension Training Centres (ETCs) were set up in the country for intensifying training related activities.

In consonance with the National Training Policy (1996), these training institutes have made a variety of programmes including participatory methods of training with a view to not only imparting skills to the trainees but also enlisting participation of people, action groups and local institutions like the panchayats. In addition, extensive support has been provided to a number of training and research institutions dealing with issues related to rural development. Training has been started for ministerial staff also. During the year 1998-99, training on responsive administration for the section officers/private secretaries, assistants and personal assistants of this ministry was conducted. More than 200 personnel from these categories were imparted training. Similarly, about 150 officers and officials of the ministry were also deputed for computer training programmes with various reputed computer training institutes as a part of their HRD activity under the career management scheme.

National Institute of Rural Development

The National Institute of Rural Development (NIRD) is the country's apex body for training, research, action research, consultancy and documentation functions in the rural development sector. NIRD is an autonomous organisation under the aegis of the ministry of rural area and employment situated at Hyderabad. It also has a regional centre at Guwahati to cater to the special needs of the north-eastern region. The NIRD's vision is to focus in the coming years on the policies and programmes that benefit the rural poor, strive to energise the democratic decentralisation process, improve the operation and efficiency of rural development personnel, promote transfer of technology and its social laboratories and technology park and create environmental awareness.

The objectives of NIRD are to organise training programmes, conferences, seminars and workshops for senior level development managers, elected representatives, bankers, NGOs and others; undertake, aid, promote and coordinate research on its own and through other agencies; study various aspects of the panchayati raj institutions and rural development programmes across the states; analyse and propose solutions to problems in planning and implementation of the programmes of rural development and disseminate information through periodicals, reports and other publication.

NIRD works as a 'think-tank' for the ministry of rural areas and employment and also acts as a storehouse of information on rural development to assist the ministry in policy formulation. There are 16 centres in the institute with about 100 well-qualified faculty members, specialised in various subjects with national and international exposure and experience. Each centre of the institute looks after specific programmes of the ministry on which groups work on a tenure basis in the respective programme areas. The Institute has a well-equipped computer centre with facilities of Local Areas Network (LAN), Internet, e-mail, NICNET, multimedia, etc. NIRD thus aims to share its resources with other training institutions and bring about improvements in training activities. It has a well-organised and growing library with a large collection of books, periodical clippings and other literature on rural development and allied subjects. It provides audiovisual inputs to the training programmes being conducted. Research activities of the institute cover a wide range of issues relating to rural development. The main aim of research studies is to enhance understanding of the changing rural socio-economic scenario and identify major constraints in the proper implementation of various development programmes and schemes.

Training is a major activity of the Institute. NIRD trains senior officers, development functionaries, representatives of NGOs etc. The training efforts of the Institute are intended to create knowledge-based development of skills and understanding of the various dimensions of rural development. During the period from April to December, 1998, the Institute has conducted 85 training programmes including NERC, Guwahati and, in total, 2,207 participants have been trained, of which 322 are women participants.

Consultancy is another important activity of the NIRD. Consultancy services offered by the institute include specific custom-made training programmes, evaluation studies, baseline studies, feasibility studies, impact assessment studies, etc. The clientele for consultancy services comprise the ministries of Government of India, the state governments and the public sector undertakings on the one side and the international organisations like CIRDAP, EEC, UNDP, WHO, WEP, World Bank, ILO, SAARC countries, UNIFEM, UNICEF, AARRO, Ford Foundation, and Konrad Adeneur Foundation on the other.

As a part of the outreach programmes, the Institute launched District Link Officers (DLOs), Ministry Link Officers (MLOs) and Programme Link Officers (PLOs) schemes. These schemes aim at improving the faculty members/institute's understanding of district, ministry and programme-related developments.

NIRD is a leading publisher of rural development literature in India. A pioneering achievement of the institute is the preparation and distribution of a monthly newsletter *Panchayat Unnati* in 12 languages, including English which is sent to over 2.5 lakh gram panchayats all over the country. The institute made sustained efforts to upgrade information handling capacities by (a) installing Local Area Network (LAN), (b) INTERNET connectivity (c) developing data base consisting of books, journals, articles, etc., and has also set up a Computerised Library and Information Clearing House (CLIC) in the Centre of Rural Documentation.

State Institute of Rural Development is a centrally sponsored scheme for strengthening/establishment of State Institute of Rural Development (SIRD) was considered vital for human resources development. This scheme was taken up for implementation during the sixth five-year plan. The scheme was continued during seventh and eighth plan to revitalise training infrastructure so as to train the rural development functionaries and implement the programme more effectively.

There are 25 SIRDs set up under this scheme in 25 states which include eight composite institutes in Gujarat, Himachal Pradesh, Jammu and Kashmir, Karnataka, Maharashtra, Manipur, Rajasthan and Tripura. Out of the 25 SIRDs, 23 SIRDs have become operational either in their own building or in rented buildings.

The SIRDs in Goa and Mizoram are yet to be operationalised. The SIRDs have the requisite linkages with NIRD and ETCs so as to function in a hierarchy to serve the vital role of imparting training to the rural development functionaries. The scheme is being monitored constantly at the various levels in order to chalk out requisite strategy/plan for further strengthening and removing constraints in the functioning of the SIRDs. A system of regional consultations has been introduced between the ministry, the NIRD and the state governments. In these consultations, emphasis is laid on improving the content and quality of training programmes.

After the enactment of the 73rd Constitutional Amendment Act, it has been decided to strengthen existing training infrastructure both at the state level as well as district level to meet the training requirements of elected panchayati raj functionaries and officials in the near future. The financial assistance by the Government of India to SIRDs is 100 per cent for non-recurring expenditure and 50 per cent for recurring expenditure. The scheme is, however, demand driven in nature. Special emphasis is being given for recruitment of core faculty members in SIRDs. Hundred per cent funding support is available to cover expenditure on procuring the services of five crore faculty members for each SIRD.

Despite fairly impressive gains, serious lacunae with regard to the tenure of the head of SIRDs continue to persist. In the annual colloquium of secretaries of rural development and directors of SIRDs which was held at NIRD, Hyderabad on 15-16 May, 1998 it was discussed that the tenure of the heads of SIRDs plays a crucial role in the functioning of the institute. It was noticed that some SIRDs do not have a regular director and in some SIRDs, directors have been frequently transferred. The general feeling was that continuity and stability in tenure are essential prerequisites for smooth and efficient working of these Institutes. Accordingly, it has been decided that the state governments should fulfil one of the three following conditions to make them eligible for getting non-recurring grants from the Government of India under this scheme.

i) The present director should have been on the post for at least one year at the time of sending the proposals for central assistance by the state governments to the Government of India; or
ii) The previous incumbent should have been there as director, SIRD for at least two years; or
iii) The average tenure of last three directors should have been at least two years.

The plan outlay for the year 1998-99 for this scheme is Rs. 3.25 crores.

Extension training centres

The scheme of strengthening/establishment of Extension Training Centres (ETCs) for imparting training to village/ block level development functionaries was taken up during the seventh five-year plan for implementation. The ETCs are expected to provide necessary training inputs for raising the professional competence of the village and block level functionaries. So far, 87 ETCs have been established/ upgraded with central assistance. Considering the increase in the number of development functionaries and rural organisations and the rejuvenation of the panchayati raj system, the role of ETCs has acquired added importance.

With the enactment of the constitutional 73rd Amendment Act, 1992 relating to the setting up of the panchayati raj institutions, the need for training for rural development/panchayati raj functionaries has increased tremendously. The Extension Training Centres are the only training set-up to reach down to the village level. Keeping all these in view, it has been decided to strengthen training infrastructure in the existing Extension Training Centres. For this purpose, central assistance is 100 per cent for non-recurring expenditure and the recurring expenditure is provided to a maximum ceiling of Rs. 5.00 lakhs per annum per ETC.

The voluntary sector plays an important role in development particularly with reference to the programmes aimed at the rural poor and for improving the quality of life in rural areas. The ministry of rural areas and employment has been earmarking funds for the voluntary sector not only in the nationally planned programmes but also for mobilising and motivating people's participation. With a view to encouraging, promoting and assisting voluntary action in rural development and with focus on injecting new technological inputs for the enhancement of rural prosperity, the Government of India, in September 1986, set up the Council for Advancement of People's Action and Rural Technology (CAPART), a registered society under the aegis of the ministry of rural areas and employment by merging two autonomous bodies, namely, People's Action for Development India (PADI) and Council for Advancement of Rural Technology (CART). The cabinet minister/minister of state (IC) incharge of the ministry of rural areas and employment is the president of the general body of CAPART. The general body comprises officials of the ministry of rural areas and employment, eminent social activists, experts in different fields in rural development and representatives of voluntary agencies. It lays down the broad policy framework within which projects under various schemes are sanctioned.

As a prelude to the preparation of the ninth plan, the government had initiated a dialogue with the Voluntary Organisations (VOs) by forming a working group to formulate a viable strategy to involve them in a big way. CAPART has taken the initiative of mobilising the efforts of VOs by decentralising its activities for a more purposeful functioning. In order to be close to the VOs in the field, CAPART had decentralised its functioning by constituting six Regional Committees in 1994 at Jaipur, Lucknow, Bhubaneswar, Guwahati, Ahmedabad and Hyderabad. During the financial year 1997-98, two more regional committee offices were opened at Patna and Chandigarh. Thus, CAPART has at present eight regional committee offices. They cater to the different regions in the country.

For ensuring the success of water supply schemes or rehabilitation of degraded lands or any capacity building project, strong people's groups with enhanced management capacities are required. Hence, the government has issued guidelines on people's participation, stressing *inter-alia* that the participation should include the notions of contributing, influencing, sharing or redistributing power and of controlling resources, benefits, knowledge and skills to be gained through beneficiary involvement in decision making. Participation is a voluntary process by which people, including the disadvantaged influence or control the decisions that affect them. It has also been emphasised that the three outcomes of participation—learning, empowerment and a vibrant organisation—need to be measured through observable indicators, which will vary from project to project. Each project must develop clearly observable indicators on people's participation, so as to judge whether they are on track or not. Such indicators should then be given to monitors and evaluators, who have to do mid-course evaluation and impact assessment. Accordingly, CAPART has constituted National Standing Committees on different subject matters for sanction of projects including one on monitoring and evaluation at the headquarters. These committees predominantly comprise eminent subject matter specialists and representatives drawn from the voluntary sector. In this manner, CAPART is trying to make its functioning more participatory and transparent.

— Regional and National Standing Committees on different subject matters formed with a larger participation of VOs to sanction projects.
— VOs are involved in monitoring process.
— Particulars of project sanctioned to be exhibited at the project site made mandatory.
— Community resource network formed for dissemination of information among VOs.
— CAPART news incorporates project sanctions.

While CAPART seeks to associate the voluntary sector in several schemes that are part of planned development and are being implemented on national basis, it also supports several innovative projects keeping in view the needs of specific areas. The main thrust of these programmes is on employment generation, houses for shelterless, conservation of water, enhancement of income and development of community assets. While CAPART receives most of its funds from the ministry of rural areas and employment, it also channelises some funds to VOs from funding agencies like DANIDA, SDC, etc. Efforts are also being made to mobilise international donations both from multilateral agencies and other international donors.

CAPART provides assistance to VOs under different programmes like Indira Awaas Yojana, Watershed Management, Social Forestry, Link Road in hilly areas, Promotion of Voluntary Action in Rural Development, Development of Women and Children in Rural Areas, Organisation of Beneficiaries, Central Rural Sanitation Programme, drinking water under the Technology Mission on Accelerated Rural Water Supply Programme and Advancement of Rural Technology. Since 1995, CAPART is also providing assistance for talking up capacity building and rehabilitation programme for persons with disability. Three per cent of the allocations made under different programmes to CAPART are being set aside to fund this programme. It has also been decided to give preference in the coverage to disabled beneficiaries under all the programmes.

A revised set of guidelines on the functioning of CAPART has been issued on 20 January 1999 so that genuine and committed voluntary organisations are brought into the fold of CAPART in its efforts towards rural development. The guiding principle "fund every VO, if there is nothing against it" for funding by CAPART has been sought to be changed to "fund only those carefully selected ones who have done or have the potential of doing outstanding work in empowerment and welfare of the disadvantaged".

Collaboration between the government and the voluntary organisation, whenever it works, always yields both qualitative and quantitative results. It is the endeavour of the government that CAPART should make all-out efforts to help growth of collaboration between the government and the VOs.

Watershed management

In a major attempt to tackle the ecological crisis and to conserve water to bring about all-round development with the government announcement of Integrated Watershed Conservation and Development Programme, CAPART, too, took it up to associate VOs in a big way. It had formulated its own guidelines and created a separate division to sanction projects. During the year under report, the division organised state-level orientation workshops to make VOs aware of the requirements, developed formats for different stages for circulation among VOs and also devised formats for capacity building. A subcommittee for setting up training institutes formulated the training content.

The broad mandate was to coordinate all efforts for advancement of technology relevant for rural areas. The thrust under this programme is to promote and support efforts for transfer of technology to the rural areas. The technologies which benefits a larger spectrum of people in rural areas are supported and the major fields are as follows:

— Construction/housing technologies

— Water conservation

— Village industries

— Primary sector fields
— Food processing
— Herbal medicine
— Energy
— Biomass utilisation
— Handicrafts

Regional resource centres are created to test technologies feasible for specific geographical area, make modifications where necessary and initiate the process of transfer of viable technologies through demonstration, training and manufacture. The CAPART has so far supported 14 VOs to establish regional resource centres involving an assistance of Rs. 5.12 crores and plans are on the anvil to create more centres under the ninth plan.

The CAPART has played a significant role in creating employment and income generation among the rural poor, through its schemes like, Promotion of Voluntary Action in Rural Development, DWCRA and IRDR. The schemes are structured so as to provide permanent source of income to target beneficiaries. The financial assistance is provided by CAPART for building infrastructure, training, assets creation, production and marketing. Under promotion of voluntary action scheme, innovative projects are encouraged as per the needs and requirements of the area. For landless labourers and persons with no employment, Jawahar Rozgar Yojana provides partial employment through such activities as house building, road construction in hilly areas, social forestry, etc. For improving the quality of life, safe drinking water and rural sanitation programmes are taken up by CAPART. The schemes called ARWSP and CRSP respectively provide financial assistance to VOs for taking up sinking of tubewells and construction of individual family latrines in rural areas through the mobilisation of local resources and contributions of enlisted beneficiaries.

Organisation of beneficiaries is given due importance by CAPART. The objective of the scheme Organisation of Beneficiaries (OB) is to create awareness among the rural poor, organise them into groups and strengthen their bargaining capabilities. The guidelines of the scheme have recently been revised to provide support to community/ groups consisting of poor people who wish to organise or have organised themselves either on their own or due to efforts of a voluntary organisation for a cause which is sufficiently just or serious and to sustain their campaign/ struggle for their betterment of economic status or social power. It has been clarified that OB was not merely a training scheme and definitely not a scheme for providing funds to organise meetings where government functionaries are invited just once to inform beneficiaries about government schemes, subsidies or projects. It is a scheme about people's struggle against injustice and should result in increased confidence of the people to fight corruption and misuse of authority. Financial assistance under the scheme is provided for mobilisation of beneficiaries, organising them into groups, holding awareness generation camps and to monitor follow-up programmes so that real benefits of development programmes reach them.

Another programme for consolidation of benefits of awareness is the training of social animators so as to create change agents in rural areas. It is expected that by such efforts, development programmes will be more effective and speedy in the thrust areas. Under this, CAPART is also providing financial assistance to VOs to take up motivation programme for the benefit of elected members of the gram panchayats. The entire programme is mainly dealt at the regional committee level as a quantum of assistance provided falls within the financial ceiling of Rs. 10 lakhs.

9

Development Paradigm

Developing countries differ significantly in history, resources, manpower and technological capability and these differences will, of necessity, require that each follows its own path of development. Their past development will have gone through stages, but these stages are not identical and the transition from one to the next will have been quite different. The implicit assumption of the time, that growth could proceed without limits being imposed by ecology, availability of resources and socio-political structure, was tantamount to defying the basic laws of nature.

The old paradigm, universally applied, also called for an internationally oriented development strategy for all developing countries, irrespective of their ability to integrate their economies with that of the world as a whole. Trade was indeed an important source of growth for many developing countries in the 1960s and early 1970s, who adopted an open-door policy to foreign private enterprise and started receiving substantial amounts of foreign aid. This outward orientation of developing economies contributed to economic growth for a period in some cases, but it could not be sustained whenever the external environment became unfavourable.

The weakness of a strategy that did not pay adequate attention to the generated growth soon became apparent. In fact, the basic problem was that agriculture was neglected. From some developing countries the resource allocated to this sector were inadequate, while for other countries problems were caused by transferring large resources out of agriculture. Some developing countries experienced a Gross Domestic Product (GDP) per capita growth rate of three per cent or more annually over the period 1965-1980. However, few countries have been able to sustain this high rate of growth and the experience of the 1980s amply testifies to the shortcomings of the old development paradigm.

Contrary to expectations, many developing countries have experienced limited growth, while a large number of rural people continue to be unemployed and underemployed and live in poverty. Furthermore, the growth of output over the period 1965-1980 did not bring about a significant improvement in the income share of the lowest twenty per cent, nor a uniform reduction in the percentage of the rural population below the poverty line.

Income inequality increases with increase in per capita income up to a certain level, before income distribution starts to become more equitable with further increases in per capita income. As a matter of fact, overall income distribution as measured by the Gini coefficient has not always worsened during this process, because of compensatory shifts of income to middle groups. It is the population at the bottom of the income scale that has suffered most, a fact further reflected in the persistence and worsening of poverty in rural areas.

There is no association between the annual rate of growth of GNP per capita and changes either in the income share of the lowest twenty per cent or in the percentage of poor people among the rural population. It does not appear to be necessary to have the inverted-U curve effect in order to achieve a high rate of growth of GNP per capita. The real challenge is to avoid both the inverted-U curve effect and the persistence of abject poverty in a large segment of the population, by involving the poor directly in the growth process.

The old dominant paradigm overlooked the requirement that growth has to serve the rural poor by raising returns to the factors of production owned and/or operated by them and by allocating an equitable share of public resources to providing rural social services and infrastructure.

A "safety net" may have to be established, to protect the most vulnerable and to encourage the rural poor to innovate, experiment and take risks. This strategy should not, however, be construed as an argument against growth itself, or against attaining a higher level of GNP per capita. Both are essential to alleviating poverty and improving the quality of life, but these ends are achieved only when growth leads to development with the participation of all segments of the population.

The concept of growing with the poor, out of poverty into sustainable development, is not yet fully understood. Past thinking was: let growth take place, then poverty will automatically be reduced and the quality of life will improve. At a later stage, policy makers were so concerned with adjustments to the economy as a whole that they did not take into account the fact that both growth and stabilisation are undermined if the poor, especially the rural poor, are bypassed. The growing numbers of the poor mean that public resources, meagre as they are, are unable to cater for basic human needs. These people remain highly vulnerable to external shocks and are easy prey to natural disasters, civil conflicts and policy, and institutional indifference.

During the 1950s and the 1960s, several countries followed a strategy of "import substitution"—rapid industrialisation, with infant industries being protected by high tariff barriers. In Asia, Pakistan joined the ranks of these countries, using tariffs and other measures, and studies suggest that the policy was costly. Domestic consumers, including the rural poor, were made to pay for inefficient industrialisation.

Quota restrictions meant that tariff barriers were non-binding, and the domestic prices of a wide range of tradables were much higher than their landed cost. During the early 1960s, many protected industries were producing negative value added. It is difficult to judge whether these strategies would have been more successful in a different domestic and international climate. Countries seeking "instant industry" tended to neglect rural areas and agriculture. Urban-based industrial activities received a very large share of development resources, and agriculture was squeezed.

Since the late 1950s large shipments of food aid have been made available of developed a vital role in and helping countries to achieve growth and social equity through the development of infrastructure. Properly used it can contribute to development. Detractors stress, however, that as a mere item of consumption outside emergencies, it can be ,a disincentive to local food production. They claim that there are political and commercial motives behind food aid and that it creates a risk of overdependence on imported commodities, especially wheat and rice. Certainly in the past, many governments of developing countries have relied on food aid to keep urban food prices low, and local agriculture has suffered. Not surprisingly, in many countries, this neglect of domestic food production by small holders has contributed to disparities in living standards between urban and rural populations, not just in incomes, but also in social services such as health care and education, and has encouraged an unstoppable tide of migration from the countryside.

In several countries, the imbalance between agriculture and industry, and between rural and urban populations, found expression within agriculture itself due to a growth in production in selected areas: the so-called Green Revolution. Asia has been the major beneficiary; its food production increased substantially between the 1960s and the 1970s. However, the distribution of benefits from this growth in output was unevenly distributed; an increase in food production did not necessarily mean that hunger and poverty were commensurately reduced. There were also problems with a negative impact on the environment due to an excessive use of fertilisers and pesticides, and irrigation-induced salinisation.

One must, however, recognise the impact of new technology in terms of a spectacular increase in the production of some basic crops. Between 1960 and 1990 the world's population increased by more than two billion, yet mass starvation in Asia has been averted. Although Bangladesh faced occasional food crises over this period and Nepal was unable to increase its food production as rapidly as has been proclaimed, India, Pakistan and South-east Asian countries achieved a rapid growth in this regard. Asia's continued success in escaping mass starvation shows the power of the technological miracle. Improved seeds, chemical fertilisers and controlled irrigation have achieved what many considered impossible even two decades ago.

During the 1960s and the 1970s, another important phenomenon was taking shape under the dominant paradigm. This was the strategy of export-led growth. Its success in the newly industrialised countries (NICs) raised hopes that other countries could use this strategy to move out of poverty and underdevelopment. However, its proponents do not seem to recognise that the NIC option, however desirable, is not available to all countries aspiring for such a status. The domestic as well as the global environment has changed. The elements of the "enabling environment" which allowed NICs are as follows:

— Higher incomes for the peasantry led to local demand for consumer goods. Industry was protected by high tariff barriers and wages were able to be kept low, partly thanks to subsidised food prices benefiting the industrial work force. Contrary to the "free market" doctrine, the state was highly interventionist. Protected markets in both the Republic of Korea and Taiwan were never challenged at any forum. Markets for their goods in industrial countries were also much more open than they are today. Over the past three decades, protectionism has increased in the Organisation of Economic Cooperation and Development (OECD) countries.

— From 1963-1973, the volume of world exports rose at an average annual rate of 8.5 per cent. These rates have not been sustained. It was projected that exports from developing countries would grow by more than five per cent per year between 1981 and 1986; instead, exports have decreased by an average of 0.4 per cent per annum.

— Early NICs still occupy all the rungs of the ladder. The initial NICs continued to export T-shirts and textiles even as they moved into microelectronics, steel or shipbuilding. Countries which succeeded in expanding textile exports were soon confronted with trade barriers. This was the case with Bangladesh, which emerged as an important exporter of garments in the early 1980s but has been facing stiff quota limitations in industrial countries under the Multi-Fibre Agreement (MFA) which governs much of the world's trade in textiles and clothing. Besides the protectionist barrier, the rate of growth of world trade—and its size—may act as constraints to the expansion of aspirant NICs.

It is true that in a large number of developing countries, for various reasons, the state has participated directly in production, distribution and services. But the developing countries have not been alone in this. Many developed countries allow a dominant state role in a wide range of activities.

Developing countries included in the past socialist economies, mixed economies and open economies. Governments have participated in industry and, to a lesser extent, in agriculture. Those countries following planned economic development have allocated most resources to the public sector, with a built-in bias for industrialisation. India's second five-year plan was famous for its emphasis on heavy industries under public sector management. Pakistan's second, third and fourth five-year plans were characterised by a relatively low allocation for agriculture and by assigning a marginal role to the private sector.

State-owned enterprises often claim an undue share of public subsidies and bank credit at the expense of both agriculture and the rural poor. Public parastatals, particularly marketing parastatals, transfer resources from agricultural producers, mostly small holders. This adds to the vulnerability of such groups in rural areas. In Ghana, direct and indirect taxes accounted for 63 per cent of agricultural value added in the 1970s. The direct intervention of the state in production, distribution and services has not always contributed much to growth, or to the alleviation of rural poverty. On the contrary, in many cases state-led growth has been found to be harmful to agriculture and the rural poor. This begs the question, what is the appropriate role of the state *vis-a-vis* local governments, NGOs and the private sector in alleviating rural poverty? In general, the state does have an important role to play in areas in which it has a comparative advantage.

CHALLENGES

The "basic needs" approach made popular by the International Labour Organisation (ILO) has presented a much stronger challenge to the dominant paradigm. It suggests that, within the framework of the growth of GNP, appropriate measures should be taken to ensure that the basic needs of the poor are satisfied with regard to food, clothing and so on. For all its merits, this strategy emphasises the consumption needs of the poor, rather than their productivity and their capacity to generate a surplus.

In any case, the necessary allocation of resources, redistribution of assets and overall policy and institutional changes have not been carried out. The real political and social challenge embodied in the basic needs approach has never been fully taken up by the international community or by national governments, with the result that the potential of this approach remains to some extent unexplored. A persistent theme in these approaches to the economics of the poor is the need for a transfer of resources from the more productive and dynamic sectors of accumulation. What is missing is the recognition that a large majority of the poor—both rural and urban—conduct their lives with very little assistance from government agencies, and that they are frequently net contributors to national accumulation.

Assistance to the poor can often be seen, realistically, not as diverting resources from growth, but as adding to it by enhancing the productive potential of an important contributor. These challenges to the dominant paradigm, however, seldom focused on rural populations and on the poor. An attempt was made to fill this gap in the 1970s through integrated rural development programmes in Africa, Asia and Latin America and also through limited programmes for the generation of employment, financed primarily by food aid. The most successful of these programmes, obtaining indigenous support, was the Employment Guarantee Scheme of Maharashtra in India. Well known though it is, it has not yet turned out to be a broad-based solution for mass poverty in India itself. These challenges and the call for a new international economic order (NIEO)—fair and stable prices for raw materials, free access to northern markets for industrial goods, regulation of the activities of transnational corporations, codes of conduct for the transfer of technology, alleviation of debt, and so on were superseded by the debt crisis. Among many reasons for this crisis was the desire of a large number of countries to borrow heavily against the future, encouraged by the growth paradigm.

The debt crisis opened the door for the strategy of "structural adjustment", yet another variant of the dominant paradigm. Structural adjustment put the major focus on internal and external balances, and in its initial years even the objective of growth was played down in favour of macro-economic balances. Only later was it recognised that in order to meet debt obligations, a high rate of growth must be maintained. The other shortcoming of the strategy is a lack of emphasis on questions of equity and poverty.

While no one denies that countries cannot live forever beyond their means, and that they must "adjust" to economic reality, the need to share resources and alleviate poverty should not be relegated to the background. Otherwise, the central objective of adjustment will be defeated. In fact, its impact on the rural poor has been mixed. Structural adjustment and the GNP growth paradigm failed to recognise that poverty alleviation and growth are complementary. Any programme for growth and adjustment must activate the productive potential of the rural poor, rather than focusing on the non-poor and merely providing welfare support for the poor during the "period of transition". This was the basic proposition put forward by IFAD, which took steps reflect its concern in project design and implementation.

The contradictions inherent in structural adjustment programmes and the difficulties faced by vulnerable groups, were concurrently brought to light by the work of the United Nations Children's Fund (UNICEF). The United Nations Economic Commission for Africa (ECA) then proposed an alternative framework for "adjustment with transformation". The Commission expressed the view that orthodox programmes were ignoring basic structural factors that had to be taken into account if economic growth and socio-economic transformation were to be achieved.

The objective of the ECA proposal was to attain sustained development by enabling countries to adjust to changes in their domestic and external circumstances, and to restructure their economies. The goal was to transform the African economy from primarily an exchange economy to a production economy. Emphasis was put on promoting production by initiating a human-centred development process.

The ECA wanted to ensure that all socio-economic groups were effectively involved. The Bretton Woods institutions themselves, and the United Nations Development Programme (UNDP) have also recognised the shortcomings of the structural adjustment paradigm. Since 1989, the International Monetary Fund (IMF) has introduced the concept of "high-quality growth". It maintains that growth should be equitable, with particular attention paid to the plight of the poor and vulnerable, and that the environment must be protected.

The World Development Report of the World Bank, 1990 introduced the concept of "poverty-reducing growth". The style of growth can be such as to reduce poverty rather than increase it, and the report recommends a two-pronged strategy:

i) broad-based economic growth which generates efficient income-earning opportunities for the poor; and

ii) improved access to education, health care, and other social services which helps the poor take advantage of these opportunities.

The strategy also includes a social safety net for the vulnerable. The UNDP, through its two human development reports of 1990 and 1991, has suggested that growth is necessary but not sufficient for human freedom of choice and human development. In its first report, it introduced a human development index which combines life expectancy at birth, literacy, and per capita income into one index. Subsequently, this index was refined to take into account such factors as standards of education attained, gender disparities and income differentials within countries. It must be recognised that "high-quality growth", "poverty-reducing growth" and "human development" are important concepts marking a shift in thinking in the development community.

The overall objective of development, around which a broad-based consensus should be generated, is proposed to be participatory and environmentally sustainable growth based on poverty alleviation. Rural populations, both poor and non-poor, can contribute in achieving this objective. The non-poor are engaged in medium and large-scale modern and traditional agriculture, livestock and fishing, and in non-agricultural activities, primarily industry and services.

The rural poor are involved in small-scale agriculture, livestock and fisheries, waged labour in all sectors, trade, crafts and services, small-scale enterprises and micro-enterprises. Outside these groups there are those who are unable, for various reasons age, physical disability, social deprivation, and marginal location, to contribute to production and have to rely on transfers from other sectors or groups. The multidimensional contributions of the rural poor to the growth process are both interactive and mutually reinforcing.

An increase in their productivity, income and quality of life increases the pace of overall growth. Not only are the number and proportion of people below the poverty line reduced but the rural poor themselves, as their income rises, purchase more of the products of other sectors and thereby contribute to their growth. This in turn leads to a growth in demand of the products of the poor and of the factor services they own, in particular, labour. Overall growth, as long as it is participatory and environmentally sustainable, will contribute to the growth of productivity and income of the rural poor, through increased savings and investments and technological progress. Given the gap between their potential productivity and their current production, the rural poor will gain proportionally more if investments, particularly in infrastructure, social services, technology and diffusion, are positively biased in their favour.

An increase in the productivity and income of the rural poor will mean that they are able to generate adequate surplus to finance their own investments, although resource transfer from other sectors and abroad can help by targeting the poor. The burden of those transfers which are necessary to support the most vulnerable, who cannot take care of their essential requirements, can be shared by the rural poor and non-poor. Such transfers are obviously not difficult to sustain, because the demands are modest.

Short-run economic calculus may show a high rate of growth, as investments are concentrated in sectors with relatively high-productivity, but such growth is not sustainable over the longer term; experience has shown that the ever increasing numbers of the rural poor are forced to overuse resources and thereby accelerate degradation of the environment. In the long term this strategy is prejudicial to growth, and leads to tension, social instability, pollution of the environment and resource depletion caused by the rich. In short, the growth-inducing linkages become growth-dampening linkages. The new paradigm postulates that this need not be the case if the poor are seen as partners in the growth process rather than passive beneficiaries of growth.

The pace of growth depends on the strength of inter-sectorial linkages; the importance of the role of the rural poor depends on their relative importance in production, market and accumulation. The poorer population groups, such as small holder farmers, account for a large share of key commodity production. Where they are closely integrated with the market, are highly commercialised, and have additional production support and infrastructure and a framework of incentives, small producers can emerge as the lead sector in the growth process.

Recent studies suggest that a 10 per cent growth in agricultural output can bring about a 13 per cent growth in non-agricultural output. Understanding the dynamics of overall growth thus requires a much higher level of attention to agricultural development than has frequently been given to it. *De facto*, small farmers constitute the agricultural "core" of many developing countries; they are responsible for the bulk of material and human productive assets, as well as a significant share of agricultural output.

To the extent to which there is any social surplus in many countries, it is because of the production of these farmers and supporting them can lead to sustainable aggregate development. Given that a large part of agriculture is in their hands, and given the importance of agriculture's role in accumulation, overall growth must always involve the growth of small farmers. Support for small farmers is also suggested by economic considerations, such as their low level of capitalisation compared with other sectors, and the important increases in production which can be achieved by investments of capital—and importantly, with little need for foreign exchange. Small farmers' consumption then rises in a way comparable to the value of industrial output at early stages of industrial development.

It is true that relatively large-scale and heavily capitalised forms of agricultural production may eventually be more efficient in terms of the ratio of production output to labour input, but, in the early stages of development this concern is of little weight, given that developing economies tend to be rich in labour, but, poor in capital: small-scale development tends to "save" capital for larger industrial activities. The displacement of small-scale producers by large-scale production essentially involves massively devaluing existing agricultural assets while the scarcity of new capital really requires their fullest possible exploitation. It should not be necessary to make a special case for subsidising small-scale producers, when one bears in mind that the development of large-scale commercial production in agriculture in developing countries over the last decades has been heavily dependent upon subsidisation while smaller-scale producers have rarely enjoyed these benefits. It is ironic that large-scale production in these countries has traditionally been seen to be at the cutting edge of efficiency and productivity, while in reality it has been heavily dependent upon transfers and protection.

In many countries, a high overall rate of growth has been sustained by a high rate of agricultural growth in which small holders have played a dominant role. There are countries such as Bangladesh and regions such as Java in Indonesia, where there is not enough arable land to support the agricultural population small holder agriculture cannot continue to be a lead sector in the growth process while at the same time absorbing a growing labour force. In Bangladesh, the agricultural sector will remain an important source of employment for the growing rural labour force but new opportunities must be created in off-farm rural activities.

Small-scale producers have a role to play in supporting the industrial and service sectors, support that can be expanded. This is clearly visible in parts of Asia, where the attainment of self-sufficiency as to food and the development of agricultural exports has led to stable urban and industrial expansion. However, alternative avenues have to be sought, through non-agricultural rural activities, to promote the productivity income and quality of life of an increasing share of the rural population so that a holding sector, awaiting the time when urban industry can absorb surplus labour. Non-agricultural rural activities can also add to the growth push of the small holder agricultural sector, making a more forceful impact on overall growth. Thus, the growth in productivity of the rural poor in both agriculture and non-agriculture becomes a principal source of growth of the economy as a whole.

The economic crisis of the 1980s has created a situation in which interest in small-scale rural production, particularly food production, has been revived in the hope that it can substitute for imports. Small-scale agriculture is no longer seen only as a source of cheap labour to be employed in the cities when economic expansion and industrial accumulation so demand; it is also perceived as a source of supply of basic commodities at appropriate prices. During the current period of economic stagnation, the small holder sector is expected to increase production for the national market and also to "hold" the rural population in the countryside pending an upswing in the urban labour market. Two groups must be distinguished: those small holders and/or elements of the rural poor who are capable of maintaining themselves as independent "farmers", making an acceptable income from the sale of agricultural surpluses, and those who are not. The latter group, which is very large, must be seen as destined for eventual integration into higher-productivity sectors as entrepreneurs or waged labourers. For them, independent agricultural activities are a means of supplementing their income until more attractive options appear.

One must also recognise that there are countries in which the population of poor people includes small holders who, while continuing to be partners in the growth process, are handicapped by physical and structural constraints and will not really be able to play the lead role. Particularly in areas where the conditions of agricultural production are marginal, small farmers cannot be expected to produce a significant surplus. Relief of poverty in these areas will have to await the expansion of other sectors, in which the assets of small-scale operators can be deployed. This does not mean, however, that supporting these producers is somehow "uneconomic".

Steady growth requires stable social conditions and cannot be attained if dramatic sectoral imbalances are allowed to develop or they will result in large migratory flows and the formation of impoverished and underemployed groups around poles of relative wealth. Long-term stability under such conditions requires investment to keep populations in the less productive areas—delaying migration until the centres of growth are capable of absorbing new contingents. Under such circumstances a transfer of resources is needed to raise the incomes of the poor but the costs of such exercises and the frequency of the need for them are much less than commonly supposed—and such emergency measures are in no way characteristic of the normal economic relationship between the poor and accumulation. In this context, one must also take into account the case of the peripheral poor in remote areas.

A special strategy for development is called for to support these groups; public resources must be used to invest in infrastructure to support the production system at minimum cost. It is obvious that agriculture cannot be dealt with in isolation from industry, nor can the problem of the rural poor be solved entirely within agriculture itself without reference to labour employment and mobility between sectors. Even rural employment outside agriculture is related to the industrialisation process and the policies that may underlie it.

A clear understanding of inter-sectoral linkages is crucial to the evolution of a new development paradigm. These linkages vary according to the stage of industrial development. However, at early stages of industrialisation the key factors are: the determination of wage rates; the mobilisation of capital; the development of market outlets; and the generation of foreign exchange. With regard to foreign exchange, it is evident that economies at an early stage of industrial development must depend heavily upon importing the industrial means of production—a fact expressed by the importance of consumer goods production in early industrial development. Given that incipient industry is unlikely to be able to generate large amounts of foreign exchange, growth will depend to a large extent upon exports from the agricultural sector—and a subsequent flow of foreign exchange from agriculture to industry. To an important extent, therefore, overall growth, and particularly the availability of modern producer goods for industry, is dependent upon the export of agricultural and mineral products, if any raw/unprocessed as well as processed.

The level of agricultural development determines wage rates and the cost of raw materials, so it has a direct bearing upon the rate of industrial growth. The need for foreign exchange to buy producer goods gives an incentive for the development of domestic agriculture and processing industries while the costs of agricultural production represent a limiting factor in national industrial growth. In the early stages of industrial development, then, agricultural development—be it based on small or large farmers—is an important contributing factor. Agricultural growth may not be as rapid as industrial growth, but it is essential to it. Sustainable development therefore requires a balance in the allocation of economic surpluses between industry and agriculture, allowing for a parallel expansion.

Industrial growth itself must also be geared to agricultural development, if rural poverty is to be eradicated by making the poor a source of growth. Such a balance has been achieved in some successful programmes for growth, for example, in Indonesia and Thailand. In cases where the agricultural surplus is perceived as a basic factor in overall development, but where it is not perceived that agriculture must retain a portion of its surplus if it is to maintain its contribution, overall growth has been much less impressive.

Poverty is thought of as stifling, debilitating, and tending to lethargy. True, but many of the processes that impoverish the poor are highly dynamic and often race ahead of efforts to keep up with them. The new development paradigm is about how to reverse these processes. Appropriate process interventions can bring about changes in the value of the traditional indicators of poverty. As a priority, such interventions have to pay attention to an equitable allocation of resources and to the design of poverty-alleviating policies and institutions. It is necessary to maximise the resources of the rural poor, especially women, and provide an enabling policy and institutional framework for them.

The new development paradigm conceives of poverty alleviation not just as a mechanism to get the poor to cross a given threshold of income or consumption, but as a sustained increase in productivity and an integration of the poor into the process of growth. For this, the poor must have access to resources and the policy and institutional framework should be such as to enable them to utilise resources effectively. Resources include land, labour and capital. Policies and institutions cover domestic policies, national, local and grassroots-based institutions and the external environment. With respect to land, the major concern is to increase the access of the rural poor to land—including forests, pastureland and fishing water—and to increase its productivity. The means are land and tenurial reform, better management of common property resources, land conservation and development, and irrigation development managed by small-scale farmers.

Technologies must also be brought into use to help poor small holders, fishermen and livestock herders, with special attention given to women. Alongside this, a supportive infrastructure is essential to give improved access to the rural poor.

Labour is an important resource of the poor and a critical concern for strategy and policy is how to create employment and increase the productivity of labour. Principal strategic elements are: labour-intensive technology (representing undistorted factor costs); improvements in the labour market; the promotion of female participation; and training to develop skills and micro-management capacity. In addition, public employment schemes and micro-enterprises will play a crucial role. An improvement in the productivity of land and/or labour is not possible without increasing the capital of the rural poor and raising their productivity.

A particular emphasis has to be placed on poor households headed by women who suffer particularly severe disadvantages. It is essential that the mobilisation of savings, public provision of infrastructure and the development of financial services have a bias towards the rural poor and towards women in particular. Technology will add to their stock of knowledge and knowhow. Finally, steps should be taken to exploit fully the traditional knowledge and wisdom of the rural poor. To turn to the policies, a positive policy environment has to be introduced in favour of the rural poor. As for institutions, it will be necessary to reorient domestic institutions and, if necessary to establish new ones to serve adequately the interests of the rural poor. It is not always appreciated that the well-being of the rural poor is affected by the international environment, over which neither the poor nor the country itself has much control. At the international level steps should be taken to increase the flow of external resources to the rural poor and to eliminate trade distortions.

The major factor determining the productivity and income of the poor is the sectoral and macro-economic environment—although their relation to that environment may be mediated to some extent by public investment. Small-scale producers, like others, produce more when the price is right. They then require modest public investments to help create a platform for higher production. If prices are not right, such investments are largely fruitless. It must be recognised that key prices in themselves are no guarantee of increased production. Supportive infrastructure is also needed. The true "cost" of supporting this group therefore is that of providing an incentive framework for production. Economic considerations need not be distorted to favour the small-scale producer; quite the contrary.

The production and income of small-scale producers are often depressed by macro-economic frameworks which are themselves distorted, to protect large-scale producers from their own inefficiencies. Rather than requiring bigger subsidies, small-scale producers require the elimination of subsidies and protection for other sectors, which distort terms of trade and pump surplus from the poor towards larger-scale enterprises controlled by the rich.

Overvalued exchange rates favouring imports take incentives away from domestic small producers, as do credit subsidies, tax relief and low charges for a range of public services. It is the large producers who normally benefit-from tax relief and have greater access to subsidised credit. The real exchange rate must be increased for rural producers if their income is to grow. Economic interventions are typically made on behalf of the more influential members of the community. Their impact upon the poor is not neutral—it is negative. It is also frequently negative for the economy as a whole: it is not subsidised assistance to the poor that has given rise to the international debt crisis and widespread economic disequilibrium in developing countries.

The "cost" of providing a more supportive environment to small-scale producers in fact means a decrease, rather than an increase, in overall public expenditure. It could well be asked whether developing countries can afford not to provide such an environment—given that one of the principal means of assistance would be to establish a "level playing field" to eliminate some fundamental distortions that have given rise to crises when following the dominant development paradigm.

Strengthening the role of poor rural women in development is a key element in the new development paradigm. If women are given direct access to resources and domestic policies, and institutions are reoriented to serve their interests, then their contribution can be significantly raised. From a situation of multiple disadvantage, poor rural women can move to one which will enable them to have a triple multiplier effect, in the household, in the community and, more important, in the future generation through their impact on children.

The pursuit of current growth often barters away the potential for future growth, through reduction of capital and the accumulation of uncontrollable debt. In contrast, investment in children, through their mothers, is an investment in the future well-being of human society. Another key element of the new development paradigm is the preservation of the environment through alleviation of rural poverty. Food security is thereby enhanced, productivity is increased and an uninterrupted supply of rural energy helps the rural economy to diversify and promote longer-term growth. If the poor are granted secure access to resources and if appropriate policy and institutional reforms are carried out, the environment is more likely to be protected. Land and tenurial reforms are needed in many developing countries, with better management of common property resources. There is also a need for investment in conservation technologies and their associated infrastructure, training, rural micro-enterprises and other off-farm activities. These have to be supported by credit, appropriate tax, tariff, pricing and exchange rate policies and grassroots-based institutions. NGOs can provide critical financial, technical and organisational inputs.

Food aid can finance investment in conservation, while compensating for the loss of income of the rural poor during a period of transition. Some groups of the rural poor are particularly vulnerable to poverty, yet are meagrely catered for in poverty alleviation programmes. They are what one might call the peripheral poor, who eke out an existence in a highly isolated and alienated state. Their special needs call for specific strategies tailored to each group. Included in this category are, for example, the rural landless poor.

Any reforms must, of necessity, affect the relationship between populations, rural energy and the environment. Population management policies will influence household size, dependency ratio, family labour and the per capita availability of land and capital in rural households. At the centre of the new development paradigm lies a concern for people as individuals. Development is about people and not just about so-called "human resources", which sees people as inputs to a process, nor is merely concerned with machines, roads, and infrastructure. Not only are people the driving force behind the development process; sustained improvement in their well-being is its desired end product.

Equitable development is not viable without the participation of people at all levels. Poverty alleviation demands the participation of the rural poor, so that their latent productive and creative instinct is utilised and their potential fulfilled. Participation—be it induced or spontaneous—must grow out of respect for human life and dignity and democratic values. Such participation can find expression at all levels: household, neighbourhood, village, community, larger communal structure, local government, provincial government, national authority and international fora.

The participating units can be individuals or representatives of individuals, communities or institutions. Participatory mechanisms should be built into the process of planning and allocating resources, delivering credit, implementing land and tenurial reform, building and maintaining infrastructure, research and extension, marketing, resource conservation and training. By this means, research and extension are no longer external to poor people, but are internalised. The rural poor both speak to, and are spoken to, by researchers and extension agents. Hence the name, "demand-driven" research and extension systems. The farmer, researcher and extension agent are partners. This concept of partnership has to be that of a network.

Participatory and environmentally sustainable development based on poverty alleviation presents a formidable task. A coalition of forces at all levels is necessary to take up this challenge. People's power must be joined by NGOs, public authorities, the private sector and the relevant international institutions such as IFAD. International cooperation is essential and increasingly has to be fostered by and between multilateral institutions. Coordination among United Nations' agencies is critical to turning the rhetoric of poverty alleviation into effective action. The new development paradigm implies that the rural poor have to be sought out and appropriate strategies have to be articulated to integrate them into the process of development. Links have to be established between the analytic framework and practical reality. The question is how to package the different elements of the new paradigm to reach the rural poor and especially poor rural women, in a project or a programme.

The basic requirements for alleviating poverty within the framework of the new paradigm will be illustrated by case studies drawing upon the accumulated experience of IFAD. National and international institutions rely on project and programme-based interventions to alleviate poverty and before choosing appropriate strategies it is necessary to assess their respective effectiveness. All strategies require a favourable policy and institutional framework to operate successfully. Targeting the benefits of development projects and programmes at the rural poor is a key operational requirement of the new paradigm. Not only must projects and programmes themselves be designed to fit into their environment, it is also vital to minimise the leakage of benefits to the non-poor, to enhance the participation of the target group in project activities and to maximise its access to resources.

Programmes have to evolve to take account of the dynamics of those processes which create and exacerbate poverty. These have to be designed in four phases, namely: project choice and development; implementation; monitoring and evaluation and policy articulation. Unless growth is internalised and made self-reliant, unless democratic and participatory values are instilled in the whole population, unless market opportunities are open to all, and unless the productivity of the poor is increased, the society will be polarised and the welfare burden—the gap between modern and traditional—will continue to grow.

There will be little contribution to savings and investment and the continued poverty of rural areas will limit the output of the advanced sector, eroding the potential for self-sustained growth; the process of internalisation will then fail. Policies require rethinking in the light of the new paradigm. Examples of a participatory approach adopted by international financial institutions (IFIs) in seeking to establish self-sustaining rural institutions mark the beginnings of a new trend. More specifically, this new paradigm relies principally on the resources of the poor to help themselves and to promote the overall growth.

The concept of growth-inducing poverty alleviation implies that increasing the production of the poor and enhancing their incomes is a viable path to macro-economic growth. In other words, "trickle-up" instead of "trickle-down". Why should a development paradigm link economic growth to participation, environmental sustainability and the alleviation of poverty? Firstly, because the old paradigm has not been successful in bringing about broadbased economic growth. GNP growth is important but it is not everything. The rural poor may not automatically benefit from macro-economic development. Secondly, the end of the Cold War and the emergence of new democracies have opened up new opportunities whose full potential cannot be realised without greater economic justice, i.e., by tackling the problem of rural poverty. Thirdly, a compelling argument for a shift in the development paradigm arises from the menace of drugs. In the absence of alternative high-return activities within a broader, more attractive, socio-economic context, the rural poor are often an easy prey to inducement to drug production. Fourthly, poverty generates population pressure, breeds social and political conflicts, contributes to degradation of the environment, undermines basic human values and erodes the status of women and the welfare of the family.

More positive reasons for introducing the new paradigm are, firstly, that the rural poor constitute a significant share of the rural population with potential for a large contribution to output and demand. Secondly, in areas where the rural poor actually account for a large share of production including food and market a significant share of this output, investments directed at them will enhance food security and accelerate economic growth. Thirdly, the rural poor are the repository of a long-tested and effective traditional technology based on local knowledge, wisdom and familiarity with the environment. With appropriate support they can contribute to both production growth and resource conservation. Finally and most importantly, the gap between the potential and actual productivity of the rural poor is much greater than that of the non-poor. Achieving an increase in productivity of the rural poor is less costly and a better use of scarce capital than investment in the non-poor. The poor in many developing countries operate at such a low level of productivity that even quite small investments in the development of their skills and knowhow and some improvement in their access to inputs and services can have a significant effect in raising their output and incomes.

Micro-projects financed by IFAD, other international financial institutions (IFIs) and WFP have shown that interventions designed to alleviate poverty can increase output, savings and investment in a cost-effective way. It is sometimes questioned, however, whether this has a parallel at the level of macro-economy, where investment in modern high-productivity sectors may possibly lead to more rapid increases in global savings and investment and, therefore, in overall growth rates. An argument put forward to support this view is that the rural poor have a lower marginal propensity to save than better-off groups, so that increased incomes and output in the hands of the rural poor lead to larger current consumption and lower savings than if the increased incomes were in the hands of better-off groups.

In countries where the rural poor constitute a large part of the population that argument is not valid. Not only is the productivity of the rural poor easily raised by modest investment, but the marginal capital: output ratio is much lower for the rural poor than for people in the capital-intensive modern sector. Marginal capital productivity may well turn out to be so much higher in the poor traditional sector than in the modern sector that the comparison between them beats the ratio of marginal savings rates between the sectors. One unit of resource invested in the traditional sector then generates greater savings than if it were invested in the modern sector.

Moreover, given the large proportion which is poor, the diminishing return to capital will not be as significant in the poor sector as it may be in the modern sector. Under these circumstances, productivity-based alleviation of poverty is a matter not of equity, but of economic efficiency. One should also bear in mind that in certain situations the rural poor on the margin save proportionally more than the non-poor and are more productive.

While the importance of poverty alleviation is now being increasingly recognised, there is still great scepticism about whether programmes to alleviate poverty, whatever their social justification, are economically or financially viable.

This lies at the root of the "trade-off" view of poverty alleviation and growth. IFAD has examined its experience of recent projects in order to assess the evidence in this regard. A study which covered 107 projects undertaken since 1985 has shown that three-fourths of these projects had an economic rate of return at appraisal of more than 15 per cent; their average economic rate of return was 23.5 per cent, with a median level of 18.3 per cent. These rates compare favourably with the returns expected from conventional investment projects and are well above the opportunity cost of capital in developing countries.

In any event, the evidence strongly underlines the economic and financial viability of programmes to alleviate poverty and the contribution they can make, both in increasing food and incomes and in generating surpluses for further investment and growth.

10

Development and Structural Change in Sri Lanka

The social components of the strategies were exceptionally successful in achieving a rapid improvement in the conditions for survival, the economic components have not been equally successful in transforming the economy and raising the economic well-being of the poor. The Sri Lankan experience raises several far-reaching issues regarding the development strategies that were pursued in the first three decades after independence and their relevance for the alleviation of rural poverty.

At the time of independence, the Sri Lankan economy had acquired many of the structural features of a colonial economy. Under British rule, the country developed a relatively large export economy based on three primary commodities—tea, rubber and coconut. This development effort was confined mainly to the south-western and central parts of the country which were in the wet zone which experienced substantial rainfall. The commercially organised plantation sector that had developed and expanded during this period existed alongside the traditional peasant sector which was based on subsistence agriculture and devoted mainly to rice and other foodcrops. The outcome of the colonial process of development was an economy which was essentially dualistic in character. One part of it was geared to the metropolitan markets of the industrial countries supplying commodities such as tea, rubber, coconut and spices. It was this part of the economy which produced the commercial urban industrial development in the coastal regions of the wet zone, based around the primate city of Colombo and its port. The other part of the economy based on subsistence agriculture was spatially distributed in the wet zone alongside the plantation sector, the intermediate zone in north-western and central parts, and almost the entirety of the dry zone in the north central, northern, eastern and parts of the southern regions.

While the economic links between the relatively developed, densely populated wet zone with its export agriculture and the sparsely populated intermediate and dry zones with their traditional peasant economy were few and limited, the rural sector in the wet zone itself had developed a wide range of economic interrelationships with the commercially organised plantation sector. Rubber, tea, coconut and spices were grown in the home gardens and highland allotments of peasant small holdings in the villages of the wet zone. Many of these villages supplied the labour force for the large-scale rubber and coconut plantations. There was a considerable rural to urban migration in this part of the country.

When Japan was excluded, Sri Lanka's per capita income was probably the second highest in the Asian region next to that of Malaysia. The export economy had created a substantial revenue base and was able to finance the development of the infrastructure and other social sectors, including state schools and hospitals. Literacy rates already stood at about 57 per cent in 1946, the crude death rate had declined to about 14 per 1,000 of population in 1947 and infant mortality to 101 per 1,000 live births. The country enjoyed a considerable current account surplus and external reserves were in the region of nearly one year's imports.

The government budget and the fiscal situation was also quite satisfactory. Current expenditure was managed well within current revenues leaving a surplus which, when combined with public borrowings, could finance a government capital budget of moderate size amounting in 1948 to approximately five per cent of Gross Domestic Product (GDP). At this stage the government did not need to have recourse to any expansionary financing of budget deficits.

The export economy which had been developed during the colonial period was exposed to all the fluctuations and instability of the world markets with which it was integrated. The effects of the recessions and the business cycles of the industrialised economies were quickly transmitted to it. The depression of the late 1920s and the 1930s had a major impact on the Sri Lankan economy. The total value of Sri Lanka's external trade was equal to about 65 per cent of its GDP at factor cost. The major part of its food requirements was imported.

The government budget was heavily dependent on the revenues generated through the export economy, with import and export duties and the corporate taxes of the plantation sector contributing more than two-thirds of total revenue in 1950. During the 1950s these structural weaknesses of the Sri Lankan economy began to manifest themselves. The terms of trade of the main primary commodities began to decline steeply after a short boom following the Korean War.

Deficits in the current account of the balance of payments began to grow. Macro-economic policies during this period continued to support rising government expenditure on social welfare. This aggravated the problems that were caused by the unfavourable trends in the country's external transactions. On the one hand, the government began to rely on central bank borrowings to finance its budget deficits and, on the other, it tried to curb the inflationary impact by drawing on its external reserves to maintain supplies. By the end of the 1950s these policies were moving the economy into a prolonged crisis. In 1950, Sri Lanka's GDP was approximately Rs. 4,000 million at current factor cost prices or approximately Rs. 6,600 million at constant 1970 prices. Its population was about 7.6 million. The per capita product in 1970 prices was in the region of Rs. 860. By 1977, GDP had increased to Rs. 16,000 million and per capita income had risen to Rs. 1,149. In a brief survey of past development trends it is useful to take 1977 as the dividing line as this year marks a decisive change in macro-economic policies.

When the three decades prior to 1977 are examined as one phase of post-independence performance, it is possible to highlight several elements of macro-economic policy which characterised this period. These are:

i) emphasis on import substitution in agriculture and industry with a high degree of protection;

ii) reliance on regulatory mechanisms and controls for economic management;

iii) promotion of a large state enterprise sector covering industry, trade, transport, banking and insurance;

iv) implementation of social welfare policies which rapidly expanded the free state services in health, and education, from the primary to the tertiary stages as well as a subsidised, and subsequently free food rationing scheme for the entire population (The small tax-paying minority was excluded from the food ration scheme in its later phases); and

(v) pricing policies and state subsidies designed to keep the prices of essential goods at relatively low levels thereby preventing significant increases in the cost of living.

From the national accounts constructed for the early 1950s, it would appear that total gross fixed capital formation in 1950 was in the region of 12 per cent of GDP. By 1977 it had risen to about 16 per cent. The share of domestic savings, however, had remained static and hovered around 11 to 12 per cent for most of the period 1950-1977. During that time, there were four alternating phases of high and low growth. The average rate of growth declined from 4.2 per cent per annum during 1950-1955 to 2.5 per cent for the period 1956 to 1964. The growth rate rose again to an average of 4.6 per cent annually during 1965 to 1970 but dropped to an average of 2.6 per cent per annum over the following seven years. These fluctuations can be attributed to several factors, both externally induced as well as endogenous, and arising from domestic policies. One set of factors originated in the openness and vulnerability of Sri Lanka's economy.

There was a secular decline in the terms of trade of Sri Lanka's main exports soon after the boom in commodity markets' during the first half of the 1950s. Although the productivity of the plantation sector rose steadily during the

1950s, this was more than offset by the steady decline in the prices of primary exports and the increase in the prices of imports. The problems of the agricultural sector were compounded by the vagaries of the weather. Prolonged droughts such as those occurring in 1965-1966 and 1972-1973 sharply reduced agricultural output.

As agriculture contributed a significant share of the GDP, this had a significant impact on the growth rate. Over the period 1970-1977 the steep increases in the price of oil, combined with droughts, seriously retarded the growth of the economy. The trends during the 1950s brought into sharp focus the vulnerability of the Sri Lankan economy as a result of its heavy reliance on a few primary commodities. The policy makers attempted to respond to this situation through various initiatives but these were unable to make any serious impact on the underlying structural problems.

What in fact the development strategies of this period did was to aggravate the problems and trap the economy into a situation in which relatively high levels of consumption were maintained and economic growth and employment creation were retarded. During this period power was shared between the two major political parties—one which advocated policies which were broadly socialist in their orientation and the other which favoured private sector development. The low phases of growth coincided with those in which socialist-oriented governments held power, state-controls over the economy were intensified and the role of the private sector was restricted and reduced. But for the period as a whole the main elements of an inward-looking strategy of development were maintained by both parties.

The policy makers were not unaware of the basic structural weaknesses of the Sri Lankan economy. From the time of independence many of the pronouncements as well as plans that were formulated stressed the need for diversification of the Sri Lankan economy to make it less dependent on a few primary commodity exports. However, the planned adjustments were inward looking and relied on import substitution both in agriculture and industry. In agriculture the government concentrated on achieving self-sufficiency in the staple food, namely, rice. This enabled the policy makers to deal with the major emerging social problems in the densely populated wet zone. The programme for rice production resulted in a large transfer of population from this part of the country to the sparsely populated dry zone. In the process, the government was able to achieve two objectives, one being to increase the level of import substitution in rice and the other to relieve the problems of rural landlessness and poverty.

The effort to diversify the economy and to deal with some of the problems arising from the country's dependence on primary exports was essentially a strategy of import substitution. Although the programme for rice production was quite successful in achieving a rapid increase in production and compared favourably with the performance of other countries in the region, the programme has recently been subjected to critical reappraisal by economists and international agencies. It has been argued that Sri Lanka would have probably obtained the foreign exchange it needed to purchase its rice requirements if it had allocated a fraction of the resources allocated for rice to the improvement of the plantation sector.

The rice programme was criticised as having been a high-cost programme producing rice at prices far above international prices. These criticisms, however, ignore a whole range of other issues. The large part of the land resources that were available to the rural population could have been readily utilised only for a programme of rice production. The peasantry itself had a long tradition of rice cultivation and it is difficult to conceive of an alternative programme which could have used available resources better to improve the productivity and incomes of the rural population. The programme could have been implemented more efficiently and higher returns obtained for the investments that were made.

The water resources could have been utilised more economically; the output per unit of land could have been higher; crop mixes which yielded higher incomes could have been adopted; and cropping intensity could have been increased. The issues that have been raised need to be examined in much greater depth before reliable policy conclusions can be drawn. This task, however, cannot be undertaken within the ambit of the present study. Another important consequence of the import substitution programme in agriculture was the demographic outcome. By transferring the rural population to new settlements and expanding the rural sector in other parts of the country, the programme promoted rural-to-rural migration and thereby relieved the pressure for rural-to-urban migration.

The priority given by the government to self-sufficiency in rice also resulted in the development of the rural infrastructure of the country as a whole. As a result the rate of urbanisation in Sri Lanka was relatively low. The urban share of the population had increased from about 15 per cent in the early 1950s to about 21.5 per cent in 1981. The programme of rice production in peasant small holdings became the centrepiece of the development agenda of almost all the governments. After independence this meant that a large share of resources allocated to health, education, transport and communication went into the development of the rural sector and thereby helped lower rural/urban disparities and produce a type of rural/urban balance which restrained the demographic pressures that might have promoted a large flow of migration to the urban sector.

In the field of industry the developments that took place years or so following independence were twofold. On the one hand, the government developed a sizeable segment of industry in the state sector. These were largely based on local resources and included cement, paper, ilmenite and rutile, tyres, steel rolling, plywood, ceramics, leather, textiles and., in the late 1960s, oil refining. Alongside these public enterprises, the government promoted private industry for import substitution in the early 1960s.

Private industry rapidly expanded and covered a wide range of light consumer goods. The public sector as well as private sector industry that grew during this period was heavily protected from foreign competition. For most products, competing imports were banned and the industries enjoyed a captive market. As a result the industrial sector was costly and inefficient and had little capacity to compete in international markets.

STRUCTURAL CHANGES

In aggregate terms the structural changes were relatively marginal, within the sectors; themselves there were significant shifts in the shares of different subsectors. This was particularly the case in the agricultural sector where the share of the export crops declined sharply, from 43 per cent in 1950 to 29 per cent in 1977, while the share of subsidiary foodcrops increased from 18.3 per cent in 1950 to 35 per cent in 1977. Altogether, the domestic agricultural sector overtook the export sector and rapidly enlarged its share of value added in agriculture. These changes are a significant indicator of developments in the rural sector. The output of the peasant economy expanded much faster than that of commercial agriculture and began to play a major role in the total economy.

Import substitution entailed substantial savings of foreign exchange and to that extent had a positive impact on the balance of payments. This does not, however, fully answer some of the critical questions that have been raised regarding the opportunity cost of the programme and alternatives that might have brought better returns. In the mid-1970s the industrial sector was largely supplying the domestic market. Foreign exchange constraints were restricting both the supply of raw materials to these industries as well as the expansion of the domestic market for their products. The structure of the external sector reflected these changes in output. The export sector remained undiversified and heavily dependent on the three main export products as at the time of independence. In 1978 they still accounted for about 75 per cent of total exports, a proportion slightly lower than that of the early 1950s.

The change was mainly due to the re-export of petroleum products—heavy oils and naphtha from the refinery—that was established in the late 1960s and the increase in the export of gems. The composition of imports, however, changed significantly. The shares of intermediate and investment goods had risen with the import substitution of both agricultural and industrial goods and the increase in domestic capital formation. The share of consumer goods declined from 50 per cent in 1950 to 38 per cent in 1978. Between 1970 and 1978, the share of intermediate goods increased from 19 per cent to 38 per cent.

Food imports declined with the increased output of rice and several other food items such as onions, chillies, potatoes and fish; the share dropped from 50 per cent in 1950 to 28 per cent in 1978. The slow pace of structural change among the three main sectors of agriculture, industry and services was reflected in the sectoral composition of the workforce. The agricultural sector employed 52 per cent of the workforce in the early 1950s and that share only declined to 47 per cent by the end of the 1970s. The share in manufacturing increased only marginally from 9.7 per cent to 11.8 per cent.

Agriculture continued to bear the main burden of labour absorption and the policies that had helped contain rural-to-urban migration resulted in mounting pressure of the rural population on the limited resources of the rural sector and a high degree of rural unemployment and underemployment. The public sector expanded rapidly during the 1950-1978 period and assumed a dominant role in the economy. Apart from its pervasive regulatory functions, the state owned enterprises in almost all important economic sectors.

Total capital investment in state enterprises was estimated at Rs. 11.3 billion at the end of 1977. The workforce in the state enterprise sector amounted to 583,000, nearly 13 per cent of the total employed workforce in the country. The state sector comprised 25 industrial corporations, 12 trading corporations, eight in transport, communications and construction, two plantation corporations and seven financial and banking institutions. These do not include the statutory authorities managing utilities such as power and water. The Business Acquisitions Act of 1971 resulted in a further expansion of the government's entrepreneurial role and about a 100 medium and small enterprises were nationalised. The land reforms implemented in the first half of the 1970s resulted in the nationalisation of the privately owned large-scale plantations in tea, rubber and coconut. By 1977 the role of the private sector and market mechanisms in the allocation of resources had been severely curbed and marginalised.

Meanwhile, the political decision makers were unremitting in their concern to protect the social welfare programme in the midst of the deteriorating economic situation. This meant not only avoiding significant cutbacks in expenditure on subsidies and social services but also making efforts to contain the cost of living and to prevent inflationary pressures from mounting and eroding the purchasing power of the poor majority. This required policies which were successful in containing the prices of essential mass consumer goods. The governments succeeded in holding the increase of the cost of living index to a mere 12 per cent from 1952 to 1967—an annual increase of 0.8 per cent. This was done despite the worsening balance of payments and the growing budget deficits.

The response was not one of managing aggregate demand and following sound fiscal and exchange rate policies, but in fact the opposite. The focus was on social welfare and not on the correction of the growing macroeconomic imbalances. Up to 1968 no adjustments were made in the exchange rate despite the fact that the rate was grossly overvalued. Governments resisted devaluation because this would have pushed up prices. After 1968 the government introduced a dual exchange rate system which was only a partial remedy and introduced other distortions to the economy which adversely affected important sectors of the economy such as the plantation sector.

A significant proportion of the rising budget deficits were financed by central bank borrowings which were essentially expansionary. The impact was cushioned, however, by running down the external reserves to maintain imports of a large range of goods at adequate levels. This prevented any steep upward movement of prices. Government expenditure had increased from about 21 per cent of GDP in 1950 to 25 per cent in 1977 while government revenue rose to approximately 19 per cent of GDP.

The budget deficit as a share of GDP had increased significantly during this period. During the 1960s and 1970s the government increasingly relied on mobilising domestic savings through captive sources of funds such as the Employees' Provident Fund and the National Savings Bank. From the late 1960s onwards foreign aid, apart from providing support to the balance of payments, became a major source of financing the budget deficit. The expanding public sector and the diversion of private savings to the government budget led to a severe contraction of resources available to the private sector. The opportunities to make adjustments to the growing imbalances at an early stage were therefore missed.

If external resources had been mobilised at an adequate level at this stage, as was attempted later, there might have been a possibility of adopting a mix of policies which would have enabled the government to carry through the adjustments without a major cutback on consumption as was the case with the post-1978 adjustments. This, however, was made impossible owing to the strategies followed by the government, particularly the nationalisation of the foreign-owned oil companies. In the latter half of the 1960s a fairly successful effort was mounted to mobilise foreign aid, which rose from a very negligible amount in 1964 to about Rs. 200 million in 1966 and about Rs. 1,000 million in 1977. By 1977 the flow of external aid had risen to approximately three per cent of GDP. A large part of this aid came in the form of grants and the concessional lending itself was based on relatively generous terms. Therefore, by 1978, the burden of foreign debt itself did not cause concern. The main outcomes of the post-independence period up to the change of direction in 1977/78 can now be summarised. The structural weaknesses of an unstable export-import economy were aggravated.

An unrealistic exchange rate, growing import demand and the relative stagnation of export earnings had produced chronic imbalances in the country's external account. The policies pursued had contributed to this by the bias against the large-scale private sector and the uncertainties within which it had to operate arising from the large-scale nationalisation programmes.

Furthermore, the policies both in agriculture and industry had geared the economy to the domestic market and the protection which was needed to nurture and maintain this production capacity had been to the detriment of the export sector and the general capacity of the economy to compete in international markets. A large public sector in commerce, industry and finance had grown which tended to restrict private sector enterprise in many areas. It operated within a political system which made it inefficient and placed a heavy burden on the government budget. Government expenditure had risen to over 25 per cent of GDP. A large social welfare programme had become almost a permanent political commitment and could not be reduced without severe social strains.

The fiscal and budgetary structure was such that resources had to be mobilised in a manner which seriously limited the resources available to the private sector. This consequently affected the level of domestic savings itself which tended to stagnate at around 12 per cent of GDP. In the period 1970-1977 the economy was growing at an annual average rate of less than three per cent and unemployment had risen to about 20 per cent of the workforce.

The period 1978-1990 covers two phases—the first between 1978 and 1983 which witnessed an unprecedented surge of sustained growth of around five-six per cent per annum; the second a phase of steady decline in which the average rate of growth fell to about three per cent per annum. A far-reaching programme of economic reforms was initiated with the government budget of 1977. These were aimed at correcting the fundamental macroeconomic imbalances and introducing decisive policy changes which would take the economy away from one dominated and regulated by an elaborate structure of state controls and interventions, to one in which market forces would operate more freely and efficiently. Since the late 1960s the economy had functioned under a dual exchange rate system, in which first, the rate of exchange itself was not realistic and second, the dualistic rate distorted incentives and resource allocation to the disadvantage of the plantation export sector. The 1977 reforms unified the exchange rate with a significant measure of devaluation, the rupee being floated in relation to a basket of currencies.

The system of exchange controls and import quotas was dismantled with the exclusion of a small component, such as the import of private cars and newsprint. Controls on foreign transactions in general were relaxed to a considerable extent and controls on interest rates also eased. The government began the process of reducing the wide array of subsidies and moving from the administered prices that governed a wide range of commodities to market prices. The food subsidy and free ration of rice, which had been available to most of the population, was restructured. It was initially replaced with a scheme which limited it to households below a specified income level, thereby reducing the number of beneficiaries to half. Later it was changed into a food stamp scheme with a fixed cash value which incorporated the various subsidies on rice, wheat flour, sugar and infant milk food.

The restructuring of the food subsidy on an income criterion was a critical breakthrough both in economic and political terms as it opened the way to phase out the food subsidies as incomes increased. The measures for liberalisation of the economy had far-reaching impacts on trade, agriculture and industry. In agriculture, private trade was allowed to operate and agricultural prices were liberalised. The guaranteed price scheme, which combined with price controls left the purchase and distribution of the produce in the hands of the state, now became a minimum price scheme which protected the farmers from excessive fluctuations.

In the traditional export sector the unification of the exchange rate brought substantial benefits, although high export taxes which were levied initially siphoned off a large part of the increase in rupee prices. These taxes, which were in the region of 40-50 per cent in 1978, were progressively reduced till they were in the range of about 1020 per cent in 1987.

In the international trade sector import quotas were replaced by tariffs and the tariff system itself was restructured in stages and the tariff bands reduced and rationalised to correct some of the distortions which arose from the wide dispersion in effective protection rates that sometimes resulted in negative effective protection. These policy changes enabled both the international agencies and aid donors to increase the volume of aid which rapidly rose to more than double the pre-1977 levels.

It was in the industrial sector that the liberalisation regime evoked mixed responses and posed dilemmas which were not easily resolved. One of the major objectives of the liberalisation strategy was to balance incentives as between import substitution and export promotion. Increasing emphasis had to be given to the promotion and diversification of exports. Policy makers were beginning to realise that industry had to play an increasingly important role in growth and employment creation and that if this were to be realised, industry had to become internationally competitive and produce for the world market. It could not expand rapidly in the limited domestic market.

By enabling industries to obtain an adequate supply of raw materials, the liberalisation policies led to better utilisation of capacities and helped the more import-competitive, efficient industries. The new policies therefore led almost immediately to a higher growth in the manufacturing sector, particularly private enterprises. Private sector manufacturing output is estimated to have more than doubled between 1977 and 1981. The new policies were able to restore the confidence of private investors and attract foreign investment.

The government established a free trade zone and was able to attract export-oriented foreign enterprises. This initiative, together with Sri Lanka's export quotas in the garment industry, resulted in a sizeable flow of direct foreign investment. The garment industry expanded rapidly and soon became one of the largest foreign exchange earners, creating a substantial volume of new employment.

One of the distinguishing features of Sri Lanka's experience in implementing the structural adjustments was that it was able to combine rapid growth with adjustment and at the same time do so without seriously cutting back on consumption and social welfare. This it was able to do for two reasons. First, after a long period in which export earnings had stagnated and the balance of payments had run into heavy current account deficits, there was an upturn in tea prices which resulted in a current account surplus after more than 20 years. More important, the policy changes cleared the way for the mobilisation of external resources on an unprecedented scale. As a result Sri Lanka's import capacity more than doubled between 1978 and 1980 as noted earlier.

As a result of large aid-financed projects such as the massive multipurpose river diversion scheme, the government capital budget expanded rapidly and the proportion of public investment in total investment rose. Aid from donor countries which came in the form of grants and concessional lending alone amounted to between seven and eight per cent of GDP. The rate of economic growth during the period 1977-1984 was the highest that the economy was able to sustain for a period of as long as six years, since independence. The rate of unemployment was also reduced from about 20 per cent in the mid-1970s to about 12 per cent in 1981-1982. The government expenditure rose to unprecedented levels. As a proportion of GDP it increased to 40 per cent by 1983. While revenue stood at about 20-22 per cent of GDP, foreign finance amounted to approximately nine per cent of GDP and the rest came from bank and non-bank borrowings.

The government capital budget which had been in the region of one-third of total government expenditure in the first-half of the 1970s had risen to 47 per cent by 1983. The expansionary impact of fiscal operations was quite high during this period particularly from 1980 to 1982, ranging from about 11 per cent of GDP in 1980 to about four per cent in 1982.

Various further far-reaching adjustments, particularly in regard to the government budget and public sector/private sector balance in the economy, were placed on the agenda but did not receive adequate attention. During the years that followed, the lack of budgetary discipline and heavy central bank borrowings coupled with the massive investment programme of the public sector had fuelled inflation which rose to 26 per cent in 1979 and 18 per cent in 1980 according to the official price index. It was over 30 per cent and 20 per cent respectively according to more realistic estimates. The current account deficit of the balance of payments (less official grants) had increased more than sixfold during the period 1978 to 1980. This by itself cannot be taken as a negative indicator as it reflected the success in mobilising external resources, which were financing investment.

The medium-term and long-term prospects of promoting structural change were as yet limited. These prospects lay primarily in a much more dynamic growth of the external sector and export industrialisation. The structural adjustments and the development effort in these directions were still inadequate. Above all, the new policies had not yet effectively dealt with the factors retarding private sector growth. The increase in the flow of external resources went to finance. A much higher level of public expenditure, particularly the public investment programme. New large-scale investments were undertaken and heavy foreign liabilities incurred by several public enterprises; for example, the Shipping Corporation, the national airline AirLanka and the Sugar Corporation. The public/private mix in investment was further tilted in favour of the public sector. The government increased its diversion of domestic savings to the government budget through its captive sources.

The external resources that became available on an unprecedented scale were not used to the best advantage.

The initial adjustments should have been followed by further improvements in the management of the budget and quicker responses in aligning the foreign exchange rate to international currency fluctuations. The liberalisation of the economy, the removal of administered prices and the steep devaluation combined with the budgetary policies and the surge in investment to produce high rates of inflation in the period 1978-1984, ranging between 11 per cent and 26 per cent according to the official consumer price index. Measures were taken quickly to control the expansionary budget deficit and to bring down inflation. The rate of inflation declined to less than two per cent in 1985.

The underlying problems relating to the macro-economic constraints which the budget imposed on the allocation of resources and the growth of the private sector remained. Neither was the conflict between policies for import substitution and those for export promotion clearly resolved. Some of the fundamental constraints to growth in the sectors with potential for growth were not fully removed. Therefore, the economic management of the 1978-1984 period which witnessed high rates of growth had many serious short-comings.

It could be argued that the failure to move forward and complete the adjustment process fast enough was already creating conditions for a significant slowing down of the economy after the first phase of relatively fast worth. But while further corrective measures were being planned and initiated, other developments of a more critical nature intervened to overshadow the economic issues. The communal violence of mid-1983 soon plunged the country into a prolonged conflict which had drastic consequences for the economy. Recurrent and capital expenditure on defence and security rose from less than 1.5 per cent of GDP in 1982 to 6.2 per cent in 1987. Tourist arrivals dropped from their peak of 400,000 in 1982 to 183,000 in 1987. Output in agriculture and fisheries in the north and the east declined.

The large population which was displaced as a result of the disturbances had to be accommodated and provided for in refugee camps. The civil disturbances in the south in

1988 and 1989 inflicted heavy damage and seriously disrupted the economy with forced stoppages of work, loss of production in the plantation sector, and destruction of physical assets such as factories, government buildings, vehicles, equipment and electrical installations. The annual rates of economic growth declined to 1.5 per cent in 1987, 2.6 per cent in 1988 and 2.2 per cent in 1989. Unemployment rose to about 14 per cent of the workforce. On the other hand, the 1988-1990 period was also able to demonstrate the remarkable resilience of the Sri Lankan economy as well as its polity. A growth rate of over two per cent per annum amidst political turbulence and economic disruption of an intense and countrywide character was maintained.

Moreover, the core political institutions and multi-party democratic system was left intact. In 1990 the economy seemed to show signs of recovery and was moving towards a growth rate of nearly five per cent. These are indicators of the underlying strength and capacity of the economic and sociopolitical system. The balance of different elements no doubt contributed to the resilience the system showed during the crisis—a fast-growing and fairly efficient small holding sector was well dispersed and could not be destabilised; a private sector which was gearing itself to make use of the new opportunities that the changes of policy had opened up for them; an educated and politically conscious population which was anxious to protect its political rights; the civil-military relations of a democratic polity; and, a state system which had acquired the capacity and power to act effectively.

During the period 1987-1990, there was a series of policy measures which attempted to take the process of structural adjustment much further in its break with the past. Much firmer disciplines for budgetary management were defined. After the 1978 reforms the government continuously set the macro-economic parameters that were essential for the management of the economy. Observance of the disciplines set by these parameters helped the government to achieve two important objectives of the restructuring.

First, a non-inflationary budget and second, a pattern of resource allocation which would leave adequate resources with the private sector to contribute an increasing share of growth and employment creation. Private sector savings had been greater than private sector investment for a long period. As mentioned earlier a large share of private saving was siphoned into the government budget. It was estimated that private savings equal to nearly five-six per cent of GDP were absorbed in this way.

The budget was trapped in a vicious circle wherein: on the receipts side it borrowed from private savings to finance nearly one-third to one-half of its public investment programme; and on the expenditure side about 20 per cent of recurrent outlays were on interest payments on accumulated domestic debt. Total government revenue ranged between 20 and 22 per cent of GDP, of which the tax component was about 18 per cent of GDP. Therefore the incidence of taxation was itself quite high by developing country standards and restricted the process of capital accumulation in the private sector. In addition, private savings were diverted to the public sector.

A restructuring of the budget by reducing public capital expenditures would have a beneficial impact on both the recurrent and capital components. It would reduce the borrowings of private savings and therefore immediately augment investible resources in the hands of the private sector; it would gradually bring down the public debt, reducing interest payments and the recurrent liabilities of the government. This would leave considerable space for government to allocate resources for improving the efficiency and quality of the services and strengthening the social and economic infrastructure for private sector development.

The overall budget deficit had been contained at about 11 per cent of GDP in the period 1985 to 1987; it had risen to about 15 per cent in 1988 and was again reduced to 11 per cent in 1989. The objective of the 1990-1994 public investment programme is to reduce the deficit to 7.8 per cent of GDP, net domestic borrowing to 2.3 per cent and the government capital budget to 9 per cent by 1994. In order to achieve these objectives the government has set itself two tasks. One is the restructuring of the administration and reduction of its surplus cadres. The second is the privatisation of public sector enterprises or their "peoplisation" as the government has designated it. The term is intended to emphasise the government's policy of broadening the base of privately owned equity and avoiding a high concentration of ownership in the process of privatisation. Privatisation will enable government to transfer commercial and industrial activities that can be more efficiently carried out in the private sector and thereby remove the burden on the budget which they will continue to impose if they are managed as at present.

The management of the two key instruments of macro-economic policy—the government budget and the balance of payments—also helped the monetary sector to keep in line with the policies of stabilisation. However, inflation which was brought under control in the mid-1980s increased in 1988 when the budget deficit rose and Central bank lending to the government expanded. But in 1989 the key budgetary aggregates were again under control.

The government had to pursue restrictive monetary policies, including the upward revision of the bank rate, the imposition of partial ceilings on commercial credit to the private sector as well as other specific measures. These contractionary policies were rendered inevitable owing to the adverse developments in 1988, reflected in the significant increase in the money supply (Ml and M2) due to the expansion of credit both to government as well as to the private sector. Sri Lanka's experience in managing the monetary aggregates demonstrate their sensitivity to the government budget as well as the balance of payments and the constant need to apply contractionary constraints which interrupt the process of growth and employment creation. These problems have risen primarily owing to the failure to coordinate macro-economic policies in relation to the management of the budget, the balance of payments and the money supply. But in designing the macro-economic policy framework, the problem of the appropriate balance between the different policy responses as well as the tolerable limits of expansionary finance and inflation has been a vexed one.

In the regulated economy prior to 1977, policies relating to interest rates and credit did not figure significantly in the management of the economy. In the periods of high inflation, particularly after 1977, rates have been adjusted appropriately. However, the total financing system both for the mobilisation of savings and for long-term lending for capital formation and development has not been reviewed and restructured in line with other developments.

There is a large variety of credit packages distributed in an uncoordinated manner throughout the system. Among them, rural credit to farmers, loans to low-income house-builders, and credit to small businesses were provided on concessional terms substantially below market rates. Some of these, particularly credit to farmers, were managed with a high degree of laxity leading to low rates of repayment and occasional large-scale write-offs. These components of the system sought to achieve the objectives of both equitable access to credit and the provision of facilities for small savers. They were therefore an essential part of a strategy of development which gave priority to poverty alleviation. But many of these schemes were not prudently administered.

Sri Lanka's experience in managing the monetary aggregates demonstrate their sensitivity to the government budget as well as the balance of payments and the constant need to apply contractionary constraints which interrupt the process of growth and employment creation. These problems have risen primarily owing to the failure to coordinate macro-economic policies in relation to the management of the budget, the balance of payments and the money supply. But in designing the macro-economic policy framework, the problem of the appropriate balance between the different policy responses as well as the tolerable limits of expansionary finance and inflation has been a vexed one.

Interest rates and credit

In the periods of high inflation, particularly after 1977, rates have been adjusted appropriately. However, the total financing system both for the mobilisation of savings and for long-term lending for capital formation and development has not been reviewed and restructured in line with other developments. There is a large variety of credit packages distributed in an uncoordinated manner throughout the system. Among them, rural credit to farmers, loans to low-income housebuilders, and credit to small businesses were provided on concessional terms substantially below market rates. Some of these, particularly credit to farmers, were managed with a high degree of laxity leading to low rates of repayment and occasional large-scale write-offs. These components of the system sought to achieve the objectives of both equitable access to credit and the provision of facilities for small savers. They were therefore an essential part of a strategy of development which gave priority to poverty alleviation. But many of these schemes were not prudently administered.

By 1989, the share of the agricultural sector had declined to approximately 23 per cent of GDP, the share of industry had risen to 28 per cent and the manufacturing component of industry stood at about 17 per cent. Although the manufacturing sector had grown rapidly, it was confined to a few sectors in which the garments industry provided the largest contribution. In the agricultural sector, the import substitution of rice and the development of new land were reaching their limits demanding new strategies for the sector. These have important implications for the peasant economy and the alleviation of rural poverty in general.

The changes in the composition of trade were also significant. The value of external trade amounted to about 60 per cent of GDP in 1989—a steep rise from 40 per cent in the mid-1970s. Tea, rubber and coconut accounted for nearly 75 per cent of exports in 1975/76. By 1989 the share of these exports had fallen to 39 per cent while industrial exports had increased to 55 per cent. These figures, however, represented the gross export earnings.

The shares of industry on net export earnings are likely to be much lower when the imported inputs are taken into account, as the two major export sectors in industry—garments and petroleum products—have high import content. The balance of payments also underwent significant structural changes. The invisibles account became increasingly important as a result of tourism and private remittances, both of which ranked high as sources of foreign exchange.

POVERTY ALLEVIATION

The governments's concern for the well-being of the poor was manifested in the first place in the social welfare programmes effected large-scale transfers through free state services in health and education; subsidies for food which provided a certain measure of food security; and macro-economic policies designed to keep the prices of essential consumer goods low and stable. Second, the concern for the disadvantaged parts of the economy was reflected in the agricultural policies which promoted peasant agriculture, established settlements for the landless poor, distributed a large extent of state land and developed traditional activities such as fishing.

Sri Lanka's social welfare programme can be traced back to the 1930s after the introduction of a substantial measure of responsible government under British rule. In the early 1930s representative institutions were introduced based on an electoral system with universal adult franchise. The British legislators who were responsible for the implementation of these measures were themselves strongly influenced by concepts of the welfare state and democratic government that were evolving in their own country. They argued that there was an urgent need to create conditions in which the local elites would become sensitive to the pressures of population demand and move in the direction of essential social reforms.

The competitive political system evolved after the 1930s fulfilled many of these expectations. Elected representatives began to articulate the demands of their electorates and promote the expansion of various public services such as health and education. The 1940s witnessed the expansion of three major components of state activity. A food distribution system with subsidised food rations came into operation during the period of the war and was retained and expanded thereafter serving the entire population. A large share of the budget was allocated for a free state health system and free education through government- and state-aided schools. In 1945, the government decided to provide universal free education from the primary to the tertiary stage. Government outlay on these services rapidly increased from six per cent of GDP in 1954 to between 10 and 13 per cent during the period 1960 to 1973. The share of the government budget for these services rose from around 25 to 28 per cent to between 32 and 36 per cent during the same period.

The social welfare programme and the programmes of economic development in the rural sector were able to improve the state of wellbeing for the population as a whole, including that of the rural sector. The social indicators during this period showed remarkable improvement. The food, health and education programmes reinforced each other and their impacts on the wellbeing of the population were closely interlinked. It is possible to trace a consequence of interactions.

Maternal and child care, family education, the increase in productivity of lower income peasant producers, the availability of a minimum food supply all combined to produce a dramatic reduction in mortality rates. The rural bias in economic development policies, which gave high priority to raising the productivity and incomes of the rural population, played an important part. The rural sector fully participated in these improvements. Rural/urban disparities in most of these indicators are negligible. Recent longitudinal studies of a cohort of pregnant mothers in the rural sector indicate that there is no significant variation in the rates of child survival among the different income strata of the rural population.

The demographic outcome of these policies has been one of the more positive achievements of this period. The average annual growth rate of the population has fallen from around 2.9 per cent in the early 1950s to 1.5 per cent in the mid-1980s. The fertility rate has declined from 3.4 per cent in 1981 to 2.4 per cent at present. It is clear that Sri Lanka has managed the demographic transition successfully and has reached a situation wherein the main problems of population growth have been brought under control. Life expectancy at birth has reached approximately 70 years—a lifespan close to that in developed countries. The crude death rate has declined to about seven per thousand, while adult literacy is in the region of 85 per cent of the adult population.

The female population has acquired the capacity to manage the reproductive part of their lives. Larger proportions of the newly reproductive female population have increasingly higher levels of educational attainment. It would therefore appear that a declining birth rate is a systemic element in the process of demographic change in Sri Lanka. The programme of liberalisation in the late 1970s, including the restructuring of the food subsidy, had adverse effects on the poorer social strata.

The removal of subsidies and administered prices along with devaluation resulted in a steep increase in the general price level. Food prices increased by 71 per cent for the period 1979 to 1982. The cost of rice increased by 100 per cent and wheat flour by 160 per cent during this same period. While the increase in prices of domestically produced food would have benefited the food-producing rural poor, the general rise in prices adversely affected the wage-earning groups in rural and urban areas as well as the poorer farmers.

11

Rural Poverty Processes

The institutional processes which tend to perpetuate rural poverty include: lack of access to land and water; inequitable sharecropping and tenancy arrangements; underdeveloped markets; lack of access to credit and inputs; and limited and ineffective extension. In discussing policy and institutional biases, the competing needs for the production of export and foodcrops should not be overemphasised. In some areas, it may be in the best interests of the rural poor to support both, or even just the export crops, in order to generate greater exchange entitlement in terms of command over food resources than they could obtain by direct local food production.

In other areas, in which there is scope for local food production, this must be exploited to the full so that areas which are relatively vulnerable because of their location are not unduly dependent on supplies from other regions of the country or abroad. This is also true of food aid, which may be costly to transport to remote areas. Policy and institutional biases strengthen, the dualistic process, accelerate population and degradation of the environment, and reinforce gender, cultural and ethnic biases.

Policy and institution-induced processes have short- and long-term impact on the welfare of poor rural households. In the short term, these households are unable to earn an income sufficient to meet minimum nutritional requirements, or to take advantage of the market, whether individually or through group initiatives. In the longer term, poor rural households continue to lag behind because they do not generate surplus for investment, nor do they have access to profitable investment opportunities which might enable them to accumulate productive assets. Moreover, the rural poor may be forced to overuse resources without being able to take measures to reverse the potential degradation of the environment which in the long run undermines their productivity and income.

Demographic processes are linked with socio-economic development and poverty in a complex manner. Rapid population growth is a consequence of the so-called "demographic transition". In fact, a reduction in mortality among the rural poor has often been a major factor explaining the increase in their numbers.

An important decline in mortality has been a linear process almost independent of improvements in the standard of living of poor people. Even in those countries where the situation of the poor has worsened, their mortality has declined. The movement of fertility, on the other hand, is much more complex to understand. The survival strategy of the poor leads them to strive for relatively large families because, traditionally, the flow of wealth is from children to parents. Once this is reversed due to increased expenditure on education and related costs, the total fertility starts to decline. However, as will be explained later, the decline in fertility has slowed down or levelled off in many regions, one main reason being that traditional survival strategies are still dominant.

Rapid population growth, and the skewed age structure and migration which result, have frequently caused and perpetuated rural poverty through increased pressure on land and other resources, social services and employment, as well as, in some cases, through a shortage of labour due to out-migration. High population growth can make land scarcity more acute. Growing population, coupled with the laws of inheritance, leads to fragmentation of landholdings and degradation of crop and pasture land. The results are marginalisation and landlessness, declining yields, and difficulties in adopting new technologies. Lack of, or ineffective implementation of land and tenurial reform combined with rapid population growth can accelerate the process of proletarisation. Reduced incomes and malnutrition follow. This process is often aggravated both by the dualistic process and by natural calamities such as drought. However, the link between poverty and fertility is noticeable worldwide.

In the process of development, the size and rate of growth of a population, its quality as to education, health and skills and the technological choices available to it, are crucial. In some cases, a dense population can create the necessary preconditions for technological innovation and the subsequent intensification of production. This has been used as an argument for large populations and rapid population growth rates, and has resulted in lack of commitment or, in some cases, outright hostility towards family planning. One should however be careful in lumping together the issues of population size and its rate of growth.

High rural population density emanating from a large population base is favourable for economic growth because it reduces the per capita cost of social and physical infrastructure. High population density is usually associated with good agricultural resources which lend themselves to a high degree of intensification. On the other hand, a rapid rate of population growth in areas of low potential can accentuate the problem of rural poverty. A high density of rural population with a low rate of growth is conducive to the success of targeted efforts to alleviate rural poverty.

The most obvious consequence of a high rate of population growth is that even with relatively high rates of economic growth, improvements in the standard of living will be limited. A young age structure and hence an increase in the dependency ratio will place a heavy burden on the economy of poor developing countries. This is particularly alarming in view of the fact that, according to the United Nations, world population is likely to grow from its present level to over eight billion in the year 2025, 7.1 billion of which will be in developing countries, representing a 74 per cent growth. With a growing population and a high dependency ratio, total saving in the economy will decline, which means fewer resources for investment in human development in the coming years.

An increasingly youthful population structure has serious implications for the budget and for GDP—even to provide minimum health and education services. In the face of competing demands from other sectors, this will generate internal, social tensions. In a situation of rapid population growth, a country has three options to deal with the problem of education: increased expenditure; smaller educational input per enrolled child; or a lower enrolment rate. In practice, a combination of the three may be adopted. Expenditure may be increased, while allocation per pupil is reduced and the quality of education is compromised.

Any reduction in the level or quality of schooling tends to affect first and foremost poor rural people living in remote areas. As the last resort, enrolment rates start to fall. Education takes up a large share of government expenditure in many developing countries. Therefore, one must make a distinction between cases where the finance for education comes entirely from the government budget and those where the cost is increasingly shared by the family and the community. The latter is an unavoidable necessity for countries with rapid population growth.

The young age structure also has implications for the labour market and labour productivity. Most new entrants into the labour market are inexperienced and poorly educated, keeping productivity as well as salary levels low. There are, thus, several ways in which the population process may perpetuate rural poverty. Most of the factors discussed above have a tendency to hit harder the poor in the marginal areas, thus increasing the gap in income and welfare between populations in different regions. The other side of the coin is the observable linkage between poverty and persistently high birth rates, a notable exception to this being seen in nomadic and pastoralist populations. The reasons for their generally lower fertility levels are mostly social and economic, relating primarily to their need for frequent and unhampered movement.

Cultural factors, such as their traditional practice of sexual abstinence, post-partum breastfeeding, also play a role. Furthermore, the polygamous unions, of nomadic and pastoralist populations tend to result in a lower average number of children per wife than monogamous unions. Physiological factors, such as malnutrition and poor health, also contribute to lower fertility—a lower number of children over the reproductive age and more widely spaced births. In pre-modern production systems, inter-generational wealth flow within a family, or an extended family, is primarily from the young to the parent generation.

Children provide wealth for the family in the form of labour and old-age security. The increased workload of rural women has tended to raise the desired family size; to attend to all of their household responsibilities, women are often dependent on the labour input of their children. Where infant mortality is high families have to produce extra children in order to ensure the survival of the required number. This economic rationale changes when children start consuming more than they produce. When children are sent to school they use up family resources in the form of school fees, uniforms, books, etc., and at the same time they are not available for farm labour. Whether or not children are sent to school is largely dependent on the perceptions of the parents regarding the utility of education. If education is perceived as useful in the medium or long run, parents have a tendency to invest more resources in their children's schooling. Where resources are limited, this favours a smaller family size.

Cultural factors play an important role here and especially, girls' education in many societies is seen as less important than that of boys, priority is given to the schooling of boys, and girls are often taken out of school before completing their studies. Nevertheless, education, especially female education, as well as women's status and participation in the labour force, is important in achieving lower rates of population growth. The mechanisms through which these factors affect fertility are an increase in female age at first marriage, improved knowledge of health, hygiene and contraceptive methods, more female independence, both economical and social, a possibility for women to gain status other than by being mothers, and a larger proportion of women remaining unmarried. Projects financed by external donors have to take these factors into account; these can affect fertility, mortality, and other demographic features by changing conditions of production, the farming system, the role of women, health, sanitation, and migratory flows.

Migration, internal and external, is another demographic process affecting rural poverty. A closer look at the effects of migration is revealing. Internal migration, which essentially converts the rural poor into urban poor, is sometimes seen as a positive influence in that remittances are sent back home and pressure on the land is temporarily or permanently eased. Migration is considered by some to strengthen market linkages between rural and urban areas.

When combined with education, migration provides a bridge for the upward social mobility of the rural poor. Besides, migration at times of economic and social stress has been an integral part of the survival strategy of the rural poor from time immemorial. However, the negative effects of a migration of labour from farms should also be noted. When young, skilled and able-bodied adult males leave for neighbouring towns and countries, they leave labour shortages behind, with the elderly and women in charge of households and local food production. Rural poverty in developing countries has to be dealt with by creating jobs in villages and market towns.

Most importantly, labour productivity on the farm must be increased and poor labourers assisted to move into better paid non-agricultural occupations, preferably in rural areas. Some countries, such as Indonesia, have tried to avoid the adverse effect of *ad hoc* migration by undertaking programmes of planned transmigration and resettlement to relieve pressure from densely populated parts of the country. However, to make such programmes successful the settlers have to be provided with the right type of assistance, including draught power.

Another aspect of demographic change is spatial distribution. As a long-term strategy to overcome rural poverty, urbanisation can be extremely important. The perception must change from one of exploitation of rural areas for urban growth to one which promotes a balanced pattern of urbanisation, keeping as its main objective the improvement of rural areas through production, service and market linkages. A rich network of urban and peri-urban centres creates better markets for agricultural products and easily accessible urban services for the rural poor.

Conceivably, a rural population can be close to urban centres which will provide them with health, education and othei services, as well as opportunities for working, selling their output and buying industrial products at a relatively cheap price. How far this model will work depends on the density and the spread of rural populations. Also, the basic condition for success is that increases in agricultural production and rural incomes must precede migration to the cities.

The availability of resources is critical in determining the extent of rural poverty and poor management can severely damage the resource base. Rural poverty, malnutrition and under-nutrition are closely linked to degradation of the environment, as poverty depletes natural resources which in turn accentuates the suffering of the rural poor. The challenge is how to reverse this negative linkage. The depletion of forest cover in search of cultivable land and/or fuelwood threatens agricultural sustainability, with serious consequences for the rural poor.

With appropriate policy and technological support, poor populations can be mobilised to promote forest regeneration and more stable fanning systems geared to soil conservation. When carried out upstream, such measures can also help solve the problems of downstream siltation and flooding which further jeopardise the life support systems of the poor. In certain situations, perennial crops such as coffee, tea, oil-palm and the like maintain cover and are much better for income and environment than cutting forest and perennial grass for annual crop production. Land degradation and desertification in arid and semi-arid areas are taking place at an alarming rate due to climatic changes, overgrasing and inappropriate agricultural practices, with poor agro-pastoralists and herdsmen cited as both perpetrators and victims. However, experience suggests that it is possible to draw on the creative potential of poor people to change deserts and semi-deserts from a "threat to life" to a "provider of life".

The adverse impact of environmental processes on rural poverty can often be traced to the internal contradiction within a development approach, which promotes savings and investment for production and accumulation but does not make adequate provision to arrest the process of capital loss through degradation of resources. Inequity in the distribution of economic and political power within and between generations makes for difficulties in reconciling present and future needs. Throughout the world, farmers large and small are putting excessive pressure on the land.

In many regions, relatively affluent large farmers and ranchers have often tried to maximise short-term profit by adopting inappropriate technology and intensive cultivation. This has led to degradation of the environment and depletion of resources. Cropping patterns also have a substantial impact on the environment. In a vast majority of cases, the degradation of the environment is a result of a combination of natural and human factors.

Extensive livestock-keeping is putting rangeland under increasing pressure. Animal survival rates being low during a drought, families tend to keep large herds for food security and for rebuilding stock. Overstocking has been aggravated by "open access" to resources and by a lack of technology to improve the carrying capacity of arid and semi-arid lands. Changes in the system of tenure, population pressure and encroachment by powerful factions in society are leading to a breakdown of the communal systems of range management, without an appropriate substitute. Take the example of the traditional *hema* system of range control in the former Yemen PDR. The control involved: no grasing and cutting of trees at certain times or seasons; specification of the kinds and numbers of animals, reservation of areas for bee-keeping; and areas set aside for forest trees.

With the gradual expansion of governmental authority into the domain of tribal control, the hema system could no longer be effectively managed. No other controls were introduced, and overstocking has been the result. In general, insecurity of tenure leads to degradation of the environment.

Deforestation has taken place in the region for centuries. But the impact has recently been multiplied by a rapid increase in human and cattle populations. Thus, desertification has taken place as the protective vegetation binding the soil and retaining moisture has been depleted. The growing populations are dependent on the trees for fuelwood and for wood for construction. The demand for fuelwood is currently one of the major crises in the area. In order to survive, the people have to cut down trees, but cutting down trees means increased erosion and desertification and every day the people must go further to satisfy their requirements. Today, three times as much wood is burned as is grown.

Degradation of the environment is strongly linked to the insecurity of the household with regard to food and fuel. The process of degradation of the environment also has socio-economic and political implications. The permanent settlement of nomadic populations, which may be the explicit or implicit policy in some countries, or just the result of modernisation, may damage the environment. Nomadic peoples frequently occupy areas which cannot support permanent agriculture because of dry conditions or meagre soils; permanent settlement may rapidly result in serious environmental problems.

Ever-increasing numbers of refugees from the zones where the desert is encroaching have resulted in concentrations of people in areas that traditionally have been thinly populated, causing degradation of the land and unprecedented problems for agriculture. In a different context, the programme to bring populations into villages has depleted resources around the villages while leaving distant lands uncultivated. This has happened mostly in the dry central and the northern regions. The most common linkage between poverty and degradation of the environment in marginal areas is caused by poor people lacking the means to keep their production systems sustainable.

National agricultural policies may also be harmful to the environment. Pricing policies favouring expansion of cereal production into marginal areas, subsidised capital to expand commercial operations, subsidies for the adoption of imported machinery or of inappropriate technologies, excessive transfer of income out of the agricultural sector—both directly, through taxes and depressed procurement prices, and indirectly, through over-valued exchange rates—and subsidised agricultural credit not targeted at poor farmers, may singly or cumulatively undermine the sustainability of small holders and pastoralists.

In effect, low public investment in rural infrastructure, a lack of price incentives and inadequate access to modern agricultural inputs and services discourage investment in land conservation. The resulting undervaluation of land may further accelerate overuse and degradation. Low investment in off-farm employment in rural areas may also contribute to further degradation of the environment by encouraging overuse of existing resources. The interlinked problems of poverty and degradation of the environment cannot be resolved within the scope of the agricultural sector alone: there is an urgent need to take pressure off the land. One way to do this is to increase investment in rural infrastructure and off-farm activities to provide employment and income for poor households.

In most developing countries, the rural poor are adversely affected when, for instance, seasonal fluctuations in food availability translate into nutritional deprivation, especially among women and children. Seasonal food shortages are often aggravated because the poor are forced to sell the harvest immediately at cheap prices so as to meet pressing needs, only to buy some of it back later at a much higher price. This means less food and money are available for savings or investments, and the small holders' long-term growth is jeopardised. Seasonal food shortages also create indebtedness. To feed themselves, the poor may have to borrow money at exorbitant interest: rates sometimes exceed 100 per cent. They then have to devote most of their energies to debt servicing, further reducing their chances of escaping the poverty trap.

In developing countries, women in rural areas are often discriminated against. In Bangladesh and elsewhere, the number of single women appears to be on the increase. And since growing poverty in rural areas has undermined traditional social bonds, women are usually left entirely to their own devices. With little or no access to land, they depend on casual labour and earn very little. Often, women farm fragmented plots of non-arable or infertile land. Their access to inputs, extension, training and credit is poor and this limits their ability to take advantage of the commercialisation of agriculture.

When droughts or cyclones strike and they can find no work, they fall even deeper into poverty. It has become increasingly clear that targeting benefits to the poor in general and hoping women will get their share, simply does not work. The impact of male migration on rural women has also been noted. In former Yemen PDR, males tend to migrate to neighbouring countries for employment or to drift seasonally into the construction sector. International migration results in diminished output from the land, while seasonal migration results in less attention being paid to routine tasks such as maintenance, and sets the stage for a long-term decline in productivity.

The rural poor are exploited by various kinds of middlemen. Landowners exploit sharecroppers and tenants, moneylenders exploit debtors and traders exploit small-scale producers. All these combine to keep millions of people in the grip of poverty. But, in some cases, cooperatives and government agencies whose task is to protect the poor, may themselves practise forms of exploitation. There are many instances where heavy levies imposed by cooperatives or government agencies have damaged farmers. Large, inefficient bureaucracies are themselves indicative of an exploitative relationship. They are paid for by the productive sectors of the community and frequently contribute to the accumulation of large budget deficits.

Political troubles and civil strife can have a disastrous impact on the rural poor. One problem is that development flows to the rural poor in disturbed areas, both from national and international agencies, become disrupted. Another is that many producers, with their productive activities disrupted, suddenly become consumers of social services, with serious consequences for production, savings, capital accumulation and investment.

INTERNATIONAL PROCESSES

Poverty is induced by both market and non-market forces. Smallholders producing for export suffer from fluctuations in international commodity prices and from the protectionist agricultural policies of developed countries. The same is true of labourers on large-scale commercial farms, or in mines. This is particularly so in countries relying heavily on one or few commodities for domestic and export income. Also affected are countries where a substantial part of rural income derives from workers' remittances from abroad. Where the remittances come from workers in oil-producing countries, they are vulnerable to fluctuations in the price of oil. Fluctuations in international interest rates also directly affect the well-being of the rural poor.

Among other international factors affecting rural poverty is the net flow of development resources to agriculture. According to the Organisation for Economic Cooperation and Development (OECD), the trend of official development funding for food and agriculture increased between 1975 and 1982, but has fluctuated irregularly since then. Moreover, concern with trade balances is diverting resources to export crops, sometimes at the expense of traditional crops grown by poor farmers.

Policy makers often fail to strike a balance in allocating resources between the production of export crops and that of traditional crops. Finally, there is the unsettled question of protection in the industrial countries, especially against agricultural imports, which militate against developing countries, often against commodities of interest to small holder farmers.

12

Human Resource Development in Sri Lanka

Rural industrialisation has not made much progress in Sri Lanka, in spite of efforts of successive governments since independence. In this scenario, it seems inevitable that unemployed and underemployed job seekers in rural areas, particularly in the dry zone, would be pushed back into their essentially paddy-based economies. In turn, this creates problems of land fragmentation as increasing populations seek satisfaction of their needs through available land which can be placed under cultivation.

Though the percentage share of the agriculture sector in total employment in the economy has declined over the years, there is no evidence to show that the dependence on agriculture of the main groups who comprise the rural poor in Sri Lanka for their employment and incomes has undergone a concurrent decline.

A number of reasons underlie the apparent inelasticity in rural labour mobility to the relative decline in the share of agriculture in terms of labour absorption.

1) Even though the labour force grew by more than 123 per cent from 2.6 million in 1946 to 5 million in 1981, and much of this increase was in rural areas, occupational diversification in rural areas continued to be slow. The urban industrial zone in the western province of the country where nonfarm employment avenues are concentrated and where such occupational diversification is relatively more marked, a substantial

volume of new sources of employment and income generation exists.

2) After an initial emergence of high inflation rates soon after the introduction of liberalised economic policies in late 1977, inflation was brought down to a low rate of 1.5 per cent in 1985, but it subsequently moved upwards again reaching about 23 per cent in 1990. One consequence has been to depress real wages, since unskilled and semi-skilled labour wages in the urban and rural sectors have not increased commensurately in recent years.

3) The inelasticity in rural labour mobility with respect to the relative decline in the share of agriculture in total employment is related to the source of growth in agriculture, namely, the growth of high-yielding variety (HYV) technology application in agriculture. This technology was considered in early writings on "green revolution" technologies to be labour intensive.

In Sri Lanka, the labour coefficient in agricultural production has declined from 0.58 in 1962 to 0.56 in 1972 to 0.55 in 1982, and to about 0.52 at present. This means that with the rural labour force growing at 2 per cent per annum, no dent is being made by agricultural growth in the overall rate of unemployment in rural areas.

Employment

The available data do not provide an accurate determination of the employment and unemployment statistics in Sri Lanka, nor does the data reveal the changing composition and characteristics of the unemployed population. Concepts and definitions and measurements of unemployment and underemployment vary widely across official surveys conducted by the DCS as well as the central bank of Sri Lanka. Problems exist with sample design, coverage, and comparability. The data sets of the different surveys can only yield a crude cross-sectional comparability.

Similarly, trends can only be vaguely discerned in relative terms, again owing to differences in concepts and definitions in different surveys. Other issues such as the inaccessibility to source material which bear upon unemployment positions in different regions and the conversion of sample data to population estimates also thwart a more detailed analysis of employment and unemployment conditions morale. However, within these limitations, a crude view of employment characteristics of the country at different times and possible indications of trends may be discerned.

According to Korale data sources on wages apparently suffer from the same malady as the data sources which pertain to employment and unemployment. For example, while wages and salaries of state employees may be derived from annual estimates of revenue and expenditure of the government, this source cannot be used to derive the gross salary or wage as the published information does not incorporate different allowances payable to different occupational categories.

The central bank since 1978 has been collecting wage data which covered the informal, unorganised sectors of the economy, including wages associated with tasks in the plantation occupations. Information on labour wages are available in the surveys conducted by the DCS every four years or so and from the labour department surveys of working hours and earnings. Wages data are also available in documents of the Public Service Salaries Commission, wage review committees in the government service.

These committees are only summoned infrequently, thus the information is inadequate for a trend analysis. The available wage data have also not been of substantial impact indetermination of minimum wages in different occupations, particularly on the lower grades of employment even within the state sector. Minimum wages in the unorganised sector particularly in food agriculture have been discussed since the Paddy Lands Act No. 1 of 1958.

However, the very complexity of issues involved including the lack of a clear empirically valid definitional separation among hired "labour", "share-tenant", and "owner-cultivator"—categories used in distribution of returns to labour in small holder food agriculture—has thwarted a legal affixation of minimum wages on the ground. Further, the producer's drive for profitability in foodcrop production in the face of insecure markets and rising inputs costs has always had a deleterious effect on even the evolution of an informally driven minimum labour wage in the country.

Consequently, while wages tended to languish in the agricultural areas, this in conjunction with the increase in unemployment and the sluggish annual addition in new employment avenues in the agriculture, industry, and service sectors, have also steepened overall poverty conditions throughout the country.

The labour force and socio-economic survey (LFSS) 1985/86 place the number at approximately six million. The consumer finances survey (CFS) of the Central Bank of Ceylon 1981/82 places the labour force at 34.3 per cent of the total population, belying the prevailing definitional inconsistencies between national census and other surveys. The Central Bank Survey 1981/82 estimates that about 50 per cent of the male population and 20 per cent of the female population were in the labour force by 1981/82. The LFSS estimated that by 1985/86,67 per cent of the labour force were male and 33 per cent female.

The overall labour force participation rates do not reveal a substantial change between 1971 and 1986 with an activity rate, which by 1985/86 was at 37 per cent. While changes in the labour force participation rate in the 1970s and 1980s indicated through the CFS and labour force surveys (LFS) reveal different rates of declines in overall participation, the decline is considered insignificant.

The CFS of 1981/82 revealed that male labour participation rates for both urban and rural sectors accounted for about 49 per cent while female participation rates accounted for 17 per cent in both sectors. The estate sector's male and female participation rates were higher at 54 per cent and 53 per cent, respectively. The rural labour force was estimated at 71.7 per cent of the total economically active population by 1985/86. With the estate sector it accounted for approximately 79.7 per cent of the total. Males accounted for about 88.4 per cent of the economically active population in rural areas, while in the estate sector, the shares of male and female labour were nearly equal. The distribution of employed population by major industries was relatively unchanged up to 1963, indicating a general stagnation in the economy affecting labour mobility.

However, since then, some changes have been observed in the distribution patterns, as different industries respond differently to prevailing investment patterns. The general upswing in the share of agriculture in the distribution of employed population in the 1980s should be primarily related to the agricultural progress arising from the Mahaweli Project, and to a lesser extent to Kirindioya, tank rehabilitation, and agricultural land alienation programmes. The Mahaweli Project appears to have reversed a general trend of a relative decline in the share of agriculture in employment generation. Generally, the popularly-held direct relationship between unemployment and poverty was not strongly borne out. Instead, an alternative notion that "the poorest cannot afford to be unemployed" appeared to be more valid with the presence of a "working poor" receiving inadequate incomes for their labour. While in the urban and to some extent the estate sectors, relatively high unemployment rates tended to be more associated with the incidence of poverty, the position was more critical in rural agricultural areas where irregular employment conditions bred underemployment. In view of the relatively low wages received, which did not readily respond to price inflation, much of the rural employed were also in abject poverty as most of them were in occupations which were largely confined to heavy manual labour and in addition were only sporadically available.

Unemployment has increasingly assumed critical proportions, since the early 1960s. Rapid population growth and higher educational attainments, especially among the youth, and the lack of a corresponding increase in employment opportunities are largely attributed to the growth in unemployment. The economic liberalisation policies of the late 1970s were expected to yield increased employment in all sectors of the economy. In fact, such an expectation appeared to have been on the way to realisation as was demonstrated by a steep decline in the rate of unemployment in the early 1980s.

The relatively slow pace of completing the economic liberalisation process, the near completion of "lead" investment projects, the dislocations resulting from widespread civil disturbances particularly in 1987, the decline in the terms of trade as a result of global price declines for primary products, and a steeply rising national debt service affecting public investment are considered the major reasons for the increasing inability of the post-1984 economy to contain rising unemployment.

The paddy sector dominates agricultural labour force absorption. Census data indicates that total employment in the paddy sector increased from 378,000 in 1953 to 784,000 in 1981. An estimate for 1986 places the number of employed in the paddy sector in the region of one million to 1.15 million persons. This is based on an estimate of approximately 2.3 million persons in agricultural employment, as derived from CFS 1986/87 data. The estimates suggest that employment per hectare of paddy crop area has increased from 1981 and is in the range of 1.11 to 1.28 labour units. Output per worker has decreased, however, from about 2.84 mt. to 2.58-2.25 mt. These rates are, however, substantially higher than the rates observed in 1971. The increased employment in the paddy sector implies that paddy production has continued to be profitable for producers, however, at a declining profit margin due to production cost escalation over the years.

A declining average product per worker, in turn, indicates that additional employment maybe approaching saturation levels, unless paddy prices increase and/or productivity levels increase to allow the employment of additional persons to be economically viable. Experience of the 1980s up to the early 1990s indicates that the increase in labour absorption in paddy agriculture has been due more to the expansion of cultivated area under irrigation. In view of sluggish growth in paddy prices and land productivities, with yields reaching a plateau condition between 3.3 and 3.6 mt./ha. coupled with rising production costs, the attainment of higher increases in labour absorption in existing lands has been thwarted.

Attainment of higher levels of labour use in the paddy sector is also being prevented due to the nature of technological innovations and policies affecting input use in the production. Current dry zone paddy agriculture is one which is moving rapidly towards cost minimisation in production. Paddy cultivated in large expanses of land simultaneously demands much labour. Yet, rising labour costs and attendant cost escalation in other inputs along with slower growth of farm-gate prices have pushed producers to save on hired labour. Thus, labour-intensive activities such as transplanting and hand weeding and other major operations are becoming increasingly mechanised. Input-use data gathered from several dry zone districts over a number of years seem to reveal that a process of task-specific displacement of labour has begun in the paddy production process. Yet, in spite of this ongoing process of technological displacement of labour, such displacement is confined to hired labour.

The intricate factor substitutions based upon cash-conserving actions that farmers, many of whom are at the subsistence level or below, take often results in a super-exploitation of family labour. This is coupled with some use of technology and practices to complete operations in time while minimising costs.

Therefore, whether the adoption of high-yielding technology *per se* has resulted in an increased labour use in paddy cultivation continues to be an unresolved question. During the last few years, substantial economic reforms have taken place in the areas of exchange rate determination and price subsidies. For example, since 1989, there have been substantive efforts to minimise the over-valuation of the rupee and remove the fertiliser subsidy. and informed observational opinion.

Farmers in settlement projects such as Mahaweli System C, Minipe, Rajangane have begun to show shifts from tractor to buffalo use in their agricultural operations to cut down on costs. Informal land transaction forms in the H and C systems of the Mahaweli reveal "owner" permit holders leasing out their holdings for a fixed share of the produce, transferring production costs to the lessees, who tend to use more labour-saving technologies than the owners of lands. However, labour is a resource that is yet available in relative abundance even though situational scarcities exist.

In settlement projects where agricultural activities tend to be compressed through adherence to strict water schedules, and short maturing paddy and other field crop varieties are used, labour scarcities exist and relative wages tend to be higher than elsewhere in the domestic agricultural sector. While the quantum of labour that will ultimately benefit from these changes is difficult to ascertain, the macro-economic adjustments being introduced in Sri Lanka are expected to lead to more efficient use of resources. How important and dynamic the other field crops (OFCs) sector will become as a source of labour absorption in the rural sector will depend on the speed with which present technical constraints can be removed and the nature of the incentive environment that producers and traders are likely to face.

Some of the important constraints of a technical nature include the non-availability of some recommended imports such as improved planting material. There is also the failure of extension services to communicate new improvements to farmers. Several projects are now in place to remedy these shortcomings. It will take some time before the technological base for OFCs is developed to a level of sophistication that the rice sector presently enjoys. However, even if the technological base is sound, expansion of these crops and other new export-oriented crops will essentially depend on the price incentives that producers face. In Mahaweli and other settlements systems where OFC cultivation is a joint response to seasonal water scarcity, prices and intensive state interventions, substantial positive responses have been noted. Yet, the minuscule nature of farm plots allocated for OFCs makes the returns inadequate to place producers along a path of higher investment. Over-production of traditional OFCs due to weak production planning often places producers at a highly disadvantageous position with respect to farm-gate prices. Weak bargaining positions of small producers of OFCs belie their lack of technical knowhow which affects post-harvest storage and ability to tide over surplus production periods. The most pervasive determinants of the domestic prices of OFCs, particularly in non-traditional varieties, are the exchange rate and the other indirect effects of trade and macro-economic policy.

In contrast to the impressive growth record of the paddy sector, the tree crops sector has virtually stagnated since the mid-1960s. The lacklustre performance of this sector has certainly affected its labour-absorption capacity. According to population census data, total employment in the tree crops sector declined from 740,325 persons in 1971 to 666,549 persons in 1981. The unemployment rate in this sector, according to the CFS of 1986/87, is around 10 per cent.

Mobility of labour from the tree crops sector to the rural or urban sectors is generally constrained by the special characteristics of the labour force in the plantations. The drop in employment in this sector has been brought about by a decline in the acreage under cultivation as well as by the neglect of a number of crop husbandry and management practices, such as weeding, fertiliser application, infilling of trees, replanting, and new planting. A range of capital developments including building and factory development and improvements in sanitation and housing has also been neglected over the years.

The disruption of activities due to the process of nationalisation and public sector management problems that prevailed after nationalisation, and a heavy tax burden—

both explicit and implicit brought about by currency overvaluation—are major reasons for the decline of the plantations. Recent steps to improve the performance of the tree crops sector include the medium-term investment plan (MTIP) primarily aimed at rehabilitation and development of the capital stock in the public sector plantations and substantial reductions of indirect taxes on export crops.

The problem of unemployment in the public sector plantations may have been drastically reduced since 1984 because of a policy decision to make it mandatory to provide six days of work to all registered persons in the public sector plantations. The fundamental issue is whether measures such as investments in capital development and rehabilitation, tax reductions to increase the profit margins in the public sector corporations and mandatory provision of employment are capable of addressing the more basic problems facing the public sector plantations.

These problems relate to the independence and management structure of state corporations and the incentive regime required to undertake efficient commercial operations and proper agronomic practices. A larger and sustainable output, commercial viability of the plantations, and more productive employment opportunities for the labour force in these plantations may not be forthcoming unless these structural problems are properly addressed.

Health and education

The Sri Lankan government is committed to health for all (HFA) by the year 2000. To this end, its key approach, since the Alma Ata Declaration, has been through primary health care. In 1980, a national strategy was set in place, its main components being the establishment of a national health development network to coordinate all health development activities; decentralisation of health administration; identification and prioritisation of PHC components; intensification and integration of intersectoral action into the health system; and provision of a family health worker for every 3,000 population with a wide range of responsibilities for maternal and child health, and family planning.

The National Health Council was established in 1980, presided over by the prime minister and comprising the minister of health services and all other ministers whose ministries are responsible for health-related activity, such as agriculture, education, and industries.

Shortage of health manpower, particularly of doctors, nurses, and public health midwives/family health workers, has been aggravated by the maldistribution of available staff between urban and rural areas; constraints in providing adequate supervision of field staff; and a disappointing level of motivation among staff. Since limited private practice was permitted to doctors there is an understandable reluctance displayed by many to accept transfers to fill-up vacancies in less densely-populated rural areas. In the end, rural hospitals and central dispensaries are not manned satisfactorily.

As important as the central dispensary is the PHC so is the School Health Education Programme (SHEP). In the background is the shortfall of staffs to visit schools at least once a school term, the SHEP has correctly concentrated on training school teachers and school children in the upper grades on the essentials of PHC, including general and personal hygiene, communicable diseases, and their containment, environmental sanitation with particular emphasis on the situation in the school premises.

The availability of pre-treated safe water on tap has long been considered vital for health. The latest dependable data on water supply come from the 1981 census of population and housing. Although wells were easily the major source of household water, 72.6 per cent of households having recourse to them, almost 30 per cent of these were unprotected, having neither a surrounding parapet nor an apron so that the dangers of these open wells serving households were ever present.

During rains, contaminations of water in open wells are most likely and diarrhoeal diseases become common in the dry zone. There is no provision to chlorinate well water. During the past decade, there occurred frequent outbreaks of diarrhoeal diseases of an epidemic order, particularly in the Mahaweli project and neighbouring districts; and these resulted in many scores of fatalities particular among infants and young children. They were, in nearly all cases, the results of water contamination. One salutary result was that the use of oral rehydration became widespread and with it the fatality rate reduced appreciably. Eradication of undernutrition in the long term depends on the success with which Sri Lanka's development raises the poverty group to levels at which basic needs are adequately fulfilled and that until then state interventions and income support would be needed to assist the disadvantaged. A comprehensive income support intervention programme is already in place. Estimates of intervention coverage indicate that not more than two-thirds of the malnourished mothers are reached, that supply and regularity leave much to be desired, that regional disparities have not been adequately taken cared of, and that abuses in the distribution system are also present.

The malnutrition has an island-wide presence. Chronic malnutrition was widespread in the dry zone, which is predominantly rural. Subsequent studies disclosed a rapid percentage decline in the "normally nourished" from infancy until the age of five and a corresponding steep rise in second and third degree malnutrition percentages during the same ages. This apparently indicates a tendency for even the "normally nourished" to slide down to the ranks of the malnourished during early childhood with its greater demand-on energy, thus calling for effective intervention programmes during pre-school years. The government has set in place a wide range of relief programmes which are intended to alleviate poverty, in the course of which the nutrition standing of the poor will also be raised.

The rising levels of education of the entire population inclusive of both employed and unemployed have had profound impacts over a wide field of the Sri Lankan economy and society, particularly in health demography, agriculture, employment, and social attitudes.

The impact of education is most pronounced on the rising generations of young persons and most visible among the female population, particularly those in the 20-29 age bracket, resulting in appreciable increases in female participation both in education and employment. The features which characterise the educational system in Sri Lanka are products of the process of history.

Despite attempts at reforming the system dating back to the later pre-independence years, the education system which was instituted by the British and Western missionaries, which the Island inherited, remains, in essence, based on the British model, the only significant changes being in the medium of instruction of all schools with Sinhala and Tamil replacing English. The curriculum has strongly favoured the academic needs of a small minority proceeding beyond secondary level to enter the higher echelons of the administrative service and the professions—principally medicine and law—rather than serving economic production-oriented and skill development learning needs of the majority, who drop out before completing secondary education.

Experience shows that sooner or later the unemployed accept any available employment. Unfortunately, the majority have a long wait of three years and more. Unlike the health system, the education system, regarded as a whole, shows very little involvement with local communities.

In short, education in Sri Lanka has deviated sharply from what might be called a basic need education strategy. It may be that not all will fully agree with this view as, for instance, health which is a basic need has made great advances due to education—particularly secondary education. The likely future consequences of the system were anticipated during the last forty years. It was fully realised that unless educational instruction was bifurcated at the appropriate stage into the academic and professional on the one hand, and technical and vocational on the other, there would be a mismatch between education and the skills the country would surely need.

Unemployment rates in Sri Lanka correlate with education, that is, at the higher levels of education the unemployment rates are seen to rise. On the other hand, the demand for the less educated, those with primary or junior secondary level learning, has been rising appreciably. This comes primarily from the expansion of the small farmer sector, automated industry and the informal sector and also through increasing self-employment. The inevitability of this outcome was envisaged over two decades ago.

Sri Lanka's health services provide extensive coverage of both the urban and rural populations equally, through primary health care facilities manned by paramedical personnel, with a strong back-up system of referral clinics and hospitals manned by physicians supported by paramedical staff.

Primary health care (PHC) has now become part of the essential wisdom of a rapidly increasing preventive system. In addition, the Western system of health care co-exists with an important government-regulated system of traditional ayurveda treatment. It can be said of Sri Lanka that due to the collaboration which exists between the education and health institutional organisation, diseases having their roots in poverty, which used to pose the most serious health risks, have been steadily reduced during the last 30 years.

Since 1953 the rate of growth of the island's population has shown a marked decline to 1.3 per cent per annum by 1989. At the same time the population has been increasing at a decreasing rate. It is now thought that the population will stabilise itself by the turn of the century or in the first few years of the 21st century.

The decline in the rate of growth was first observed when the free education scheme just got under way; subsequently a number of other factors combined to raise the age of marriage and lower fertility. The first is the rise in unemployment among the educated and in consequence the postponement of marriage. Another is that the rapidly rising cost of living, especially during the 1980s, led young couples to realise that both partners needed employment to set up a house, leading to a further postponement of marriage. At present the average age of marriage for females is 25 years and for males, 29 years.

13

Poverty and Income Distribution in Bangladesh

Periodic Household Expenditure Surveys (HES) carried out by the Bangladesh Bureau of Statistics (BBS) remain to date the major source of information on income distribution and poverty. The HES form the main source of information for most of the studies on rural poverty. Diversity in the methods of imputation, lack of panel data at the household level, uniform methods of recording data flow, and careful time sampling, and shortcomings of the memory recall method are some of the limitations of these surveys. Moreover, the problem of missing cases needs to be emphasised particularly. As the HES data are focused on those who comprise household units, it seems plausible that these surveys might have excluded those household units which may be lost in the reference population due to distress migration. One may also classify as missing cases those landless households which do not possess even homestead lands.

As these households are major elements in what may be called the hardcore poor, their exclusion from the HES sample frame would invariably entail considerable underestimation of the severity of poverty. Various approaches have been used in studies on rural poverty which are carried out over the last decade.

In general, most studies have used either the 'fixed-bundle' approach or the 'graph-fitting' method. The methodological review presented in this section concentrates on 'fixed bundle' studies only. Most studies have used the headcount ratio as a measure of poverty. If one considers only those operating under the fixed-bundle approach, there appears to be substantial discrepancies among the head-count estimates recorded for the same year.

Variations in the estimates are attributable to differences in underlying assumptions such as those relating to minimum caloric requirement for physical survival, items to be included in the minimum diet, and the prices to be used for its costing. It may be argued that these discrepancies do not matter as long as the interest is in capturing the trends in rural poverty.

However, no single study has estimated a head-count ratio for a specific time-point—starting from 1973/74 and ending with 1985/86, the last year for which the HES data are currently available. This obviously necessitates comparison among studies, a task rendered difficult because of conflicting findings about movements in rural head-count ratios, especially in the late 1970s and early 1980s.

The set of prices used for costing of the minimum diet constitutes the major source of discrepancy among various headcount estimates. This is not to say that other elements, such as minimum calorie requirement, items to be included in the minimum diet, provision for non-food items, and choice of current as opposed to constant prices, are factors of negligible importance in explaining the discrepancies. However, even after adjusting for these factors, substantial differences may arise from the choice of inappropriate prices by which the minimum calorie bundle is converted into value terms.

There is, indeed, surprisingly little discussion in the poverty literature of Bangladesh on this score. Rahman and Haque, for instance, assumed the rural poverty line for successive years of observation to be a constant 90 per cent of the respective urban poverty line. In effect, then, their procedure involved the costing of the minimum diet using urban retail prices for individual items and then deflating the result by 10 per cent to arrive at an estimate on presumed rural consumer prices.

Muqtada, on the other hand, used prevailing prices for the rural low-income groups without, however, providing insights into how those prices had been derived from the available statistics. The problem is exacerbated by the fact that a proportion of the consumption bundle is met from household production. Whether allowance should be made for such expenditure saving possibilities, in costing the minimum diet, remains methodologically unsettled. For instance, Ahmad and Hossain assumed that 50 per cent of vegetable and fruit consumption is met from production in kitchen gardens.

Naturally, the cost of vegetables and fruits calculated by them would be less than in cases where imputation of these items are carried out on a full cost basis. It appears that both the choice of items to be imputed and the values to be applied for imputation are determined in a quite arbitrary manner.

The more important problem relating to the costing exercise originates from the uncertainty regarding the commodities to be proxied for a generic item, say fish, that has been included in the minimum diet. The statistical year books published by the BBS (Bangladesh Bureau of Statistics) provide urban retail price series for rohu fish only. Hence, in most cases, in costing the calorie share derived from the consumption of fish, prices of rohu fish were used.

Similarly, in the costing of vegetables and potato, prices were used, and in case of pulses of all kinds, the prices of a superior quality of pulses (*masur*) were used. As a result, not only has the costing of the minimum diet failed to take into account the scope for cost-saving at rural household level, but also has yielded a distorted picture of the poverty line income/expenditure.

In general, the aggregate effect of inappropriate costing seems to have resulted in an upward bias in determining the poverty line. Moreover, in so far as urban retail price data are used as a base, possibilities exist that a movement in such prices over time may generate certain, often unpredictable, fluctuations in the estimates of poverty line income/expenditure, eventually resulting in conflicting perceptions about trends in rural poverty. Given the limitations of the previous estimates of rural poverty, and in the face of difficulties in forming a clear idea about trends in poverty from existing studies using different methods of computation, the need for developing an alternative set of estimates on poverty ratios can hardly be exaggerated. To this end, an attempt has been made to recalculate the poverty line for each of the successive observations for which the data are available, and to re-estimate on that basis the corresponding headcount ratios and other poverty indices.

One of the major issues to emerge from recent discourse on poverty is whether the nature and extent of poverty can be best captured by defining it mainly as a unidimensional phenomenon or viewed primarily as a complex multi-dimensional process. The multidimensional approach would lead to the consideration of a range of quality of life variables such as health and sanitation, housing, access to the state distribution system, crisis-coping capacity, and personal security.

The HES data provided by the BBS do not adequately address various non-income dimensions of poverty. With a view to achieving a more informed analysis, a repeat survey of the 62 villages that were the subject of an earlier study on the differential impact of agricultural modernisation, was undertaken by the BIDS over the period November 1989-February 1990.

The repeat survey attempted to generate data on various qualitative dimensions of poverty. Some of which are discussed here.

Being distinct from the approach whereby a predetermined yardstick of a minimum consumption standard is used to demarcate the poor from the non-poor, households can be asked to self-categorise themselves in terms of deficit/ sufficiency in relation to the household's perception of its consumption needs. Four broad categories can be identified: (i) chronic deficit; (ii) occasional deficit; (iii) self-sufficient; and (iv) surplus. As is known, poverty is not a routine feature of all families all the time. The economic position of a household may vary with a year due to seasonality of employment and earnings.

Housing status is another living standard indicator which is sensitive to the poverty scale. The distribution of rural households desegregated by five housing categories:

1) *Jhupri* (matchbox-type houses made of leaves);
2) Single structure houses;
3) Houses with one or more structures with thatch roofs;
4) Semi-durable structures with one or more rooms; and
5) Durable structures with one or more rooms.

Combining the first three categories, the share of the vulnerable segment of the rural population would constitute about 60 per cent of households. In addition, the housing indicator identifies two further levels of differentiation.

Jhupri and single structure categories together constitute 32 per cent of the rural households which compares with the 24 per cent of the 'chronic deficit' households by the self-evaluation criterion and possibly constitutes a hardcore poor group within the broader ranks of the absolute poor households.

The annual per capita availability of cotton textiles per head of population appears to have been broadly stagnant since liberation. Per capita availability on a national scale, including non-cotton and second-hand clothes, was about 9.96 yards in 1986/87. As regards to health and sanitary conditions, the situation appears to be generally precarious.

The BBS figure for 1982 previously indicated that 54 per cent of the rural households did not have access to toilet facilities. The situation seems to have improved only marginally by 1989/90, the proportion having declined slightly to 44 per cent of rural households. Even among the well-off segment of the rural population, only 25 per cent of households maintain sanitary toilets which may indicate a problem of sanitary awareness as distinct from the problem of inadequate resources.

Primary health care deserves to be much improved. In the absence of viable risk-insurance mechanisms, sudden deterioration in the health status of poor household members often leads to a crisis situation for the household as a whole in terms of steep decline in income and welfare. As revealed by the 1989/90 survey, about 35 per cent of all the various types of crisis experienced by rural households are related to health hazards which rank immediately after vulnerability to natural disasters as a matter of concern.

Available data also suggest limited access of the rural population to education. Abdullah et al., for instance, observed that 32,000 villages, nearly one-half of all villages, do not have even a single school, even though on average there is nearly one primary school per 3.2 sq km. Yet other evidence suggests that government expenditure and subsidy per student at the primary level are restricted to less than two per cent of the corresponding figure for the university level. About 23 per cent of children of primary school age do not attend school at all; while a smaller proportion drop out from the system.

The cross-sectional data base derived from the 62-village survey carried out by the BIDS during 1987/88 forms the major source of information on the profile of the rural poor.

Two broad categories of poor households have been identified:

1) Extreme poor households whose average income constitutes 60 per cent of the poverty line income;
2) Moderately poor households whose average income falls in the range of 60-100 per cent of the poverty line income.

The estimated poverty line income for 1987/88 was about Taka 4,300 per person per annum. These two categories may be contrasted with the nonpoor group with respect to some selected socio-economic variables. Landless and functionally landless households represent 59 per cent of the deficit households while marginal and small farmers together make up an additional 31 per cent. This indicates that about 90 per cent of the deficit households are in land-poor categories.

Because of resource scarcity, however, the spread of new seed-fertiliser-irrigation technology is comparatively low for the extreme and moderately poor categories compared with the non-poor group. For instance, the rate of adoption of modern rice variety expressed as proportion of total cultivated area steadily increases from 31 per cent in the case of the extreme poor to 37 per cent for the moderately poor and 45 per cent for the non-poor. Limited access of the poor to land and to new agricultural technology is further exacerbated by some adverse implications of the demographic processes that tend to characterise poor households as distinct from non-poor households.

The extreme and moderately poor households are found to have greater family size, higher child-woman ratio, and a lower male labour force ratio compared with the non-poor households. For instance, in the case of the extreme poor only 24 per cent of family members were adult males as against 33 per cent for the non-poor. The proportion of male members above age 10 is also lower for the poor. Thus, potential earning capacities of poor households would be limited even if only due to the relatively low proportion of male-earning members compared with the non-poor group.

Education is generally considered a means by which the rural poor can aspire to achieve higher social mobility and ensure greater access to income earning opportunities, but, the actual achievement of the poor as a group lags well behind their non-poor counterparts in this respect.

14

Income Distribution in India and Sri Lanka

Income Distribution in India

The economic welfare of the population depends upon aggregate GNP growth, its distribution and a host of other variables like access to education, health and safe drinking water. Therefore, a comprehensive analysis of growth performance and welfare change requires scrutiny of various other welfare indicators. The total income of an individual and hence, personal income distribution, depends upon factor prices and the distribution of ownership of factors of production.

The sample survey data collected by the National Sample Survey Organisation (NSSO) in different years, however, provide some information on the distribution of ownership holdings and operational holdings in rural India. The NSS surveys for the years 1953/54, 1960/61, 1970/71, and 1981/82 show a steady increase in the number of operational holdings but a steady decrease in the total as well as average area of operational holdings in rural India.

The Lorenz ratios, on the other hand, do not show any improvement in the distribution of operational landholdings over the years. Regarding operational holdings, their number increased from 44,354,000 in 1953/54 to 71,043,000 in 1981/82. This is mainly due to the natural growth in population and number of households, and consequent fragmentation of older holdings and also because of land distribution policies of the state governments.

The NSSO has collected data on the distribution of six major types of assets, viz., cattle, buffalo, other livestock, agricultural machinery, non-farm business equipment and transport equipment across 15 size classes of operational holdings in 1971/72. The assets considered here do not include land and buildings. In terms of Lorenz ratios, these assets are much more equally distributed than operational holdings. Cattle is the most important asset of the rural community, accounting for 45 per cent of assets. Agricultural machinery is the most unequally distributed asset, but it has only a modest share in total assets, even though it is important in enhancing productivity in agriculture.

There is a wide inter-state variation in the average value of asset per hectare of operated area and in its distribution across size class of holdings. An unequal asset distribution generates an unequal income distribution which accentuates the skewness in the initial asset distribution further via the saving function.

The National Accounts Statistics (NAS) provides data on net domestic product by four principal categories:

1) Wages and other compensation of employees;
2) Interest;
3) Rent;
4) Profits and dividends.

India has a large unorganised sector where many households are self-employed and work on their own account, simultaneously earning all the four categories of income in different proportions. These are called mixed income and are shown as such in the NAS. About 80 per cent of the rural work force is employed in the primary sector. Even the non-primary sector is largely informal in character in the rural areas. Primary and private unorganised sectors are not mutually exclusive sets; a large subset of the primary sector is a subset of the private unorganised sector. Mixed income and compensation of employees together constitute nearly 90 per cent of the net domestic product in the primary sector. Their share has tended to decline over the years whereas the interest, profits and dividends categories have increased their shares. But there has been a phenomenal increase in the absolute size of the work force depending upon wage and self-employment.

The National Council of Applied Economic Research (NCAER) has conducted nationwide surveys at irregular intervals. The Lorenz ratios for the NCAER data on rural income distribution are 0.463 for 1967/68 and 0.388 for 1975/76. But it is difficult to make any judgement about the underlying income distributional changes.

The NCAER concepts of income vary between surveys; sample size is inadequate; and the concept of income does not include imputed rental value of owner-occupied houses. In the absence of time series data on income distribution, studies on income distribution in India have used the NSS data on consumption distribution as proxy and have drawn conclusions on that basis.

The use of consumption as proxy for income is justified on the grounds that they are highly correlated in a poor country like India and that consumption is a better proxy for permanent income distribution than income. Whether consumption can be used as a proxy for income depends upon relative income increases of the different income groups and the shape of the consumption function.

It is quite possible that, at least in the short run, a decrease in consumption inequality may accompany an increase in income inequality. The degree of inequality in rural consumption distribution as measured by the Lorenz ratio does not show any sustained trend either for India or for any state. They show a pattern of fluctuations over time. The data, which are at current prices, are not adjusted for the differential impact of inflation which has hit the poor more adversely than the rich.

Price-adjusted distributions show an increasing trend in inequality up to 1977/78 for states like Kerala, Tamil Nadu and West Bengal. Consumption does not capture other aspects of welfare such as health, life expectancy and access to public goods. Also, simple measures of consumption inequality like Lorenz ratios are mean independent.

Poverty estimates are generally made on the basis of the NSS consumption data. For such estimates, the choice of a norm is very important. A working group set up by the Planning Commission in 1962 recommended a national minimum consumption level of Rs. 20 per capita per month at 1960/61 prices. This estimate was based on the balanced diet recommended by the Nutrition Advisory Committee of the Indian Council of Medical Research. Based on the NSS data, Dandekar and Rath have estimated Rs. 15 and Rs. 22.5 per capita per month at 1960/61 prices as the poverty lines for rural and urban India, respectively, corresponding to a per capita daily intake of 2,250 calories. A similar approach was adopted by the Planning Commission when it estimated the poverty line as the midpoint of the monthly per capita expenditure class having a daily per capita calorie intake of 2,400 in rural areas and 2,100 in urban areas. These poverty norms are based on average calorie requirement of the population.

Calorie requirements vary depending upon the age, sex and occupation of the individual. But, age, sex or occupation, specific poverty lines have so far not been estimated. Therefore, the same all-India poverty norm is applied for states as well, after suitable adjustments for inter-regional price variations. Updating of the poverty lines is generally done using relevant price deflators.

For rural India/state, the corresponding Consumer Price Index Numbers of Agricultural Labourers (CPIAL) are used as deflators. For urban India/state, the Consumer Price Index Numbers of Industrial Workers (CPIIW) is used. The Planning Commission has been using CSO's national income deflator for both rural and urban sectors. The CPIAL and CPIIW relate to certain subsets of the rural and urban populations; and hence are considered inappropriate for updating the poverty lines for the general population. The Planning Commission approach is inappropriate because it assumes the same price movements for both rural and urban sectors.

Minhas *et al.* have constructed a Consumer Price Index for middle rural population using NSS rural retail prices and the NSS weighting diagram for the corresponding population. For the urban sector, a deflator as a linear combination of CPIIW and Consumer Price Index for Urban Non-manual Employees was obtained using total expenditure weights. The NSSO and the CSO are the two most important data sources for poverty estimates. The NSSO provides distribution of population across per capita expenditure (PCE) classes with monthly PCE corresponding to each class. The CSO provides national aggregate private consumption expenditure.

In addition to direct estimates based on the NSS data, poverty ratios have also been estimated superimposing the NSS distributions on CSO aggregates. The estimates of poverty based on these two data sources differ with respect to both level and trend. This, in turn, is due partly to conceptual and methodological differences between the NSSO and CSO estimates of PCE and partly to differences in methods and deflators employed in poverty estimation. The NSS is a socio-economic survey conducted in the form of successive rounds, wherein information on household consumption by commodities is collected. Thus, the NSS estimates are direct estimates unlike those of the CSO where consumption estimates are made using the 'Commodity Flow' method.

Both the NSS and the CSO are estimates of some unknown parameters. The population parameters being sought to estimate are not the same conceptually. The NSS seeks to estimate all expenditures incurred by the household sector exclusively towards non-productive purposes. The CSO estimate, in addition, includes (i) consumption of private non-profit institutions, and (ii) imputed values of rentals in owner-occupied houses.

Further, there are also other factors like differences in reference period, in the definition of consumption, in methods of valuation and in coverage which have caused differences in the NSS and CSO estimates of total as well as commodity-wise consumption. In fact, studies on poverty in India differ with respect to many such aspects as the basis of definition of the poverty line, methods of its calculation, methods of estimation of poverty, and the database. In 1986/87, the absolute size of the poor in rural India was approximately 153 million, which means a decline of 25 per cent in absolute size from about 203 million in 1970/71 even though the poverty ratio has come down by 45 per cent during the same period.

In rural India, absolute poverty among the scheduled castes declined from 64.6 per cent to 53.1 per cent. For the scheduled tribes, the decline was from 72.4 per cent to 58.4 per cent. Poverty is not a regular feature of all families all the time. The economic position of a household varies between years depending upon a good or bad harvest and within a year due to seasonality of employment and wage earnings.

A study by the International Crops Research Institute for the Semi-Arid Tropics of agricultural households in central India during 1975-1983 showed only 12 per cent of the households to be above poverty all the time. Forty-four per cent were poor for six or more years while 19 per cent were poor every year. The NSS in 1983, on the other hand, has shown that only 81 per cent of the rural households got adequate food throughout the year; for 16 per cent this was true during some months only; and finally two per cent did not get adequate food throughout the year. The incidence of poverty is the highest among agricultural labour households as is their share in total rural poverty. One important reason for this is the high incidence of unemployment. These households account for 60 per cent of total person-days of rural unemployment, even though their share in all rural households is only 30 per cent. Even at the disaggregated level, it is found that poverty is the highest among the agricultural labour households. A household type is defined by reference to the major source of livelihood for the household in the year preceding the date of survey. All households with per capita total consumer expenditure of less than Rs. 76.65 per month constitute the set of poor households. The poverty norm of Rs. 15 per capita per month at 1960/61 prices, when adjusted by the consumer price index for rural agricultural labourers, works out to Rs. 76.65.

In 1986/87 only 16 per cent of the rural population in India had access to tap as a major source of drinking water; about 37 per cent used tube well/handpump and 39 per cent depended upon *pucca* well. About 26 per cent of the rural population reside in electrified dwellings, but only 16 per cent of the rural poor do so. As for sanitation, about 34 per cent of the rural population and an equal percentage of the rural poor-live in dwellings sprayed with disinfectants.

In order to stabilise the general living standards of the population and insulate them against rising prices, the government sells some basic items of daily use to the public at controlled prices through outlets like ration shops and fair price shops. For commodities such as rice and wheat, about 25 per cent of those who depend exclusively on the PDS are poor. The bottom 20 per cent of the rural households account for about 98 per cent of the rural poor. These households get less than 15 per cent of their total purchases of foodgrains from the PDS. The PDS has an urban bias in the sense that more than 80 per cent of the total foodgrains supplied under this scheme goes to the urban sector. But the latest data published by the NSS show quite a different picture. PDS is no longer urban-oriented. In a few states, in terms of total quantity supplied as well as percentage of total food purchased from PDS, it has a rural bias. PDS does provide income support but since both the rich and the poor get the same entitlements it does not really redistribute income significantly. For items such as foodgrains and kerosene, the rich depend on the PDS as much as the poor to meet their consumption requirements.

Since per capita purchases of the rich are more than that of the poor, it would follow that in absolute terms the rich might be getting benefited more than the poor, at least in the urban sector. The poor allocate on average about 80 per cent of their total expenditure on food. Yet, they do not get enough nutrition in terms of calories and fat. This picture holds good at the state level also, with varying intensity. The problem is serious with respect to the children whose development gets stunted because of malnutrition. The poor have little formal education. Low investment in human capital prevents them from taking up jobs in the formal sector. Instead they end up entering the informal sector as casual labourers or self-employed. Illiteracy was highest (75.83 per cent) among labourers, followed by self-employed (61-56 per cent) and the least among others (41.88 per cent).

Rural common property resources (CPRs) are broadly defined as resources to which all members of an identifiable community have inalienable use rights. Historically, the maintenance of these resources reflected people's concern for their collective sustenance and for protection of fragile land resources by keeping them under grass, bush, or trees. CPRs often helped generate multiple earning options and the flexibility required by farmers to adjust their farming systems to variable agroclimatic conditions.

Traditional farming systems in dry tropical regions of the developing world are currently passing through a transitional phase. Having evolved during times of low population pressure and absence of rapid technical and institutional interventions, such systems were land-extensive. In the face of increased population pressure, increased integration of agriculture into the monetised market economy, and a variety of external interventions, however, traditional resource-extensive farming is becoming less feasible. As elsewhere in agriculture, the strong trend is toward increased intensity of use of land resources. This is reflected in ploughing of low-productivity submarginal lands, reduced duration and frequency of fallow, and emphasis on short duration or multiple cropping.

In India, community pastures, forests and wastelands—the major focus of extensive resource use in the past—now bear the burden of land use intensification. It happens in several ways. First, CPRs are privatised and converted into crop lands irrespective of their use capabilities. Second, the use intensity of CPRs, even when they are not ploughed, is increased. The latter happens because of shrinkage of CPRs and reduced availability of periodically followed crop lands. The final consequence is physical degradation of CPRs.

Public interventions including institutional reforms, welfare measures, and production-promoting activities can have adverse effects on CPRs. They tend to accentuate the roles of other factors mentioned above in depleting CPRs. For instance, land reforms in India encouraged privatisation and shrinkage of CPRs. By disrupting the traditional management systems, they also contributed to over-exploitation, poor protection, and degradation of CPRs.

CPRs contribute to employment, income, and as accumulation. They are an important component of people's self-provisioning systems. Because they are taken for granted, however, these contributions are seldom recognised and quantified. In certain areas employment on CPRs exceeds employment generated through antipoverty public programmes. Furthermore, CPR income accounts for 14 to 23 percent of household income from all other sources in the study villages—and it is likely this is a significant underestimate.

More importantly, the inclusion of CPR incomes in total household incomes from all other sources reduced the extent of rural income inequality, as indicated by lower values of the Gini coefficient. Despite their valuable contributions to the economy of the rural poor, CPRs are one of the most neglected areas in development planning in the country. The consequence is their depletion both in terms of decline in area and in terms of physical degradation.

The information relates to 82 villages from 21 districts from dry regions of seven states in India, which was a watershed in the agrarian history of independent India. During the early 1950s, comprehensive land reforms were introduced. The status and management pattern of CPRs underwent drastic changes following land reforms and subsequent public interventions. Because they were a major event in the memory of villagers, the land reforms also served as an important reference point to facilitate recording an oral history of CPRs.

The benchmark situation was compared with the status of CPRs, when fieldwork for the study was conducted. The impact of this change is clearly visible in terms of both decline in proportions of CPR lands in total village area and increase in population pressure on CPRs. In the absence of recorded information with which to assess degradation or decline in productivity of CPRs over time, a benchmark had to be constructed from oral histories and scattered village records.

The variety of CPR products declined because a number of plant and tree species disappeared from common lands. Local names of a limited number of CPR plots indicated their coverage by specific vegetation in the past. Few of these species grow there any longer. Similarly, a number of selected CPR plots that were traditionally used for grazing more productive animals like lactating cattle and working bullocks are no longer able to sustain such animals. With their depleted forage potential and changed vegetative composition, they are now grazed by sheep and goats.

The difference in the number of species found on protected and unprotected CPRs is an important indicator of vegetative degradation and associated resource depletion. Certain CPR areas are protected through religious sanctions against removal of live trees and shrubs from them. The number of trees and shrubs recorded per hectare was three to six times higher oil protected CPRs than on unprotected ones. The number of watering points, an important component of common grazing lands, has also declined.

Although public policies did not explicitly advocate privatisation, in practice virtually all the programmes designed to provide land to the landless and to small landholders have reduced the area of CPRs, because little other land for redistribution could be acquired through land ceiling laws or through voluntary donations. Privatisation involved distribution of land to the landless and the rural poor under various welfare schemes, and legalisation of encroachment on CPR lands.

Although privatisation was supposed to benefit the rural poor, in practice, the benefits to relatively better-off households exceeded the benefits to the poor. Similarly, despite the mention of rehabilitation and protection of grazing lands and village forests in the government's planning documents, very little was done in practice. Moreover, development programmes for these resources were highly "technique"-dominated, with little attention given to user perspectives.

Further, such institutional changes in village administration as the abolition of the feudal system, the decline in the authority of the traditional village headman, and the introduction of formally elected village councils (panchayats) led to slackening of the traditional arrangements for conservation and regulated use of CPRs.

The proportion of poor households among the total recipients of CPR lands was generally the highest; however, the proportion of land received by the poor was much lower than that received by other social groups. The average land area received by the poor barely exceeded one hectare per household; the area received by "others" ranged from two to three hectares. A detailed inquiry into the current status of CPR lands received by the rural poor revealed that the poor could not sustain the gains from land distribution programmes. This happened despite legal restrictions in several areas on transactions in land belonging to the poor.

The area so disposed amounted to 23 to 45 per cent of the land received in different states, excluding Tamil Nadu. Nine to 36 per cent of lands so disposed were submarginal and unsuitable for cropping. Most of the households that disposed of land did not have the necessary resources—like bullocks and ploughs—to cultivate it. Lack of resources to develop the land, inadequacy of the land to sustain the family, and pressing needs for cash induced the poor households to give up the land. The evidence suggests that policies and programmes to help the rural poor through privatisation of CPRs have not worked as intended. It is quite doubtful whether poor people's collective loss from reduced CPR areas has been compensated by private ownership of CPR lands given to them.

The latter is partly an indirect consequence of shrinkage and overcrowding on CPRs. More importantly, as a by-product of public interventions, including land reform and introduction of democratic institutions at the village level, the traditional formal or informal arrangements regulating the use of CPRs have weakened or disappeared. For instance, the abolition of grazing taxes and levies and of compulsory labour to fence and trench CPR lands and to desilt ponds has led to significant declines in the private costs to CPR users. Similarly, the replacement of the informal authority of the village elders by elected village councils and the replacement of conventions by formal laws relating to land have eroded the traditional social and religious sanctions protecting CPRs. This in turn has led to over-exploitation and poor upkeep of CPRs.

Public policies and programmes encouraging privatisation of CPRs affected all villages. But the actual decline in CPRs differed from village to village even within the same state or district. These differences call for examination of other factors that might influence CPRs independently or in association with public policies. These factors can be grouped into three categories. Population size or its density, growth of population, and village size in terms of number of households represent the demographic factors.

The ecological factors comprise such variables as area of the village, extent of submarginal lands and number of livestock. The role of market forces is reflected in such variables as distance from a marketing centre. Historically, even in the context of a micro unit like a village, higher population pressure-implied land scarcity. Once the supply of better lands had been exhausted, any additional demand could be met only through occupation of submarginal lands, including CPRs. Increased population pressure induces a shift from land-extensive to land-intensive farming.

CPRs bear the maximum burden of land use intensification. As observed during the fieldwork, smaller villages were relatively isolated from major markets. They were located in ecologically less favourable environments with greater proportions of submarginal lands. They were also found to have greater social cohesion and respect for conventions relating to use of CPRs. These attributes of smaller villages, originating in ecological, social, demographic, and market-related factors, helped protect the CPRs. This explains both the greater initial availability of

CPRs and the lower decline in their area over time in smaller villages.

Submarginal lands and livestock rearing have a long historical association. Viewed in the context of the traditional practice of reserving submarginal lands for common use, this explains the positive association between the importance of livestock and the extent of CPRs. Furthermore, in the villages with higher livestock populations, people had greater stake in CPRs—a factor that also slowed their decline since the early 1950s.

Villages with higher initial extent of CPRs lost more of CPR area because it was easier to execute land distribution programmes in them. In addition, villagers had a greater awareness of the status of CPRs where the total CPR area was smaller. This prevented encroachments on CPRs by fellow villagers as well as by the state. This sort of safeguard against the decline of CPRs was rarely found in the villages with large and widely scattered CPR lands.

We expected that the size of the CPR area would be negatively influenced by the size of the population and positively influenced by total village area, distance to market, the area of submarginal land, and livestock density. The extent of submarginal area significantly influenced the extent of CPRs, in both periods. The size of the village population was another significant determinant of the extent of CPRs.

Other factors such as the importance of livestock and the distance from a market centre did not emerge as significant determinants of CPR area. Demographic factors declined in importance in the 1980s, while the area of submarginal lands remained the only highly significant determinant of CPRs in that decade. The only factor limiting the privatisation of CPRs for arable farming was the submarginal quality of land.

The initial extent of CPR area was the most significant factor influencing the decline in CPR area. This could be partly due to inter-regional differences in the relative size of villages, the impact of which could not be captured in the regression analysis.

INCOME DISTRIBUTION IN SRI LANKA

The egalitarian trends in relative income distribution and social indicators in Sri Lanka, viewed rather unambiguously at first as effects of policies of intervention, received the attention of a number of Sri Lankan researchers. In addition, an international effort was evident at the time to combine growth with redistributive justice, and the Sri Lankan case came to be examined with some interest. The "uniqueness" of the Sri Lankan experience in this regard has come to attract a wider attention and also to cause much controversy from around 1977 with the appearance of a series of studies, most of them in international publications.

A careful reading of these literatures suggest certain underlying ideological overtones. Yet this debate has helped much in clarifying issues pertaining to the theoretical and empirical analysis of the matters concerned. The initial heat in the debate now appears to have cooled off. Whatever are the interpretations offered, the studies in this chapter do not seem to question seriously the proposition that the reduction of poverty-targeted intervention under liberalisation policies after 1977 has produced adverse impacts on the poor and led to a worsening of the pattern of distribution of income, wealth, and opportunities. Moreover, the research work carried out by the ministry of plan implementation and other government agencies on trends in malnutrition and such other issues have provided additional support to household survey data in showing the short-term ill effects of market-oriented policies on poverty and equity.

Perhaps it was the interpretation of the government itself that the social discontent emanating from these developments was, at least partly, responsible, as in some other countries under similar policy programmes, for the emergence of violent political movements in Sri Lanka since about the mid-1980s. The United National Party, which introduced these policies in 1977 and supervised their implementation through 1988, thus, rather ironically, had to contest the presidential elections of the latter year on basically a wide-ranging poverty alleviation programme.

Due perhaps to the commitment of the newly elected government to this new poverty alleviation programme, the World Bank also has commenced work on a Sri Lanka poverty alleviation and employment project. Other external agencies like the USAID are also studying poverty in Sri Lanka and its socio-economic dimensions. In all these instances, it is methods of extra-market poverty-alleviating intervention which are being studied. In spite of voluminous research already available, there are still unexplored or inadequately explored viewpoints and policy perspectives which can guide further studies of recent trends in poverty and equity in Sri Lanka.

Until the results of the Consumer Finances Survey (CFS) of 1978/79 were made available, relative income distribution in Sri Lanka was widely considered to have moved towards greater equality over time. The statistical basis for this argument was provided by the earlier CFS, particularly those of 1963 and 1973. Except for occasional dissenting views of some writers like Lee, the almost unanimous view in this regard was that there was a movement towards relative equality in income distribution in Sri Lanka during this period. In comparison with the CFS data of 1973, on the one hand, and those of 1978/79 and 1981/82, on the other, shows that there was a reversal of this earlier trend towards greater equality during the 1970s. The Lorenz type analysis of income data from the CFS shows that there was, in a relative sense, an equalising trend till 1973 and a reversal of this trend some time after that year. Since there was no similar survey between 1973 and 1978/79, it is not possible to be precise about the time of this trend reversal. Since the structural and institutional changes and various redistributive policies of the early 1970s continued till 1977, with a major reform effort in the form of nationalisation of company estates added to that package in 1975, it is quite probable that this trend reversal occurred around the time of the policy reforms of 1977.

The highest of income receivers, declined from 1973 to 1978/79 and from 1978/79 to 1981/82. For the highest decile on the other hand, the income share had gone up from 30 per cent in 1973 to 42 per cent in 1981/82. The income share of the lowest 40 per cent was, in the four years, about 12 per cent. In 1973, the income share of the highest decile was slightly less than the share of the lowest 60 per cent of income receivers. In 1978/79 and 1981/82 the highest decile had a higher income share than the lowest 70 per cent of income receivers.

Income distribution is better analysed in terms of the units which would be spending the incomes received. This is of particular significance in a society like that of Sri Lanka, where many spending units have more than one income receiver. Moreover, at a time like the period 1977 to 1982 in Sri Lanka when there was some speeding up in the creation processes of job opportunities, income distribution data by income receivers are likely to show a more inegalitarian pattern than those by spending units for two reasons: one is that new workers at the beginning of their working life would have been at initial points in their wage scales, and the other that the average number of income receivers per family (or household) is likely to have increased at this time of rapid creation of employment opportunities.

In terms of the Gini coefficients, the spending units data for all four survey years show a lower degree of concentration than income receivers data. The increase in the degree of income concentration between 1978/79 and 1981/82 also appears smaller for spending units than for income receivers. All these support the preceding *a priori* reasoning about the distribution patterns likely to be shown in the two data sets. Yet even in terms of spending units data, the income share of the lowest 40 per cent declined from 19.3 per cent in 1973 to 16.1 per cent in 1978/79, and 15.3 per cent in 1981/82.

A possible interpretation of the income data from the CFS is that policy regimes of Sri Lanka till about 1977 contributed to produce an improvement in relative size distribution of income and those of the period since 1977, a tendency towards greater concentration of income. The strength of this argument, of course, depends on the quality of the income data from the surveys. No doubt, these data have to be used with extreme care. The CFS data can also be used to examine the behaviour of mean income levels of different income groups. Average incomes have registered significant increases in the case of all income groups, but the benefits from this income growth were eroded substantially by price inflation. Because of possible sampling and non-sampling errors in the current price income estimates and the doubtful reliability of the implied GNP deflator, one need not place too high a degree of confidence on the reliability of the rates of real income growth. Those rates of growth nevertheless bring out a few interesting points. First, the decline in average real income of the lowest decile of income receivers from 1973 to 1978/79 seems to indicate that the immediate impact of the 1977 change of policy was strongly unfavourable to the lowest income group. This decline, however, was compensated by developments in the following period, and the average real income of this group rose up to the 1973 level in 1981/82.

Second, during both periods under consideration, real income growth of only the highest decile exceeded that of the mean and the median for the total population (disregarding the case of the two lowest deciles during 1978/79-1981/82). As a result of this highly unequal income growth, income differentials between, for example, the lowest and the highest deciles had widened substantially. In 1973, the average real income of the highest decile was only 16 times that of the lowest, whereas in 1978/79 it was 33 times and in 1981/82, 35 times that of the lowest decile. Income growth achieved during this period was thus heavily concentrated in the high income groups, particularly those of the two highest deciles. Except perhaps in the case of the lowest decile from 1973 to 1978/79, there was some trickling down of the benefits of growth to low-income groups by way of real income gains.

Yet, given the widening disparities and the widespread availability through imports of numerous consumer goods of luxury type, it is questionable whether the low-income groups were satisfied with the rate of income growth which they were able to enjoy. It is known that the central bank had conducted the next in the series of its CFS in 1986/87, but its report has not yet been published, although some studies are available using the unpublished data from this CFS. For any analysis of the country's income distribution pattern in more recent times, one has to, therefore, turn to information in the Labour Force and Socioeconomic Surveys (LFSS) of the Department of Census and Statistics (DCS). The LFSS data are not fully comparable with those of the CFS. According to the LFSS, the higher the decile, consistently higher has been the rate of increase in incomes. The highest decile registered a 107 per cent income increase as contrasted to the lowest where the increase was a negligible three per cent. Though the data sets are very different from one another the question is whether the rate of increase in inequality in income distribution accelerated further in the first half of the 1980s as compared with the second half of the 1970s.

The post-1978 trend towards greater inequality in the size distribution of income has apparently continued even after the last available CFS. As between the two LFSS of 1980/81 and 1985/86, the income shares of all income deciles other than the highest have declined. The share of households in the highest decile increased by 11.4 percentage points—from 27.4 to 38.8 per cent. The Gini concentration ratio went up between the two survey years from 0.31 to 0.43 for the All Island data.

Very sharp increases in the sectoral Gini ratios (for income receivers, since relevant data for households are not available) had taken place with respect to the urban and estate sectors. Though at a lower rate, the Gini ratio for the rural sector too had gone up, in terms of per capita income deciles, the distance in per capita monthly household income between the lowest and the highest deciles has increased—11.8 times in 1980/81 as against 23.6 times in 1985/86.

In a developing country with a rather underdeveloped database, reliable and adequate information to classify national income by sources or types in terms of factor shares—wages, property income (interest and rent), profits, and dividends from incorporated businesses and income from unincorporated businesses—is, not surprisingly, very difficult to come by. The Department of Census and

Statistics in Sri Lanka prepares a national accounting time series on such a classification. The basis of calculation of these aggregative data is not known and, therefore, the limited information as available in the LFSS of 1985/86 on a classification of incomes by sources has been used in the following analysis in preference to the former set of aggregative time series data.

Though not in terms of identical conceptual categories, the CFS of 1978/79 and 1981/82 also seem to support the two hypothesised tendencies. In the first place, there has been a drop in the share of wages and salaries in total incomes. The CFS referred to indicate a drop in the share of the number of regular employees among income receivers from 39 per cent in 1978/79 to 33 per cent in 1981/82. A rise in the share of casual employees, however, was also shown from 27 to 39 per cent. While the relevant ratio for the estate sector remained the same, it rose by 17 percentage points in the urban sector and five percentage points in the rural. In terms of the numbers of income receivers, the CFS report a tendency of employers and the self-employed to increase since 1978/79—employers from 1.5 to 2.3 per cent and the self-employed from 24 to 24.6 per cent from 1978/79 to 1981/82.

The consistent policy emphasis on the promotion of self-employment and small enterprises seems to have produced some results during the period under consideration. In terms of the degree of concentration, employment income appears more equally distribute than enterprise/profit income and the extent of concentration in the latter type of income has increased over time more rapidly than the former. In so far as this enterprise sector includes small businesses of the self-employment type, this heavy concentration of profit income tells us that the relevant sector included a great variety of businesses with widely varying degrees of profitability.

An examination of changes in the structure of employment and in wage trends may, to some extent, help in the understanding of some of the factors behind the observed changes in the pattern of income distribution. The period under consideration witnessed a high policy priority placed on employment. It is believed that employment opportunities expanded more rapidly than did the labour force until about 1983. The CFS data support that belief. The rate of unemployment (as a percentage of labour force) declined from 15 per cent in 1978/79 to 12 per cent in 1981/82. Since 1983, however, the rate of growth of employment opportunities appears to have suffered a serious setback.

The LFSS of 1985/86 estimated that the rate of unemployment had risen to 14 per cent and there were, in more recent times, references in the literature to unemployment rates as high as 18 per cent. This increasing unemployment has basically been a phenomenon prevalent among the relatively young and the more educated members of the labour force. Those with eight years and more of formal education among the unemployed amounted to 63 per cent of the total in 1985/86, with those in the age group of 15-29 years forming 76 per cent. The type of employment which appears to have grown most rapidly during this period probably has not been of the type demanded by these young and more educated job seekers.

The bulk of the working population in Sri Lanka is engaged in non-plantation agriculture and they are not at all covered by the available real wage indices. These indices are, moreover, based either on minimum wages set by wages boards in the corporate sector or on initial commencing wages in government service. Although the statutory and living allowances are included, these minimum and initial wages exclude income supplements like annual increments, overtime payments, bonus earnings and other incentive payments. They also do not show the behaviour of various non-employment incomes of those employed in private and public sectors arising from their holdings of land and other property, tuition earnings of teachers outside normal school hours and so on. It is, in these circumstances, very risky to come to strong conclusions about trends in real earnings of wage workers purely on the basis of available wage indices. On top of all these, there are questions arising from the reliability of the

Colombo Consumer Price Index (CCPI) deflator as an indicator of inflation.

There was a consistent rise in real wages in wages boards sectors since 1970 reaching a peak in 1979/80. Since then real wages in industry and commerce declined or at best remained stagnant and in services clearly declined. Along with real wages of government employees, those of the estate workers consistently increased even after the above peak. Of the groups, teachers seem to have fared worst in terms of real wages which, in 1989, appear to have been even less than what they were in 1970. The wages scene, after 1977 in the formal sectors of the economy, shows the existence of attempts to keep wage increases at bay at a time when incomes from other sources like profits, rents, and interest appear to have been rising rapidly.

The conditions pertaining to wages in the informal sector present some special features for consideration. In the years immediately following the policy reforms of 1977, there were sharp rises in informal sector nominal wages. This was helped by heightened economic activity, following these policy reforms, within sectors like construction, trade, transport, tourism, and so on and increased outflows of workers to the Middle East at and around the time of the second oil shock. Apart from impressionistic evidence, there is some statistical information in the CFS of 1981/82 which can be interpreted as supporting this idea of a significant increase in informal sector wages. To what extent this relative rise in informal sector wages continued into the subsequent period is difficult to know. The impressionistic evidence seems to suggest that, after the initial spurt, the increase in these wages has become more moderate.

Sri Lanka was more successful than many other developing countries in keeping the rate of rural-to-urban migration under restraint through various village-targeted programmes. Yet, Sri Lanka also has had its urban bias in development policy with consequent concentration of incomes, opportunities, and power in urban areas, particularly in and around Colombo. How and to what extent the above patterns have been influenced by more market-oriented policies of the recent past is an interesting as well as a relevant question, but to find an adequately well-substantiated answer to it is extremely difficult given the prevailing data limitations. The spatial issue under consideration here may be viewed as having at least two dimensions: distribution by agro-climatic or administrative regions, and distribution according to the common urban/rural dichotomy.

In the case of each of these two dimensions there is the additional question of intra-regional distribution. The first aspect of distribution by agro-climatic or administrative regions is extremely difficult to analyse quantitatively due to lack of data.

As the country's administration has been until recently, that is, until the establishment of Provincial Councils in 1988, highly centralised within a strongly unitary system of government, the country's national accounting system does not as yet have any regional accounting component. Any analysis of inter-regional distribution at the level of agro-climatic or administrative regions also has to therefore depend on the family budget surveys that are available. The CFS present some of their data in terms of five agro-climatic zones into which the country was divided for purposes of survey sampling and data collection. These are:

Zone 1: Districts of Colombo (excluding the Colombo Municipality), Gampaha, Kalutara, Galle and Matara.

Zone 2: Hambantota, Monaragala, Amparai, Polonnaruwa, Anuradhapura and Puttalam.

Zone 3: Jaffna, Mannar, Vavunia, Mullativu, Trincomalee and Batticaloa.

Zone 4: Kandy, Matale, Nuwara-Eliya, Badulla, Ratnapura, Kegalle and Kurunegala.

Zone 5: Colombo municipality.

Assuming there was no significant difference from one zone to another in price trends over time, these data, however, present some interesting features with respect to changes in regional distribution over the two inter-survey periods.

Economic growth that took place over these periods appears to have been strongly biased towards the Colombo metropole.

The northern and eastern province districts in Zone 3, which, in terms of average incomes, appear to have enjoyed conditions comparable to those of the Colombo municipality in the early 1970s, had witnessed a substantial relative decline by the end of that decade and the early 1980s. A similar development is observed for the dry zone districts belonging to southern, eastern, and north central provinces in Zone 2. No doubt, the median income data in the table, even if they were sufficiently reliable, are clearly not adequate to establish the regional biases in economic growth which operated during the period concerned. Yet, they appear to corroborate the impressionistic evidence that development patterns under more market-oriented policies since 1977 have, in general, been rather skewed spatially and in particular, very highly urban biased.

Inequality in income distribution in intra-regional terms had become perceptibly worse during the period 1973 to 1978/79 in the case of all regions concerned. Except in the case of the up-country regions of Zone 4, no significant further worsening of inequality during the subsequent period of 1978/79-1981/82. As for Zones 2 and 3, there was a mild decline in the degree of income concentration during this period. In terms of the other regional classification noted, namely rural/urban/estate trichotomy, however, more information is available in CFS reports than for the zonal classification.

Poverty, in a rather fundamental sense, is both a relative and a subjective phenomenon. People in developing countries capable of enjoying what would constitute the average living conditions of the poor of the advanced countries may be seen as non-poor in their own environment. Even within the confines of an under-developed society people are used to different lifestyles, whether they are local or foreign, they may see poverty differently from one another. These relative and subjective aspects of poverty perceptions are obvious enough.

The extensive and rapidly growing literature on poverty in the developing world clearly shows the wide acceptance of another view—a concept of absolute poverty—which is based on the perception of "an irreducible core of absolute deprivation... which translates reports of starvation, malnutrition and visible hardship into a diagnosis of poverty without having to ascertain first the relative picture". Needless to say, however, this irreducible core of basic life-sustaining requirements will also have society-specific, culture-specific and climate-specific elements.

Much research effort has gone into poverty measurement work in Sri Lanka, some of which even utilising the original data tapes from the pertinent household surveys. Yet almost all the work done so far on this subject have been restricted to deriving the so-called head-count ratios, except for the calculations of a poverty gap measure and the Kakwani poverty index, made by Gunaratne by way of passing for the two survey years he has examined. The confusing picture of Sri Lankan poverty statistics is merely a reflection of the variety of ways available for handling four essential steps involved in the calculation of poverty ratios for a society over a number of years:

i) What entitlement/deprivation measure has to be used-income, consumer expenditure, food expenditure or a non-monetary commodity/service basket?

ii) Below what specific level of the adopted entitlement measure should someone be treated as being poor?

iii) Should the head-count ratio be worked out as a population percentage or a household/family percentage?

iv) How could compatibility be guaranteed in the ratios so computed across sections of the society at a point of time and also over different points of time, particularly when one begins to work from one poverty line norm for the whole society?

The arbitrariness involved in both the minimum nutritional requirements approach and the minimum basic requirements approach to poverty measurement and the consequent objections to them are quite well known. A direct commodity approach would have eliminated any need for price indices to achieve inter-sectoral and inter-temporal comparability with respect to the adopted poverty measure. Yet as they have all decided to adopt the indirect approach, it may rightly be asked whether the price indices used have been sufficient to achieve the necessary degree of inter-sectoral and inter-temporal comparability.

Guided by considerations such as the seasonality of incomes in predominantly agrarian societies, the unreliability of stated current income as a guide to permanent income and the very high likelihood of income understatement in household surveys, there has been a rather general tendency to adopt consumer expenditure or food expenditure as better welfare indicators than income. However, the first two of these points can be also made with respect to expenditures. Overstatement biases are found in expenditure declarations in household surveys as much as understatement biases operate with respect to income declarations.

Some have defined the poverty lines in terms of entitlement per household and others in terms of entitlement per capita. As a result, the poverty line figures adopted for any given year in different studies cannot be brought to a comparable basis without making arbitrary assumptions about things like the number of persons per household, food expenditure proportion in total average family expenditure and so on. At one end appear to have fixed their poverty level entitlement so high that, for the years concerned, they come out with unusually high headcount poverty ratios.

Yet the range of variation in even the remaining set of ratios is also not that negligible. Even when one works on the same methodological premises, Gunaratne clearly shows that any slight variation of the poverty threshold can produce significant variations in the poverty ratio. Of the various studies under consideration, three formed parts of the same overall research project and therefore, used the same basic poverty cut-off point of a monthly food expenditure of Rs. 69 rounded off to Rs. 70 as derived by Gunaratne. There are no principles on which the average food expenditure of the bottom 40 per cent can be called adequate by any absolute standard of living. For the benchmark year, then, Gunaratne's poverty threshold, adopted also in two other studies, is at best a relative poverty measure. There are two objectionable aspects of these exercises. First, what is in effect a relative measure has been presented as an absolute measure with respect to the benchmark year and, second, it was used as such, of course in constant price terms, as the absolute poverty threshold for the other survey years examined. The reader is left wondering why the average for the bottom 40 per cent in 1978/79, rather than in any other year, was chosen as the norm.

On the one hand, the approach adopted had a built-in tendency to come out with a poverty ratio of around 20 per cent for the years close to the benchmark year. On the other hand, the quite valid relative aspect introduced through this method into the poverty measures with respect to the benchmark year was lost sight of when the benchmark year's relative magnitude was applied as an absolute magnitude for other years for purposes of inter-temporal comparison.

Understanding the nature of poverty in terms of such characteristics, even by way of "causally inexplicit relationships" or mere "characteristics-poverty links", is considered helpful in formulation of policies toward alleviation of poverty. Moreover, much efforts have gone into making such classifications of poverty groups and thereby developing a taxonomy of poverty in Sri Lanka. Perhaps, the feature of poverty in Sri Lanka, laid bare most consistently in all the statistical analyses so far, is the overwhelming dominance of the rural sector as a repository of that poverty. Over time, this feature does not appear to have undergone any significant change. Given the predominance of the rural economy in the distribution of the country's population, the fact that the rural sector holds the largest proportion of the poor is not surprising. The important fact, however, is that the ratio of the poor in the rural sector has consistently been found to exceed the rural share of total population.

The rural sector in the threefold classification system, adopted in the normal tradition of Sri Lankan statistical practice, is smaller and narrower in its spread than what one would mean by the rural sector within a more usual twofold rural-urban classification. The estate sector in Sri Lanka, which in terms of locational and certain other characteristics, is also rural as that word is normally understood, but excluded from the rural sector for purposes of most socio-economic analysis in Sri Lanka. To bear in mind this peculiarity in the sector classification is useful in understanding the overwhelming dominance of the rural sector in the distribution of poverty.

One of the conclusions coming out from the poverty studies cited so far, as consistently as the above characteristic of rural sector dominance, is that the estate sector has been in a better position in terms of poverty incidence than both other sectors. A person having seen the poor facilities found in most of the living quarters provided by estates to their resident labour forces may indeed find the above conclusion surprising. It is basically the adoption of a "minimum nutrition" or "minimum needs" type of poverty definition which leads to such conclusions. The bulk of the estate sector population, employed as they are in plantations, do have some regular employment opportunities and often, a number of members in such families could be in employment, receiving regular incomes. In addition, the plantation system has over the years developed mechanisms to prevent hunger among estate workers. No business obviously could remain profitable with a hungry labour force.

The rural sector, on the other hand, does not have sufficient conditions for providing regularity in work opportunities available for its people. As most of these rural folk do not have income sources other than work, there is extreme variability and irregularity in their incomes and other receipts. This characteristic transforms, over a period of time, like say a month, to one of low incomes, low nutrition and, on even the most stringent criteria, poverty. This irregularity of work opportunities or, in other words, the underemployment characteristic of the work practices in rural areas also comes out of the pattern of poverty in terms of economic activity or employment.

No doubt, unemployment has been noted to have increased in recent times and in so far as this tendency applied also to household heads, unemployment would have been closely related to poverty. In fact, a number of writers already referred to hypothesize such close links between poverty and unemployment. Yet it is perfectly possible that a fair proportion of the country's underemployed got recorded as unemployed in the household surveys and census reports. Furthermore, the consistent evidence provided by these surveys is that the unemployed in Sri Lanka have been concentrated among the young, and they would not have been household heads, poor or non-poor.

Strictly speaking, much of the poverty identified must be linked more to underemployment than to unemployment. This conclusion is strengthened by a consideration of the type of economic activity areas generally identified as those where the poor are concentrated. The landless agricultural workers, small landowning peasants cultivating foodcrops using family labour, workers in small-scale rural industry, small traders, and individually operating craftsmen like carpenters, have been seen as forming a dominant proportion of the poor. A person falling into any of these categories need not necessarily be poor in the sense of being unable to maintain even an absolute minimum level of nutrition, if he was in a position to obtain full-time work. This is particularly so in the 1980s when the informal sector wage rates, even in the rural economy, increased as compared with the preceding decade, at rates higher than some formal sector wages. Even casual workers in rural areas working for daily wages have benefited from this general rise in informal sector wages. Even with full-time work well spread over the month, some of these wage rates may not have entitled a worker to as high a poverty line monthly income as Rs. 1,600 assumed in Korale. But these informal sector wages of the 1980s would have easily provided a minimum nutrition level income of Rs. 300-400, if the workers concerned had regular employment for at least two weeks a month. The available literature attempts to see the links between poverty and many other economic, social and demographic variables—household size, age and sex, educational attainment, ethnicity, religion, employment, and so on. Quite often contradictory relationships come out from different studies, as well as from the same study when it analyses the data for different survey years.

The very survival of Sri Lanka's social fabric would depend on positive and quick achievements in this poverty alleviation struggle. Support from donor agencies and countries is being sought for poverty alleviation programmes. Given this policy prioritisation, studies of poverty are bound to be extremely useful. The valid question is whether, after gaining the knowledge embodied in all these studies, we know what causes poverty and what perpetuates or reproduces it in the Sri Lankan context. None of the studies cited seem to try to give concrete and definitive answers to this question. The most these studies do in this respect is to identify certain relationships without necessarily implying causality.

Studies with a quantitative bias, focusing on poverty measurement rather than explanation, are perhaps not the ideal type to explain why poverty reproduces itself. Without knowing how many families were able to get out of poverty and how many continued to remain there, say, between two surveys, and why those who emerged out of poverty and those who continued to be in poverty did so, mere knowledge about their cross-sectional characteristics and the peculiarities of their social conditions in a given survey time may not be able to say much about social conditions and mechanisms which help or hinder social progress. Intensive micro research at the village/community level is probably the best way to understand the forces behind poverty reproduction and thereby also the mechanisms through which poverty could be eliminated.

Sri Lanka was seen as an "outlier" or an "aberration", in the sense that the country has attained a higher stage of social development with respect to many welfare indicators than one would predict it to have on the basis of its relatively low per capita income.

The available information concerning social indicators obviously is aggregative in character and is, therefore, of limited direct use in a discussion of distributional trends or of conditions prevailing in selected social groups. Indirectly, however, time series information on these indicators can be very useful in examining the trends in the conditions of the poor in a country, as an improvement in a social indicator over time must necessarily reflect the improvement of the relevant conditions among the poor. Most of these indicators have theoretical maxima or minima, and even in the least developed countries, the rich must be very much closer to these maxima or minima than the poor. From the time the Physical Quality of Life Index (PQLI) was introduced, the relatively high living standards in Sri Lanka attracted attention.

The package of Sri Lanka's so-called welfare policies, which presumably brought about its "outlier" status in inter-country comparisons had undergone certain perceptible changes since the introduction of the policy reforms in 1977 aimed at liberalisation of markets and promotion of growth. Particularly important is the fact that the proportionate emphasis accorded to welfare purposes in the allocation of government funds has been made to undergo a decline, initially, in order to transfer more funds for growth and in addition to this, in more recent times, to accommodate the growing defence expenditures. These policy reforms, even before the latter became a significant problem, have begun to work towards greater concentration of wealth and incomes and to exacerbate poverty conditions.

Although published information is not readily available, nutrition levels, morbidity conditions, and so on among certain poor strata of society are considered to have deteriorated in recent years. The CFS of 1981/82 showed a mild yet widespread decline in literacy rates from 1978/79 and high school avoidance rates for children from low-income families. The main reason for school avoidance has been noted as inability to provide basic requirements. The proportion of the population with no schooling at all had increased between 1978/79 and 1981/82 for the whole country and for all its sectors.

Similarly, indicators like the proportion of population reported ill, average number of days absent from work due to illness per person have all registered increases for the country and its different sectors between the same years. One used to come across ideologically tinted arguments like there is no strong reason to suppose that welfare goals Sri Lanka had reached in 1977 were severely compromised when economic controls were lifted. But the evidence gathered by government statistical agencies and independent researchers were so overwhelming that such arguments are not presented so strongly anymore.

On the whole, social indicators also have begun showing signs of a gradual deterioration, which presumably means a deterioration of living conditions particularly among low-income groups. For a number of reasons, the deterioration in social indicators in the recent past has not been as sharp as the increase in the incidence of nutritional-criteria-based poverty.

Sri Lanka has a widely spread network of schools, hospitals, and clinics, mostly state funded. No doubt, facilities available in most of these institutions leave much to be desired and with relative decline in government expenditures on education and health in the recent past, these facilities may have even deteriorated over time. Traditionally, it has been the state which provided these services free of charge but certain elements of privatisation had seeped into even these service sectors over the recent past.

The "free" component of available health and education services thus deteriorated, adversely affecting the benefits they could provide to the poor. All this plus the weakening nutritional conditions are bound to have had their toll on social indicators, but the impact is unlikely to be felt quickly. Once a society at large gets accustomed to individual and social practices which provide safeguards against things like infant mortality, maternal mortality, illiteracy, and so on, it may try to maintain those practices even if it requires some diversion of resources from other uses. Sending their children, particularly the primary school-age children, to school in spite of poverty is not a very rare practice among many poor families.

Though public funds channelled into social sectors declined in relative terms, that is, in relation to total government expenditure or GNP, it did not appear to have led to drastic cuts in basic services. In fact, the number of institutions like schools and hospitals is recorded to have gone up. Yet as poverty starts pressing against growing numbers of households, social indicators will also start showing signs of deterioration, unless, of course, the policies which initially worsen distribution and poverty conditions eventually begin to show strong dynamism in terms of output growth, combined with extensive and productive participation of the people in that growth.

15

Role of SAARC in Poverty Eradication

A large number of successful programmes were launched several decades ago by South Asian governments to tackle the problem of poverty widespread in the region. Recent South Asian history is full of local as well as sectoral experiments, that have helped alleviate some of the worst consequences of poverty in selected areas. Many of these experiments have provided models for other countries and regions around the world. Estimates of the incidence of poverty vary widely in the region. Even if the extremes in estimates are left out, poverty in the region in 1991 would have affected approximately 30 to 40 per cent of the population.

Given the present trends in population and economic growth and in the absence of a concerted effort at poverty alleviation, the number of poor in the region is likely to increase substantially. Despite decades of planning for development in most South Asian countries, they failed to make a significant dent in the problem of poverty. It was in recognition of these concerns that the heads of state or government of SAARC countries decided to set up an Independent South Asian Commission on Poverty Alleviation (ISACPA) and directed the commission to examine the causes and consequences of the resilience of poverty in South Asia, to distil the positive lessons from successful and sustainable experiences on the ground, to diagnose what went wrong with past development interventions and to identify critical, concrete and practical elements for a coherent strategy to alleviate poverty.

The SAARC leaders accorded the highest priority to the alleviation of poverty in all South Asian countries. They affirmed that South Asia's poor could constitute a huge and potential resource, provided their basic needs were met and they were mobilised to create economic growth. This requires that the poor are empowered and are irreversibly linked to the mainstream of development.

The SAARC leaders, recognising that the great majority of these people remain below poverty line, evinced a keen interest in a "daal-bhaat" or assured nutritional standards approach towards the satisfaction of the basic needs of the South Asian poor. The SAARC leaders authorised the commission to conduct an indepth study of diverse experiences of the seven countries on poverty alleviation and then submit their report to the seventh SAARC summit.

The main recommendations of the report of the Commission (ISAPCA) contained in the section entitled "An agenda for action: A plan for the poor". It strongly recommended that each SAARC country should prepare, immediately, a national level plan for the poor using the pro-poor prospective and premises for action identified in the report. The implementation of such a plan for the poor in their respective countries should build on the success cases, on poverty alleviation on the ground and other innovative macro processes currently being initiated in all their countries.

The whole process should be monitored with built in self-corrective measures so that coherent process of poverty alleviation that will now be initiated will result in poverty being eradicated by the year 2002, leaving only residual number of poor who would need to be carried by the respective societies through safety nets or welfare programmes. In the implementation of such a pro-poor plan each government should take the following specific action:

— Support, financially and administratively, establishment of independent, nongovernmental and national level support mechanisms to catalyse formation of organisations of the poor in both rural and urban areas, building on the success cases on the ground;

— Commit adequate financial resources on a long term basis to these support mechanisms to enable them to provide the required services to the organisations of the poor.

— While using existing successful support mechanisms and creating new support mechanisms where necessary, other organisations of the state system and the banking system should be reoriented, *inter-alia*, by devolving appropriate powers and responsibilities to decentralised and participatory local bodies, with the aim of providing the necessary support to the pro-poor plan.

— Ensure the direct and full participation of the poor, including poor women, in these organisations, as well as in decentralised government bodies.

— Provide the enabling policy framework for agricultural development and food security at the household levels, small-scale labour-intensive industrialisation, physical infrastructure development, employment guarantee and human development.

— Commit to transfer a fair proportion of clearly identified development resources.

— Involve all these organisations in the mobilisation of savings and investment in programmes to improve the productivity of investment. Mobilise public and private resources to the fullest for this strategy of poverty eradication.

— Ensure selective use, with appropriate adoption and social control of the technology choices available—enabling a new people/nature/technology mix to inform the poverty-alleviation process.

— Provide necessary resources and encourage the support mechanisms to train the large cadres of animators/catalysts, facilitators, leaders and managers who will stimulate and assist the process of social mobilisation and institution building through awareness creation and help the poor to overcome practical barriers that presently or event contribution to growth and self-development.

The monitoring process must involve at the national levels an assessment of the state-of-the-art for measuring poverty, including an improved and more relevant statistical information base, as well as exploration of methodologies of innovative monitoring and evaluation of the whole process of poverty alleviation.

The governments should involve institutions, action-research groups and think-tanks in the preparation of the state-of-the-art and evaluation repots. The Commission emphasised that "success in preparing, carrying out and monitoring this pro-poor plan would require re-affirmation of the underlying assumption in the report of a deep political and administrative commitment by each of the South Asian governments to the urgent task of poverty eradication within the given timeframe".

A relativity and productive potential are eroded by chronic poverty, the leaders reiterated their commitment to empowering the poor for enhanced growth, consistent with human development and equity. They committed their governments unequivocally to the eradication of poverty in South Asia, preferably by the year A.D. 2002 through an agenda of action which would, *inter alia*, embody:

— A strategy of social mobilisation involving the building of organisations of the poor and their empowerment through appropriate national support mechanisms with the assistance of respective governments;

— A policy of decentralised agricultural development and sharply focused household level food security through universal provision of 'daal-bhaat' or basic nutritional needs;

— A policy of decentralised small-scale labour intensive industrialisation with the choice of efficient and cost-effective technology;

— A policy of human development, including the enhancement of the social role and status of poor women, the provision of universal primary education, skill development, primary health care, shelter for the poor and protection of children;

— A policy to support the above initiatives with adequate financial resources.

They underscored the critical link between the success of national efforts aimed at poverty alleviation and the external factors affecting growth and development. They urged all major actors in the world economic scene, particularly the industrialised countries and multilateral and regional financial institutions and non-governmental organisations, to create an enabling international atmosphere that is supportive of poverty alleviation programmes in South Asia. This would require, they felt, a new dialogue with donors. The leaders agreed to the follow-up action which were:

— A national level pro-poor plan to be drawn up by each member state. This plan was to be harmonised with the open economy and structural adjustment strategies;

— To share during the next summit, information regarding the progress achieved.

The Council felt that a meeting of finance ministers of SAARC countries may be held to address the issues of harmonisation of national pro-poor plans with open economy and structural adjustment strategies, including the broadening of international macro-economic policies to respond to developing countries' concerns which were highlighted by the seventh SAARC summit. The council of ministers also noted that the seventh summit consensus on eradication of poverty in South Asia had evoked keen interest both in the region and among the international donor community.

The informal workshop on poverty reduction in South Asia held in collaboration with the World Bank in October 1993, highlighted the broad poverty reduction strategies and experiences of South Asia and international organisations in this field. The Council recognised the importance of a coordinated approach in the formulation of national pro-poor plans and felt that the meeting of finance/planning ministers would discuss, *inter alia*, a mechanism for developing such a coordinated approach. The regional cooperation among SAARC countries on the task of poverty alleviation began with the SAARC finance/planning ministers meeting hosted by Bangladesh in Dhaka in July 1994.

The ministers recognised the unique opportunity provided by SAARC for sharing country experiences in poverty alleviation and noted that all the member states have long experiences in dealing with poverty that emphasise access to credit, investment and social development sectors, rural infrastructure that is relevant to poverty eradication, and employment generation, particularly in the rural areas through self-employment, wage employment and agro-based and labour-intensive micro-enterprises.

They agreed that steps should be taken to bring about a closer interface between government agencies, NGOs and community organisations engaged in poverty alleviation, so as to bring about convergence in action at all levels, particularly at the grassroots levels. This process, the ministers felt, could be strengthened by sharing and exchanging relevant studies carried out by institutions, experts and NGOs. This mechanism would be in the form of a three-tier institutional structure that would meet once a year. This three-tier would be:

— the group of secretaries to the government in the ministries/departments that are essentially concerned with poverty alleviation and social development;
— the finance and planning secretaries of the SAARC countries; and
— the finance and planning ministries of the SAARC countries.

Regional cooperation among SAARC countries began to gather momentum in 1995 with the brainstorming meeting on pro-poor planning and social mobilisations, in New Delhi in January, the recommendations made and decisions taken during the eighth SAARC summit in New Delhi as well as other SAARC workshops and seminars related to poverty alleviation.

A group of former poverty commissioners and South Asian scholars and professionals made an independent assessment of where the implementation of the 1993 SAARC summit consensus on poverty eradication stands. The issues highlighted in the communique were:

— the need for each country to develop national level pro-poor poverty eradication strategy and a coherent time- based action programme specifying prepared policies and programmes and identifying appropriate roles for the public, private and peoples' sectors, in the social mobilisation process;
— the need to improve the effectiveness of the governments role in strategic thinking and implementation through greater decentralisation, devolution and social mobilisation;
— the need to improve the enabling environment for the development of organisations of the poor; and
— the development of independent research; dialogue with the World Bank and other donors; support the establishment of an independent research-cum-focal point in each country.

The heads of state or government reaffirmed their commitment to the eradication of poverty in South Asia, preferably by the year A.D. 2002 through an agenda of action. The leaders endorsed the recommendations of the SAARC finance/ planning ministers meeting held in Dhaka in July 1994 and directed that the next meeting of finance/ planning ministers consider the efficacy of such mechanism towards eradicating poverty in the region. They agreed that the governments of SAARC countries will have to play a lead role in promoting the support structures needed for poverty eradication. The leaders decided to declare 1995 as the "SAARC year of poverty eradication".

The objectives of the plan are, *inter alia*, making poverty eradication the centre of national development plans, policies and budgets; planning strategies and schemes for poverty eradication; promoting self-help structures of the poor and their support structures; promoting exchange of information and experiences among SAARC countries on issues related to poverty eradication and developing innovative norms for monitoring and evaluating all policies related to poverty eradication programmes.

The plan lists a number of strategies and activities for implementation by the member states during the "SAARC year of poverty eradication, 1995". The SAARC leaders at the Delhi summit had endorsed the recommendations of the finance/planning ministers' meeting in Dhaka in July 1994, which recommended that a mechanism should be set up which would act as a forum for exchanging information on poverty eradication programmes. Pursuant to this decision of the SAARC leaders, a meeting of the group of secretaries to the governments/departments concerned with poverty eradication and social development in SAARC countries was held in New Delhi on 6 and 7 September, 1995.

All member states informed the meeting that they had incorporated substantially pro-poor programmes and strategies in their national development plans, as well as various measures being undertaken by their respective governments to protect the poor from any possible adverse impact of structural adjustment and the commitment of their countries to make all efforts to make the markets friendly to the poor. The group was of the view that member states should evolve an appropriate mechanism to evaluate the efficacy of pro-poor plans. The delegates exchanged information and experiences on innovative programmes being implemented in their countries such as food for education (Bangladesh); integrated approach to agricultural development (Bhutan); employment assurance scheme (India); rural credit scheme (Maldives); let-us-build our-village-ourselves programme and programme for the rehabilitation of the landless (Nepal); social action programme (Pakistan); and prosperity programme (Sri Lanka).

The delegates also informed the meeting about the steps taken by them in creating and strengthening various support structures to facilitate poverty eradication. They discussed in detail structures such as Palli Karma Shahayak Foundation (Rural Employment Support Foundation) and rural development board in Bangladesh; constitutional amendment for creation of three-tier local self-government (panchayati raj) and council for advancement and promotion of rural technologies in India; national rural support programme and Aga Khan Rural Support programme in Pakistan and Samuodhi Authority in Sri Lanka. After an indepth deliberation on various aspects of poverty eradication strategies and programmes, the group of secretaries made the following recommendations:

— Social mobilisation of the poor should be an important component of the strategy for poverty eradication.
— Pro-poor plans should have top priority and distinct status by ensuring specific commitment of adequate resources and organisational support.
— The poor should be fully involved in formulation and implementation of pro-poor plans through participatory institutions and processes at the grassroots levels.
— Pro-poor plans should have maximum impact through an efficient delivery system minimising administrative and organisational expenditure.
— Pro-poor plans should be timebound, target-oriented and their impact monitored annually to ensure the objective of poverty eradication by the year A.D. 2002.

Member states should evolve an appropriate mechanism to evaluate the efficacy of pro-poor plans. In this context, a set of social and economic indicators should be developed taking into account the cultural and social uniqueness of the region. Poverty eradication programmes concerning specific sectors such as employment, health, education, family welfare, shelter and other basic needs should be strengthened by following an integrated approach taking into account the critical linkages among various sectors. The second tier of the three-tier meetings, consisting of the finance and planning secretaries, that followed the meeting of the group of secretaries, made the following observations:

— Poverty eradication should be reviewed in the overall context of accelerating economic growth resulting in employment generation in an environment of macro-economic stability with emphasis on overall human resources development.
— In respect of pro-poor plans, the finance and planning secretaries felt that it may be strengthened further through devolution of power and appropriate decentralisation.

The effectiveness of pro-poor programmes depend substantially upon the financial sustainability of these programmes, especially in terms of their recurring costs. The information on the exchange of experiences on poverty eradication of the member states needs to be disseminated on a regular basis. The recommendations of the first and second tiers of group of secretaries would be considered by the third-tier meeting, i.e., second meeting of finance/ planning ministers expected to be held in India.

The recommendations of the finance/planning ministers' meeting was then to be submitted to the heads of state or government at the ninth SAARC summit during 1996 in the Maldives. The ninth SAARC summit was also expected to review the progress in the implementation of the "plan of action for the SAARC year of poverty eradication, 1995" and take decision on future course of action for eradicating poverty by A.D. 2002. The removal of poverty has been one of the cardinal objectives of most governments of the South Asian nations. Amelioration of hardcore poverty is one of the most crucial elements in the socio-economic agenda of all member states. The constitutions of most South Asian nations enjoins poverty alleviation as a fundamental responsibility on the state.

The sheer magnitude and complexity of poverty required a firm commitment to take immediate measures to alleviate it within a certain timeframe. Therefore, the Dhaka consensus on eradication of poverty has great significance to the peoples of the SAARC region. All the leaders of the South Asian nations, collectively committed their governments unequivocally to the eradication of poverty in South Asia, preferably by the year A.D. 2002, through an agenda of action, which identified policies and strategies required for this purpose. The SAARC initiative at the Dhaka summit has continued to gain momentum with the governments of the member states incorporating substantially pro-poor programmes and strategies in their national development plans.

The SAARC leaders reaffirmed their commitment to the eradication of poverty at the eighth SAARC summit at New

Delhi in May 1995. To reinforce their commitment, they also decided to declare 1995 as the "SAARC year of poverty eradication", and endorsed the plan of action for the SAARC year of poverty eradication. Eradication of poverty is a complex and difficult task for any nation or regional grouping.

The SAARC leaders recognised that poverty is a complex, multidimensional problem with origins in both national and international domains. They felt that country-specific programmes to tackle poverty and international efforts supporting national efforts and the parallel process of creating a supportive international environment conducive to economic growth and social development of developing countries, are crucial for a solution to this problem. Subsequently, the collective position on poverty alleviation was presented to the summit by the prime minister of Bangladesh and chairperson of SAARC. The SAARC focus on poverty eradication has evoked keen interest among donor countries, multinational financial institutions, UN agencies, particularly the World Bank, IMF and UNDP, and NGOs.

Since the Dhaka summit, several seminars and workshops between SAARC and UN agencies, NGOs and multinational financial institutions have been held. These meetings led to exchange of information and experiences and raised new concepts and strategies to tackle poverty in South Asia. The World Bank expressed its willingness to help the poverty alleviation programmes of countries, provided the areas could be effectively identified. The WB-SAARC workshop made a number of findings in areas of agreement among the participants, which could be useful and relevant to member states for preparation of their national programmes and strategies on poverty eradication. These findings were:

— Poverty is multidimensional: the poor not only lack adequate income to meet their basic needs but are also deprived in other ways—social, economic and political.
— The indirect effect of macro-economic, sectoral and trade policies in limiting the growth of employment opportunities, as well as returns to the non-labour assets of the poor, have been substantial in South Asia.

— The primary thrust of any effective poverty reduction strategy is to enable the poor to climb out of poverty and stay out of poverty.

— Economic growth is necessary for sustainable poverty reduction. However, the quality of growth is a crucial ingredient: it must be broadly-based and labour intensive, and incentives must be in place that encourage efficiency and reward competitive activities.

— Investment in people, in health, education, family-planning, etc., must accompany growth if it is to lead to sustained poverty reduction.

Participation of the poor in the design and delivery of basic service as well as in specific, targeted programmes, is crucial. There is abundant evidence of successful and effective participation of the poor in South Asia. Even so, much work needs to be done to analyse empirically the circumstances under which participation is most effective and when it is not and how successful schemes can be scaled up or replicated. Immediately after the world summit for social development, a round table on poverty alleviation in South Asia was organised by the German foundation for international development in mid-March, 1995.

The round table recognised:

— the need for involving all important actors in development at the national level in the task of poverty alleviation;

— the important role of the government in any poverty alleviation strategy and programme;

— the need to make the development structure "people worthy";

— the donor countries/agencies should give high priority to poverty eradication measures directly targeted at the poor; and

— both the national government and the donors have to play a proactive role in the field of poverty alleviation. This would give structural adjustment reform a "human face".

Bangladesh has a very rich experience with rural development programmes aimed at poverty alleviation.

Vulnerable Groups Development (VGDP) Programmes; Comilla Cooperatives; Swanirvar (self-help); Grameen Bank; Small Farmers' Development Project (SFDP); Comprehensive Village Development Programme (CVDP); Rural Maintenance Programme; Bangladesh Rural Development Board (BRDB) programmes; Bangladesh Rural Advancement Committee (BRAC); Food for Works Programme (FWP) and Food for Education Programme (FEP) are only some of the major programmes which have achieved considerable success.

The relevant authorities learnt that the poor are extremely difficult to reach through budget-supported governmental programmes. They do not often represent a cohesive and homogeneous interest group and are weakly organised. Benefits intended for them tend to get appropriated by the middlemen and the powerful sections of the population in poorly administrated institutional settings. The organisation and management style needed for a successful implementation of programmes for the poor is missing in the traditional bureaucratic apparatus.

The bureaucratic and centralised organisations of the government manage poverty alleviation programmes for which their functionaries have neither the motivation and commitment, nor the training or incentives. It may be inexpedient and counter-productive to impose too many rules, regulations, by-laws, etc., for smaller groups and poorer beneficiaries. However, they must be left reasonably free to use the credit on activities which they are familiar with. NGO's activities have not been well orchestrated or coordinated. In some fields, they, are overcrowded. But they can be a very vibrant and an effective supplementary force to help alleviate poverty, as part of the national effort. The poverty situation in the SAARC region has reached alarming proportions. Massive and well-coordinated measures have to be taken by the governments of the member states in order to eradicate poverty by the year A.D. 2002, as committed by the SAARC leaders in the Dhaka summit and reiterated at the New Delhi summit.

The South Asian population is widely dispersed but concentrated mainly in the fertile plains and valleys and in over-congested cities and urban areas. People living in far flung, remote areas are largely deprived of the benefits of credit and social services. Extensive erosion of the natural resources base and environmental degradation have further marginalised the poor. Floods and droughts are directly linked to pressure on the ecosystem, while global warming and sea-level rise pose a threat to the densely populated lowlying coastal areas and overall food production in the region. Poverty is aggravated by various social deprivations and discriminations. The social position of women is generally weak and women have to bear a greater burden whenever there is scarcity. The region's growing foreign debt burden, the reverse flow of resources and the emergence of regional blocs in the developed countries have marginalised South Asia in the global economy.

The structural adjustment policies, economic liberalisation and open market policies of most SAARC countries have put further pressure on the poor, at least in the short term. The world's resources are not scarce, but they are cornered and controlled by the developed nations. Less than a quarter of the global expenditure on arms would be enough to finance programmes for universal primary health care, vaccination against killer diseases, safe drinking water and primary schooling. There are occasional utterances by donor countries and international financial institutions about their desire to help the developing countries, especially the LDCs, but they are hardly translated into action. ODAs are actually decreasing in real terms and debt servicing is depleting meagre reserves. The World Bank president and the IMF managing director, speaking at the formal opening of the annual meeting of IMF and World Bank, said they would do more to help member nations cope with vast changes sweeping across the world economy. The World Bank president was reported to have said that developing countries deserve their support for moral and social reasons. We shall have to see the terms and conditions and the amounts that World Bank would make available to developing countries following the annual meeting. But it is likely to be below expectations. Some funds would be available but it would be inadequate to cover the required amounts. Resources have to be mobilised internally for this purpose and for which priorities have to be drastically changed.

Structural adjustment programmes should include social development goals, in particular, eradicating poverty, promoting full and productive employment and enhancing social integration. The governments of SAARC countries need to accelerate and widen economic reforms and liberalisation which would facilitate eradication of poverty and generate employment.

The state should withdraw in a systematic manner from production and trade of goods and services because the private sector does it better. It should continue to provide social services and infrastructure. There is only room for the private sector to play some role in human resources development and formation of domestic savings which are essential for faster economic growth. The benefits of rapid economic growth trickle down to the majority of the people and this benefits the chronic poor as well.

The eight high performing countries of East Asia have not only grown fast but they are quickly eradicating poverty. We need to learn from their economic strategy and adopt them to our requirements. The need to focus on women's enhancement and improvement as a means to eradicate poverty has to be pursued with vigour. Moreover, education and health to women and girl-child are among the most critical requirements for sustainable development in the region. South Asia has been a pioneer in the development of community-based organisations and poverty alleviation programmes. The whole region has numerous success stories of programmes that have helped the poor. The South Asian nations have enormous resources, the greatest and most potent is human resources.

Bibliography

Abayawardene, H. A. P. (1969) "Systems of Education in Ancient Sri Lanka", in *Education in Ceylon: A Centenary Volume.* Colombo: Ministry of Education and Cultural Affairs.

Abbott, John C. 1990. "Marketing and the Rural Poor". The State of World Rural Poverty Working Paper 18. Rome: International Fund for Agricultural Development.

______________ , 1987. *Agricultural Marketing Enterprises for the Developing World.* Cambridge: Cambridge University Press.

Abdullah, Abu Ahmed 1976. "Land Reform and Agrarian Change in Bangladesh". *The Bangladesh Development Studies.* 4 (1): 67-114.

______________ , Rita Afsar and Anwara Begum (1990) *Regional Social Devolvement Strategy, through the year 2000 and beyond (Phase II)-Bangladesh Country Report* (Dhaka: Bangladesh Institute of Development Studies, Draft).

Adelman, Irma, and Cynthia T. Morris. 1973. *Economic Growth and Social Equity in Developing Countries.* Stanford, California: Stanford University Press.

Afsar, Rita 1991 "Struggle for a better future". Paper presented at the International Institute of Development Studies, 27-29 July.

______________ , 1995a "Causes, consequences and challenges of rural-urban migration in Bangladesh". Ph.D. dissertation, University of Adelaide.

______________ , 1995b "Rural-urban migration and its impact on women's roles and status". Empowerment: *A Journal of Women for Women* [Dhaka] (2): 1-29.

______________ , 1997 "Onus of poverty on women in the poorer settlements of Dhaka city". Dhaka: *Women for Women.*

Ahmad, Kalamuddin, and Nazmul Hassan (eds.). 1983. *Nutrition Survey of Rural Bangladesh 1981-82*. Dhaka, Bangladesh: University of Dhaka, Institute of Nutrition and Food Science.

Ahmad, Nessim, and Caroline Lucas. 1990. "Environment and IFAD Projects 1986-1990: A Review of Selected Issues". The State of World Rural Poverty Working Paper 26. Rome: International Fund for Agricultural Development.

Ahmad, Qazi Kholiquzzaman and Mahabub Hossain (1984) *Rural Poverty Alleviation in Bangladesh—Experiences and Policies,* Food and Agriculture Organisation/ WCARRD Follow-up Study Series.

Ahmed, Iftikhar. 1981. (ed.). 1985. *Technology and Rural Women. Conceptual and Empirical Issues.* London: George Allen and Unwin, for the International Labour Office.

____________, 1981. "Farm Size and Labour Use: Some Alternative Explanations". *Oxford Bulletin of Economics and Statistics.* 43 (1): 45-67.

Ahmed, Raisuddin and M. Hossain 1990 *Developmental Impact of Rural Infrastructure in Bangladesh,* Research Report No. 83. International Food Policy Research Institute.

____________, and Mahabub Hossain. 1990. *Developmental Impact of Rural Infrastructure in Bangladesh.* BIDS Research Report 83. Washington, D.C.: International Food Policy Research Institute in collaboration with the Bangladesh Institute of Development Studies.

AIDWA (1994) State Reports prepared for fourth national conference of All-India Democratic Women's Association, Coimbatore.

Aiyappan, A. (1965) *Social Revolution in a Kerala Village.* Bombay.

Alamgir 1974. "Some Analysis of Distribution of Income, Consumption, Saving and Poverty in Bangladesh". *The Bangladesh Development Studies. 11* (4): 737-818.

____________, 1980a. *Famine in South Asia: Political Economy of Mass Starvation.* Cambridge, Massachusetts: Oelgeschlager, Gunn and Hain.

____________, 1980b. "Income Distribution and Nutritional Status of the7 Agricultural Population: A Case Study of Bangladesh in the Year 2000". A study commissioned by FAO. Rome: Food and Agriculture Organisation.

____________, 1980c. *The Dimensions of Undernutrition and Malnutrition in Developing Countries: Conceptual, Empirical and Policy Issues.* Harvard Institute for International Development Discussion Paper 82. Cambridge, Massachusetts: Harvard University.

____________, 1984a. "Agricultural Pricing Policy in the Context of Poverty-alleviating Development Strategy". Rome: International Fund for Agricultural Development.

____________, 1984b. "Formulation and Implementation of Rural Credit Programmes". Rome: International Fund for Agricultural Development.

____________, 1987. "Institutional Arrangement for Managing Policies, a Review of the Operational Effectiveness of Credit and Savings—Marketing and Distribution Institutions as Instruments of Household Food Security". Rome: International Fund for Agricultural Development.

____________, 1988. "Some Lessons from IFAD's Approach to Rural Poverty Alleviation". In Lewis, and contributors. 1988.

____________, Mohiuddin, and Poonam Arora. 1991. *Providing Food Security for All.* IFAD Studies in Rural Poverty 1. New York: New York University Press.

Albin, Alice 1990 "Manufacturing sector in Kerala: Comparative study of its growth and structure", *Economic and Political Weekly,* 25(37):2059-70.

____________, 1992 "Kerala economy at crossroad", *Economic and Political Weekly.*

Alderman, Harold. 1990. *Nutritional Status in Ghana and Its Determinants.* Cornell Food and Nutrition Policy Programme Working Paper 1. Ithaca, New York: Cornell University.

Amin, Galal A. 1978. "Project Appraisal and Income Distribution." *World Development.* 6 (2): 139152.

Anand, S. and C. Harris 1985 "Living Standards in Sri Lanka 1973-1981/82: an Analysis of the CFS Data Central Bank" (mimeo). Colombo.

Anderson, Dennis, and Mark W. Leiserson. 1980. "Rural Non-Farm Employment in Developing Countries". *Economic Development and Cultural Change.* 28 (2): 227-248.

____________, Mark W. Leiserson, P. Suebsaeng, and M. de Tchihatchef. 1978. *Rural Enterprise and Nonfarm Employment.* Washington, D.C.: World Bank.

____________, 1987. *Economic Growth and the Returns to Investment.* World Bank Discussion Papers 12. Washington, D.C.: World Bank.

Arulpragasam, L.C. 1990. "Land Reform and Rural Poverty in Asia". The State of World Rural Poverty Working Paper 21. Rome: International Fund for Agricultural Development.

Asaduzzaman, Mohammad 1989 "Feeding our future towns an overview of urbanisation and associated food policy issues". In Planning Commission ed., *Food Strategies in Bangladesh: Medium and Long Term Perspectives* Dhaka: University Press Limited.

______________ , M. Hassani, and K.S. Bimal. 1984. *Performance of the Special Public Works Programme in Bangladesh, 1979-84.* Research Report New Series 40. Dhaka: Bangladesh Institute of Development Studies.

Asari, V. Gopalakrishnan 1994 "Population change in Kerala and its socio-economic implications", in A. K. G. Centre for Research and Studies (1994a).

Asian Development Bank, Economics and Development Resource Center (1991) *Key Indicators of Developing Asian and Pacific Countries*. Vol. 22 Manila: The Bank.

Azam, Jean-Paul, Gerard Chambas, Patrick Guillaumont, and Sylviane Guillaumont. 1989. *The Impact of Macroeconomic Policies on the Rural Poor: Analytical Framework and Indicators.* UNDP Policy Discussion Paper. New York: United Nations Development Programme.

Banerjee, Biswajit 1981 "Rural-urban migration and family ties: An analysis of family considerations in migration behaviour in India". *Oxford Bulletin of Economics and Statistics.*

______________ , 1983 "Social networks in the migration process: Empirical evidence on chain migration in India". *The Journal of Developing Areas.*

______________ , 1984a "Information flow, expectations and job search: Rural-to-urban migration process in India." *Journal of Development Economics.*

______________ , and S. M. Kanbur 1981 "On the specification and estimation of macro rural-urban migration functions: With an application to India data". *Oxford Bulletin of Economics and Statics.*

Bangladesh Bureau of Statistics (BBS) 1980 A *Report on the Household Expenditure Survey of Bangladesh* 1973-74, vol. 2 (Dhaka).

Bardhan, Pranab K. 1980. "Interlocking Factor Markets and Agrarian Development, a Review of Issues". *Oxford Economic Papers.* 32 (1): 80-98.

______________ , 1984. *Land, Labour and Rural Poverty: Essays in Development Economics.* Delhi: Oxford University Press.

Becker, Gary S. 1974 "A theory of social interactions". *Journal of Political Economy.*

Beneria, Lourdes (ed.). 1982. *Women and Development. The Sexual Division* of *Labour in Rural Societies.* New York: Praeger, for the International Labour Office.

Benjamin, McDonald P. 1985. *Investment Projects in Agriculture: Principles and Case Studies.* London: Longman.

Benor, Daniel and James Q. Harrison, 1977. *Agricultural Extension: The Training and Visit System.* Washington, D.C.: World Bank.

Bentley, W.R., G.B. Singh, and N. Chatterjee. 1987. "Tenure and Agroforestry Potentials in India". In John B. Raintree (ed.). 1987. *Land, Trees and Tenure.* Madison, Wisconsin: Wisconsin University, Land Tenure Centre.

Berger, Marguerite, V. DeLancey, and A. Mellencamp. 1990. *Bridging the Gender Gap in Agricultural Extension.* Washington, D.C.: International Centre for Research on Women.

Berry, Brian J. L 1967 *Geography of Market Centers and Retail Distribution.* Englewood Clifs, NJ: Prentice-Hall.

Bhalla, S. and P. Glewwe 1985, "Living Standards in Sri Lanka in the Seventies—Mirage and Reality" (mimeo). Washington, DC: World Bank.

Bhattacharjee, P. J. and G.N. Shastri (1976) *Population in India: A Study of Inter-State Variations,* New Delhi: Vikas.

BIDS-IFPRI 1985 *Devolvement Impact of the Food for Works Program in Bangladesh* (Dhaka: Bangladesh Institute of Development Studies and Washington, D.C.: International Food Policy Research Institute).

Bilsborrow, Richard E., A. S. Oberai, and Guy Standing (1984) *Migration Surveys in Low Income Countries: Guidelines of Survey and Questionnaire Design.* London: Croom Helm.

Birdsall, Nancy, 1980. Population and Poverty in the Developing World. World Bank Staff Working Paper 404. Washington, D.C.: World Bank.

Bose, Ashish 1991 *Population in India: 1991 Census Results and Methodology.* New Delhi: D. K. Publishing.

Burman, B.K. Roy 1984. "*Social Dimensions of Development*", *Social Change,* Vol. 14.

Cain, Mead, Syeda Rokeya Khanam, and Shamsun Nahar (1979)

"Class, patriarchy and structure of women's work in rural Bangladesh". Centre for Policy Studies, Working Paper, no. 43. New York: The Population Council.

Caldwell, J. C. 1986 "Routes to low mortality in poor countries", *Population and Development Review.*

______________ , and Pat Caldwell 1985 "Education and literacy as factors in health", in Halstead *et al.* (1985).

Centre for Development Studies 1977 *Poverty, Unemployment and Development Policy: A Case Study of Selected Issues with Reference to Kerala.* Madras: Orient Longman.

______________ , 1990 *The Urban Poor in Bangladesh. Vol. 1 Comprehensive Summary Report.* Dhaka: Centre for Urban Studies, Dhaka University.

Chakrabarti, A. (ed.). *India Since 1947*, Bombay: Allied publishers, 1967.

Chambers, Robert 1983 *Rural Development: Putting the Last First,* London: Longman.

______________ , 1988 'Poverty in India: concepts, research and reality.' Discussion Paper *241,* Institute of Development Studies, Sussex.

Chan, Kok Eng 1983 "Socio-economic implications of population ageing in a developing country: The Malaysian case". Kuala Lumpur: University of Malaya, Population Studies Program.

Chandrasekhar, C.P. and Abhijit Sen 1996 "Statistical truths: economic reform and poverty", *Frontline*, 23 February.

Chaudhari, Pramit 1978. *The Indian Economy: Poverty and Development*, New Delhi: Vikas Publishing House Pvt. Ltd.

Chaudhuri, Salma and Pratima Paul 1991 *The Conditions of Garment Workers in Bangladesh. An Appraisal.* Dhaka: Bangladesh Institute of Development Studies.

Chen, Ali Ju and Gavin W. Jones (1988) *Ageing in ASEAN: Its Socio-Economic Consequences.* Singapore: Institute of Development Studies.

Chowdhury, Nuimuddin 1989 'The changing food system: storage marketing and distribution issues.' In Planning Commission, ed., *Food Strategies in Bangladesh:* Medium and long Term Perspectives (Dhaka: University Press Limited).

Chowdhury, Rafiqul Huda 1978 "Determinants and consequences of rural out-migration: Evidence from some villages in Bangladesh". *Oriental Geographer* 22 (1 & 2): 20.

Damodaran, A. D. and V. Govindarajulu 1994 'Ecstasy and agony of Kerala development model', in A. K. G. Centre for Research and Studies (1994b).

Dasgupta, Biplab and Roy Laishley 1975 "Migration from villages." *Economic and Political Weekly* 10 (Oct. 18).

Davy, J. 1821, reprinted 1969 *An Account of the Interior of Ceylon and of its Inhabitants.* Dehiwela: Tissara Prakashaya.

de Silva, G.V.S. et. al. 1979, "Bhoomi Sena: A Struggle for People's, Power" *Development Dialogue,* 1979:2.

Department of Census and Statistics (1969) *Socio-economic Survey 1968/69.* Colombo: Government Press.

Department of Census and Statistics 1981 and 1986 *Labour Force and Socio-economic-Survey:* 19801-81 and 19851-86. Colombo: Government Press.

______________ , 1990 *Household Income and Expenditure Survey: 1990.* Colombo: Government Press.

______________ , (various years) *Annual Statistical Abstract.* Colombo: Government Press.

______________ , (various years) *Food Balance Sheet.* Colombo: Government Press.

______________ , (various years, 1990-95) *Labour Force Participation Quarterly Surveys.* Colombo: Government Press.

Desai, A.R. 1987. *Recent Trends in Indian Nationalism,* Bombay: Popular Prakashan.

Dreze, Jean and Amartya Sen (1989) *Hunger and Public Action.* Oxford: Clarendon Press.

______________ , 1995 *India: Economic Development and Social Opportunity.* Oxford and Delhi: Oxford University Press.

Dube, S.C. (ed.) 1977. *India Since Independence; Social Report on India 1947-1972,* New Delhi: Vikas Publishing House Pvt. Ltd.

Duvvury, Nata 1994a *Report on the Discussions on the Status of Women,* International Congress on Kerala Studies, Thiruvananthapuram.

______________ , 1994b *Social Security in the Unorganised Sector: A Study of Labour Welfare Funds.* Thiruvananthapuram.

Eames, Edwin 1954 "Some aspects of urban migration from a village north central India". *The Eastern Anthropologist.*

Elizaga, Juan C. 1972 "Internal migration: An overview". *International Migration Review.*

EPW Research Foundation 1993 "Poverty levels in India: norms, estimates and trends", *Economic and Political Weekly.*

Food and Agriculture Organisation of the United Nations (FAO). 1990b. "Gender Issues in Rural Food Security in Developing

Countries". Paper prepared for the 15th Session of the Committee on World Food Security, Rome, 26-30 March 1990. Rome: Food and Agriculture Organisation.

______________ , World Health Organisation (FAO/WHO). 1973. "Energy and Protein Requirements. Report of a Joint FAO/ WHO Ad Hoc Expert Committee". Rome, 22 March-2 April 1971. FAO Nutrition Meetings Report Series 52. Rome: Food and Agriculture Organisation.

Franda, Marcus 1979, *Small is politics: Organisational Alternatives In India's Rural Development*, New Delhi, Wiley Eastern Ltd.

Frankel, Francine R. 1978. *India's Political Economy: The gradual Revolution*, Delhi: Oxford University Press.

Garbett, G. Kinglsey 1972 "Circulatory labour migration in Rhodesia Towards a decision model". Paper presented at the Twelfth International African Seminar, University of Zambia, September.

George, Jose 1980 *Politicisation of Agricultural Workers in Kerala: A Study of Kuttanad*, M. Phil. Dissertation, Jawaharlal Nehru University, New Delhi.

George, K. K. 1994 'Whither Kerala Model?' in A.K.G. Centre for Research and Studies (1994e).

Ghatak, Subrata 1975 "Rural Interest Rates in the Indian Economy". *Journal of Development Studies.*

Gopalankutty, K. 1981 "The Integration of the Anti-Landlord Movement with their Movement against imperialism: The case of Malabar, 1935-39" *Studies in History*.

Gore, M. S.. 1968 *Urbanization and Family Change*. Bombay: Popular Prakashan.

Government of Bangladesh 1990, *Draft fourth five year plan in Bangladesh,* Planning Commission, Ministry of Planning, December 1990.

Government of Kerala 1985 *Report of the Survey on Socio-economic Conditions of Agricultural and Other Rural labourers in Kerala: 1983-84*. Thiruvananthapuram: Department of Economics and Statistics.

______________ , 1992 *Economic Review*, 1991. Thiruvananthapuram: State Planning Board.

Government of Pakistan, undated. *Pakistan Census of Agriculture, 1960*. Vol. I. Karachi: Government of Pakistan, Agriculture Census Organisation.

Griffin, Keith 1974 *The Political Economy of Agrarian Change: An*

Essay on the Green Revolution (Cambridge: Harvard University Press).

Herring, Ronald 1983 *Land to the Tiller: The Political Economy of Land Reform in South Asia*. New Haven: Yale University Press.

______________ , 1992 Contrasting the "Great transformation": Land and Labour in South India". Ithaca: Corncll University.

Hirashima, S., and M., Muqtada (eds.). 1986. *Hired Labour and Rural Labour Markets in Asia: Studies Based on Farm-Level Data*. New Delhi: International Labour Office, Asian Regional Team for Employment Promotion.

Holzer, Harry J. 1988 "Search method use by unemployed youth." *Journal of Labour Economics*.

Hossain, Mahabub 1985 "A note on the trend of landlessness in Bangladesh". The *Bangladesh Development Studies* 13 (3).

______________ , Atiur Rahman and Hossain Zillur Rahman (1988) "The economic impact of the 1988 floods: report from a field tour". Dhaka: Bangladesh Institute of development Studies, Mimeographed.

Houtart, Francois and Genevieve Lemercinier 1978 "Socio-religious movements in Kerala: a reaction to the capitalist mode of production", *Social Scientist*

Howe, John, and Peter Richards (eds.). 1984. *Rural Roads and Poverty Alleviation*. London: Intermediate Technology Publications.

India 1989: A Reference Annual, Research and Reference Division, Ministry of Information and Broadcasting, Govt. of India, New Delhi: 1990.

India Since Independence 1971. New Delhi: Publications Division, Ministry of Information and Broadcasting, Govt. of India.

International Fund for Agriculture Development (IFAD). 1979. Report of the Special Programming Mission to Sri Lanka." Rome: International Fund for Agriculture Development.

International Labour Office 1960 *Why Labour Leaves the Land: A Comparative Study of the Movement of Labour out of Agriculture*. Studies and Reports, new series no. 59. Geneva.

______________ , (ILO). 1977. "Poverty and Landless in Rural Asia". A World Employment Programme study. Geneva: International Labour Office.

______________ , 1988a. *Rural Employment Promotion. International Labour Conference*, 75th Session, Report VII. Geneva: International Labour Office.

______________ , 1988b. *Yearbook of Labour Statistics*. 1988. Geneva: International Labour Office.

______________ , 1989. *World Labour Report*. Geneva: International Labour Office.

______________ , 1990. *The Challenge of Employment, Rural Labour, Poverty and the ILO*. Geneva: International Labour Office.

______________ , and P. K. Michael Tharakan 1986a *An Enquiry into the Historical Roots of Backwardness of Kerala: A Study of Travancore Region,* Working Parer 215. Thiruvananthapuram: Centre for Development Studies.

Jain, L. R. and Minhas, B. S. 1991 "Rural and urban consumer price indices by commodity groups (States and All-India: 1970-1 to 1983)" *Sarvekshana*.

Jones, Ian. 1990. "Training and Rural Poverty Alleviation". The State of World Rural Poverty Working Paper 14. Rome: International Fund for Agriculture Development.

Joshi, V. H. 1966 "Economic development and social change in a South Gujarat Village: Social consequences of industrialisation and urbanisation in a village in South Gujarat with special reference to tensions between groups and classes". Thesis; M. S. University of Baroda Research Series.

Kothari, Rajni 1988. *Rethinking Development*, Delhi: Ajanta.

Mason, Philip (ed.) 1967. *India and Cylon: Unity and Diversity*, London: Oxford University Press.

Maxneef, Manfred, et. al. 1989, "Human Scale Development: An Option for the Future", *Development Dialogue*, 1989:1.

Mehta, S.R. 1984, *Rural Development Policies and Programmes: A Sociological Perspective*, Now Delhi, Sage Publications.

Mincer, Jacob 1978 "Family migration decisions". *Journal of Political Economy*.

Minhas, B.S. and L.R. Jain 1990 "Incidence of rural poverty in different states and All-India: 1970-1 to 1983", in *Agricultural Development Policy: Adjustments and Reorientation*, Oxford and IBH, New Delhi

______________ , L.R. Jain and M.R. Saluja 1990 "State-specific urban consumer price differentials relative to All-India for middle fractiles and total population: 1961-1983" *Indian Economic Review*.

Morris-Jones, W.H. 1974 *The Government and Politics of India*, Bombay: B.I. Publications.

Murray, Christopher J. L. and Lincoln C. Chen 1992

"Understanding morbidity change", *Population and Development Review.*

Naik, J. 1976. *An Alternative Policy for India:* New Delhi: S. Chand & Co. Pvt. Ltd.

Nath, Rabindra 1977, "The Strategy for Planning", *Yojana*, 21,7,1-14 May.

National Sample Survey 1979 "Consumer expenditure, NSS 27th round (October 1972-September 1973)" *Sarvekshana*, 2(3).

____________, 1986a "Some results on the second quinquennial survey on consumer expenditure, NSS 32nd round,' Sarvekshana, 9 (3).

____________, 1986b "Results on the third quinquennial survey on consumer expenditure: NSS 38th round", *Sarvekshana*, 9 (4).

Palmer, Narman D. 1961. *The Indian Political System*, New York.: Houghton Mifflin Co. Boston.

Rahman, A. and Dilip Kumar Roy 1990 "Rural employment generation in Bangladesh: a regional perspective". BIDS Research Report No. 123, Bangladesh Institute of Development Studies.

Rahman, Hussain Zillur 1988 "Monitoring rural poverty: conceptual framework and organisational options". Dhaka: Bangladesh Institute of Development Studies, Mimeographed.

____________, and Binayak Sen (1990) "Preliminary findings from a 62-village survey". In Omar Haider Chowdhury et al., *The face of Rural Poverty in Bangladesh: Trends and Insights* (Dhaka: Bangladesh Institute of Development Studies, Mimeographed).

Rao, M. S. A. 1970 *Urbanisation and Social Change: A Study of a Rural Community on a Metropolitan Fringe.* New Delhi: Orient Longmans.

Ravallion, Martin 1990 "Impact of Policies since 1982". HIID/ESEPP Working Paper, Planning Commission, Dhaka, Mimeographed.

Report of the Task Force on Poverty Alleviation 1991 A Report prepared for the Adviser, In-charge of the Ministry of Planning, Mimeographed.

Reports of the 'Five-Year Plans' (5th, 6th & 7th), Planning Commission, Govt. of India, New Delhi: 1990.

Sen, Amartya 1984 "Rights and Capabilities", A. Sen, *Resources, Values and Development.* Oxford: Basil Blackwell.

Sen, Binayak 1990a *NGOs Role in Green Revolution, Rural Development and Employment Generation: A Comparative Study of Government and NGO programmes*. Report prepared for the Planning Commission, Dhaka.

Shah, A. M.. 1974 *The Household Dimensions of the Family in India: A Field Study in a Gujarat Village and a Review of Other Studies*. Berkeley University of California Press.

Shiva Kumar, A.K. 1991 "UNDP's Human Development Index: a computation for Indian states", *Economic and Political Weekly*.

Social Information of India: Trends and Structure 1983. ICSSR. Delhi: Hindustan Publishing Corporation.

Sovani, N. V. 1966 *Urbanisation and Urban India*. New York: Asia Publishing House.

Stark. Oded 1975 "Utility technology change, surplus and risk: The micro-economics of rural-to-urban migration of labour in less developed economics", Ph.D. dissertation, University of Sussex.

Stern, Nicholas 1977 "On labour markets in less development countries". Paper prepared for the Development Research Center, The World Bank, Washington. D.C.

Todaro, Michael P. 1969 "A model of labour migration and urban unemployment in less developed countries". *American Economic Review*.

United Nations Conference on Trade and Development 1989 *Trade and Development Report* 1989 New York.

Work Bank 1983 Bangladesh: *Selected Issues in Rural Employment*, Washington, D.C.

__________, 1986 *World Development Report 1986* (New York: Oxford University Press).

__________, 1987 *World Development Report 1987* (New York: Oxford University Press).

__________, 1990c *Bangladesh: Managing the Adjustment Process- An Appraisal* Report No. 8344-BD (Washington, D.C).

Zeitz, Joachim and Alberto Valdes 1988 "Agriculture in the GATT: An analysis of alternative approaches to reform". Research Report 70, International Food Policy Research Institute.

Index